PROPERTY RIGHTS IN CONTEMPORARY GOVERNANCE

# PROPERTY RIGHTS IN CONTEMPORARY GOVERNANCE

Edited by **Staci M. Zavattaro,**
**Gregory R. Peterson,**
and **Ann E. Davis**

**SUNY**
PRESS

Published by State University of New York Press, Albany

For information, contact State University of New York Press, Albany, NY
www.sunypress.edu

Library of Congress Cataloging-in-Publication Data

Names: Zavattaro, Staci M., 1983- editor. | Peterson, Gregory R., 1966- editor. | Davis, Ann E., [date] editor.
Title: Property rights in contemporary governance / edited by Staci M. Zavattaro, Gregory R. Peterson, Ann E. Davis.
Description: Albany : State University of New York Press, [2019] | Includes bibliographical references and index.
Identifiers: LCCN 2018012994 | ISBN 9781438472898 (hardcover) |
ISBN 9781438472904 (e-book) | ISBN 9781438472881 (paperback)
Subjects: LCSH: Real property—Economic aspects—United States. | Land use—Law and legislation—United States. | Real property—United States—History.
Classification: LCC KF572 .P76 2019 | DDC 346.7304—dc23 LC record available at https://lccn.loc.gov/2018012994

10  9  8  7  6  5  4  3  2  1

# CONTENTS

# ILLUSTRATIONS

# PREFACE

We sat together in a classroom at Marist College in Poughkeepsie, New York, during Summer 2014, looking out the window to see a gorgeous view of the Hudson River, green hillscapes, and rumbling trains below. The three of us would not have met otherwise—an economist, a philosopher, and a public administration scholar. We had come together to participate in the National Endowment for the Humanities summer institute, "Meanings of Property," developed and led by Ann Davis to foster interdisciplinary approaches to the study of property and ownership. Attendees affectionately called our summer together "Property Camp." About thirty scholars from various disciplines such as economics, law, history, public administration, political science, and bioethics gathered for six weeks to study, debate, and exchange ideas about how property and its various interpretations guide our everyday lives. The viewshed outside our classroom window, as we learned, was critical in the area for both real property and social contract reasons.

The work of John Searle, particularly the book *Making the Social World: The Structure of Human Civilization* (2010), opened our analysis that summer. In that work, Searle argues that the relevance of the term *property* would be its meaning in particular social institutions. There would be language statements regarding how the term, and its referent, would be understood and used in social and cultural contexts. There would be "status function declarations," which designate certain persons to have particular powers with regard to the object. Those declarations could be public and verifiable with official documents. For example, the registry of motor vehicles would verify that this 1968 Volkswagen Beetle is "my" car, that I had a title, that I had purchased the car from a legitimate dealer, and that its safety inspection verified it for road use. Further, it would be necessary to supply evidence that I was an authorized driver with car insurance and a driver's license, for which I had been tested in a uniform procedure.

Work from Stuart Banner proved useful in the exploration in the historical variation property types, particularly his book *American Property: A History of How, Why and What We Own* (2011). Banner explored diverse historical and cultural contexts to demonstrate the wide variation in forms and types of property. Mary Poovey and Hendrik Hartog elaborated on the epistemological and institutional contexts of property. Alan Ryan provided the long-term history of property, citing Greek and Roman law, as well as liberal political theory. Robert Goldstein discussed the ecological implications of the definition of property, and Kenneth Pomeranz guided us in examining property variations in China as historically compared with the West. As readers can tell, the scope of our deliberations regarding such a seemingly simple construct as property was wide-ranging, including philosophical, economic, historical, cross-cultural, social, linguistic, and contextual factors.

During the institute, participants raised important questions regarding the importance of language. We challenged Searle's foundation of all institutions in language statements, and proposed other forms of nonverbal communication that conveyed important social understandings. We questioned whether land was a particular kind of property, which existed prior to legal understandings and judicial proceedings. Others challenged the way that the human body has been conceptualized as property, not only in Locke's famous argument for self-ownership but also in the historic institution of American slavery and contemporary medical practices that impinge particularly on the rights women have over their own bodies. Fellow scholars brought references to other literature and other disciplines, such as anthropologists David Harvey and Arjun Appadurai. We list the variety of authors here not to show how many books we read. No. Instead, we list them purposefully to underscore the interdisciplinary foundations that led to this volume.

Searle's position on human rights was challenged, as well as his view that negative human rights, such as private property, were more enforceable than positive rights, such as adequate nutrition (Searle 2010). The role of property in the foundation of the liberal state, and its role in economic production and income distribution were other aspects that were mentioned. The rich discussions and debates provided much of the foundation for this book. To round out the volume, we invited in scholars from areas not as well represented at the seminar, and this led to the inclusion of interesting contributions about water rights and drone regulations. The intention is to share with the reader some of these questions, debates, and resources on this important issue of the "meanings of property," including terminology, authoritative statements, and social institutions.

# INTRODUCTION

## Property, Governance, and a Plan for the Book

STACI M. ZAVATTARO, GREGORY R. PETERSON, AND ANN E. DAVIS

Imagine this scenario. A woman leaves her corporate job to open her dream bakery. She quits to enroll in pastry school. She takes out traditional loans yet also turns to GoFundMe, an online, crowdsourced fundraising platform, for assistance. There, she knows strangers can contribute to her online campaign for books and other school supplies. Upon graduation, she decides to start her own business but cannot immediately afford a storefront with kitchen equipment, so she rents space from a local corporation that makes a business of such ventures. She is there daily with other chefs preparing food for delivery. She then opens her virtual storefront, turning toward a free website hosting service. She does not need to pay a fee to use their templates to create a business website.

The orders come pouring in once her website goes live and word of mouth spreads. She expands to create an Instagram feed, a social media application focused on sharing photos. She posts pictures daily of her latest creations to increase business so she can finally buy a storefront. To deliver her baked goods, she relies on ride-sharing services such as Uber and Lyft. She has both apps for busy times so she can find the best price for her rides. Her own car is too old to travel the distances her customers require. Each day, she takes the rides at least fifty miles back and forth, all while still baking on her own without an assistant.

Where does property fit in? In our all-too-real example, there is a mix of real and social property—all of which come with different social contracts. When our fictional baker takes an Uber to her delivery, no taxes are going toward driving on those roads as would happen if she rode in a taxicab. Who pays for repairs? Is there a commons problem emerging with overuse? If someone contributes to her GoFundMe account, do they expect a portion of her royalties—or at least free cupcakes? If something happens in the kitchen, who is responsible? When she posts photos and someone takes them for their own blog, have they violated her intellectual property even with proper photo credit?

In today's ever-connected, fast-paced society, we see these tensions regularly. Our book uses property as a lens through which to explore these changing relationships via our understanding of governance across disciplines. Practically, we see policy disagreements based on social aspects of property—environmental protection, (de)regulation of industry, and health insurance, to name a few. Governance is indeed a cross-cutting construct influential across intellectual and practical discussions, but we borrow here a broad definition from the public administration literature given that discipline's ability to undergird most of the chapters within the volume. We use the term *governance* to show the interconnectedness between actors in our social, economic, political, and governmental systems. Governance implies a networked relationship rather than a hierarchical one, though there is no agreed-upon definition of the term (Keefer, 2004). In governance scenarios, state and nonstate actors assume equal footing in deliberative spaces to arrive, ideally, at a consensus-based decision. Now, we see perversions of this ideal regularly, and many of the chapters herein illustrate the tension between public-private interactions. Governance and property are inextricably linked given the theoretical foundations of self versus other inherent within philosophical and practical debates about the individual's role in society and rights to ownership.

We need to be clear up front: our book is not a legal text dedicated to the nuances of admittedly complex property law. That is for other volumes. Instead, we take a purposefully interdisciplinary approach to show how one concept—property—manifests in daily governance issues. By governance, we mean a shift from top-down, government-led policies and practices to a system that, ideally, embraces collaboration, dialogue, and the commons. In systems practicing good governance, there is shared discussion among stakeholders who set the rules and evaluate processes along the way (Bovaird & Loffler, 2003). As some of the chapters show, we see breakdowns in governance processes in favor of top-down policy provision and implementation.

All of the writing involves a mix of public, nonprofit, legal, and corporate actors struggling with some aspect of property as a concrete thing or abstract concept. The authors in this volume show not the limits of property but instead its power across disciplines in theory and practice.

## WHY A BOOK ON PROPERTY AND GOVERNANCE?

There exist myriad books on the varied aspects of property, so why do we need another volume? Property is its own wide-ranging area of expertise, especially in law schools. But changing theories of property influence law school curriculum. For example, a recent legal studies text cites five alternative theories of property and four key debates (Alexander & Penalver, 2012). Books also exist that delve into nuanced aspects of property, such as intellectual property. Again, we emphasize the importance of those volumes, but our goal is to take property out of its traditional legal home into one that is more recognizable in daily life. Reflection on property regimes is integral to political philosophy, and ethicists, biologists, and legal experts continue to weigh in on the issues raised by efforts to patent life forms, either in whole or part. Historical studies of property and its significance abound, and much of history can be reduced to claims to property and disputes thereof. Women and slaves were once widely considered property, but are no longer so (in some regions of the world anyway). Children are, strictly speaking, no longer considered property, although their legal status remains different in many respects from that of normal adults.

The distinctiveness of the present volume is twofold. First, it is a uniquely interdisciplinary volume in an area where research across disciplines is sorely needed. No one field owns the study of property, and real progress in reflecting and understanding the significance of property for the past, present, and future increasingly requires knowledge of multiple areas of inquiry. Understanding the history of property requires some foundation in economics and economic systems, as well as the philosophical distinctions that explicitly or implicitly impact the decision making of historical actors in their context. Second, the chapters that jointly comprise the volume collectively raise issues of the various meanings of property and the ways these meanings become concretized in the intersection of economics and governance. The embodiment of meanings of property is a clear concern of both the historical chapters comprising the first half of the volume and the policy and theoretical chapters of the second half.

## THE CHANGING FACE OF PROPERTY

This book is timely—yet can stand the test of time—given the contemporary discussions surrounding the expansion of property rights, rules, and regulations. In one example, the election of Donald Trump as U.S. president presented a tangled ethical web related to his global properties. As one news article describes, the Trump name on buildings throughout the world could cause extra security concerns and even make the properties terrorist targets (Crowley, 2016).

In another example, many readers are familiar with the sharing/gig economy mentioned at the outset of this introduction. Services such as Airbnb, Lyft, and Uber fall under this umbrella. People have created enterprises that circumvent traditional economic practices within this model. Uber and Lyft are ride-sharing applications that go around the heavily regulated taxi companies, while Airbnb does the same for hotels. Another aspect of the sharing economy is temporary workspaces. Startups might not need full office spaces—or cannot afford them—so they enter into basically rental agreements akin to gym memberships (Broderick & Kuschel, 2016), as our baker did in the opening scenario. The person occupying the space is not listed as a tenant usually but as a member, thus lessening the property rights and even privacy rights they have related to the shared space. Regarding privacy rights, shared spaces mean no doors and no protection for potentially sensitive information. One slip, and a breach could be potentially disastrous.

Ongoing developments in science and technology constitute one obvious driver of changes in the conception of property, and the history of technology in particular is deeply intertwined with evolving definitions of intellectual property and patent systems. Although intellectual property as a concept has roots in the ancient period (Moore, 2001), legal protections of intellectual property (Queen Elizabeth I in England in the early seventeenth century) are now a crucial modern phenomenon, and the protection of intellectual property enshrined in the first article of the U.S. Constitution is a remarkable exemplification of this fact. The Constitution's phrasing is itself indicative of another important dimension, since its protection of intellectual property conceptualizes such property as a right, but one that exists only for a limited duration and with a particular justification: the "progress of science and useful arts." From the outset, arguments concerning the status of intellectual property have attempted to balance the rights of creators, which inherently limit access to creators' inventions, and the rights and the needs of the community, for whom the inventions hold promise for improving their quality of life. Achieving this balance has become increasingly difficult as new technologies have made some forms of intellectual property such as music and software exceedingly cheap to reproduce and share (Banner, 2011; Lessig, 2006; Moore, 2001). Advances in biotechnology raise a different kind of issue: To what extent can living things, including their genes, be patented, and is this even a wise practice to pursue (Andrée, 2007; Koepsell, 2015)?

While science and technology constitute one driver of changing conceptions of property, it is important to acknowledge distinctly social ones as well. Indeed, the economic shifts that accompanied the transition to the early modern period and laid the groundwork for the emergence of capitalism, however much they may be explained by other factors, were associated with large-scale shifts in society and institutions. The emergence of joint stock companies and the genres of documentation that gradually developed to support the new world of commerce (Poovey, 2008) had little initially to do with science and technology and much to do with the shifts in first British and eventually European and American society. In these developments, the contingent discovery and exploration of vast lands beyond the confines of Europe played no small role. And while it is easy to focus on the significant responses, highlighting for instance the need to balance risk and profit (Bernstein, 1998), it is important to acknowledge the more subtle impacts, including exposure to an American frontier for which British property laws were less than optimally suited to its Native American inhabitants.

As three of the chapters in our volume testify, issues of environmental protection raise their own set of property and ownership dilemmas, and it is no accident that the most famous example of free riders exploiting a public good—the tragedy of the commons—concerns the way environmental goods such as clean air and water are subject to exploitation (Hardin, 1968). This may seem paradoxical at first, since ownership of land is considered the paradigmatic form of property, and it is the primary referent for Locke's (2003) influential labor theory of property ownership. But while we often think of land under our feet having a sort of permanence immune to change, this is far from true, as all landscapes change over time, usually very slowly, but, as in cases of massive erosion from hurricane landfall, sometimes quite suddenly, with deep implications for those who thought their property permanent.

Although advances in science and technology provide some of the most obvious examples changing conceptions of property, they are not the only ones, and motivations for reconceptualizing property can arise from basic societal shifts as individuals and communities react to and interpret their immediate environment. The emergence of new forms of property coinciding with the rise of capitalism in the early modern period provides one obvious example, giving way to the corporation, stocks, tradable public debt futures, and more.

Another source of property's changing conceptions can be found in the European encounter with what they considered to be the American frontier. Europeans arriving in the New World brought with them legal frameworks of ownership that did not always apply equally well to a frontier whose property boundaries were still being determined and where traditional solutions to European problems did not always apply. The idea that property rights, empirically speaking, are not just one thing but really a "bundle of sticks" that can be arranged in different ways depending on need and context becomes more than apparent as we contemplate the sweep of history and the shifting demands placed on us by technology and societal change.

At the end of the day, we are interested in not only how the bundle of sticks we call property rights were arranged in societies past but also how they ought to be arranged now and in the future. The concept of property is inherently connected to questions of justice and fairness, and the most influential conceptions of property, such as those put forth by John Locke and Karl Marx, are deeply tied to specific ethical justifications. While such justifications have been and continue to be societally impactful, questions remain concerning the arguments supporting them. Indeed, the divide between the two major works of late-twentieth-century American political philosophy—John Rawls's *A Theory of Justice* (1971) and Robert Nozick's *Anarchy, State, and Utopia* (1974)—can be understood in no small way as a divide over the fundamentals of property rights and the extent to which the Lockean paradigm should remain dominant. Forty years of subsequent debate have not settled the matter, prompting a search for new avenues of conceptualization and justification. In this volume, Peterson applies in a preliminary way the capabilities approach of Amartya Sen (1999; 2009) and Martha Nussbaum (2000; 2007; 2011) to the subject of intellectual property, and in the conclusion we return to the capabilities approach as a way of thinking about property as a natural versus constructed phenomenon. Their work helps us to think about property regimes not only in terms of exclusive rights to be protected but also in terms of human goods and conceptions of well-being. While the Lockean paradigm can and should remain an important conversation partner as we reason through particular conceptualizations of the bundle of sticks that constitutes property rights, the limitations of the paradigm—manifest in its near-exclusive focus on historical justification and the ease with which Locke's important provisos are forgotten or pushed aside—become apparent. Ongoing changes in society and technology and the relation of both to the natural environment dictate, we suggest, exploration of alternative philosophical frameworks.

## ORGANIZATION OF THE VOLUME

We chose to divide the book into two broad sections: historical explorations of property rights, and contemporary views of property issues. As noted above, we interpret the word *property* broadly to showcase the different ways in which the concept drives our everyday interpretations of the world.

In the first section, authors capture the roots of some of property's more lasting features. Our historical survey begins with the role of conceptions of property in the development of modern economic systems, and in chapter 1, Ann Davis places one particular innovation in the conception of property, the corporation, at the heart of a narrative that begins with the Italian city-states of late medieval/early Renaissance period and extends to the formation and flourishing of capital markets in the modern period. To understand this innovation and the other innovations associated with it—joint stocks, banking systems, and national debt—Davis uses Searle's conception of status function declarations. On this account, economic systems and institutions are real precisely because we declare them to be real, with the result that, while common coinage reserves the term *real property* to tangible assets such as land, stocks, futures, and options are not less real, however ephemeral they may otherwise appear.

The grounds of judicial reasons constitute a basic issue for the determination of legal property rights, and in chapter 2, R. Ben Brown examines this issue as it emerges in the context of competing rights claims by landowners and the owners of animal stock. The issue of what to do when roaming stock (one form of property) damaged land or crop (another form of property) was a common one on the American frontier, and Brown demonstrates how contrasting rulings appealed either to principles of common law or to more relevant American practice and legislative act. At heart, Brown argues, is the question of the priority of an abstract conception of law versus that of democratic will, and Brown shows how deeply embedded commitments to legal genres end up privileging the former over the latter.

A central contemporary issue of property law concerns the ability of government to expropriate or otherwise regulate or modify land privately owned. With chapter 3, Jill Fraley clarifies the history of one particular form of such action, the taking of private land for use as public roads, examining in particular the seeming contrast between British and early American legal traditions. Although the British had developed a tradition of strong protection of private property that aimed to avoid unnecessary taking by constructing roads on "wasteland," American law and politics has appeared to be more willing to take land in such instances. As Fraley argues, however, the contrast may be more apparent than real, since such cases of American takings tended either (1) to involve land that had been vested but not cultivated or (2) to fall within the common understanding in the American context that grants of land that included wastelands did not calculate the wastelands as part of the value of the land and, importantly, it was expected that roads would eventually be built there, following the British custom. Partly behind this American understanding can be seen, Fraley argues, the Lockean labor theory of value, which implied a duty to cultivate land at least in part, and which treated unimproved land as also unowned, a way of thinking that proved important in colonial context and which worked to the significant detriment to the land's native inhabitants.

While Fraley's chapter addresses one of the central issues involving the most paradigmatic form of property—land—Tyson Leuchter in chapter 4 draws attention to the turns of fortune of the Paris stockbroker Vincent Perdonnet and his effort to recoup substantial losses from Comte Forbin-Janson after investing on his behalf. The dispute between Perdonnet and Forbin-Janson eventually worked its way to France's highest court, and, as Leuchter explains, the central question between them concerned whether or not futures contracts properly constitute property or are merely fictions with no legal status. The debate reveals the shifting norms and conceptions of property in postrevolutionary France, shifts that retain considerable importance for understanding today's highly financialized economy.

While Section One of our text approaches basic questions of property historically, Section Two provides a cross-section of contemporary issues emerging as a result of contemporary institutionalizations of property. In chapter 5, Donald Richards considers the impact of property regimes on proposals for climate mitigation. Central to Richards's account is the distinction between environmental and ecological economics. While environmental economics understands the natural environment as merely one exchangeable resource among others, Richards favors the ecological economics argument that we should understand the human economy as a subset of the natural ecology, rather than the other way around. Richards charts the course of events following the Kyoto Accord, and notes how different property regimes associated with each approach impacts what we think of as a satisfactory basis for international agreement. Whereas environmental economics would favor a system that treats carbon emissions and stock as private property to be managed through a potentially intractable international cap and trade system, an approach based on ecological economics would favor one that treats the environment as common property that is the possession of all humankind. This approach, Richards argues, could draw stronger involvement from less developed countries, since such a common property approach would necessarily take into account the size of relative populations and the burdens each must bear.

Karen Consalo in chapter 6 shifts the level of analysis from the "meta-commons" of the atmosphere to the slippery issue of water rights. Consalo provides a useful overview of the factors leading to contemporary patterns of water rights in U.S. law, highlighting in particular the distinctive approaches taken in the American West, where "first in time, first in line" became the basis for a legal framework that inadequately addresses issues of overuse, and the East Coast approach to riparian rights that inadequately addresses pollution issues. As Consalo notes, neither of these approaches engages the water needs of nonhuman organisms, and she charts the development of Earth Jurisprudence as one approach that may more adequately address these issues.

While Richards analyzes issues of climate and property and Consalo provides an overview of basic issues of property and water rights, Chad McGuire in chapter 7 brings these considerations together as he analyzes the issue of coastal property rights in the face of rising sea levels caused by climate change. In doing so, McGuire contrasts a Lockean natural rights approach associated with the Fifth Amendment of the U.S. Constitution with a "modern" approach associated with the Tenth Amendment that aims to balance competing interests in the interest of maximizing outcomes according to contemporary norms. McGuire argues that the unprecedented nature of the sea level rise caused by climate change will necessitate a modern approach as governments find themselves forced to act in order to preserve the public good.

Chapter 8 from Staci Zavattaro takes property in the linguistic sense and uses it as a metaphor to explore developments in place branding. Her chapter is theoretical, showing the sociorelational side of property and how it matters for people and their place. For people, a place becomes part of them. People take a sense of pride in their community or *not*. Both matter for the success of place making, crime rates, economic increases, and social safety. Zavattaro argues this process of developing a place-based identity as personal property involves the interaction of borders as social constructions, as well as place cultures, and the interaction of individualism and geographic collectivism.

In chapter 9, Gregory Peterson shifts the focus to another contemporary governance issue: intellectual property. He explores the topic using an international lens, with a case study of South African pharmaceutical companies battling for rights to produce and sell drug treatments. His chapter is philosophical in nature, highlighting what he terms the State of Plenty. In this state, there is enough of everything to go around, potentially avoiding large-scale commons conflicts known to modern society. Peterson provides us with what is essentially a thought experiment to shift our focus from property as singular to property as communal and mutually beneficial.

Finally in chapter 10, Timothy Ravich details the emergence of property rights related to drones. The air is commonly seen as a public highway above five hundred feet, but below that the air becomes a bit thicker. With drones, anyone can fly them anywhere without regard to these airspace rights. As Ravich explains, law enforcement agencies, in one example, could take advantage of this legal imperfection to conduct unwanted aerial searches, thus violating constitutional protections. He deftly details how laws, rules, and regulations related to drones need to catch up to common practices, given the problems the devices can be and are causing.

With the variety of topics, we know the volume will have wide appeal to readers generally interested in the topic. We envision the volume spurring deep discussions in legal seminars and undergraduate courses alike. Instructors could also pick and choose chapters to share with students based on the course content and subject area. The chapter on drones, for example, would work well for public policy classes, while the chapter on branding could work in an urban planning context. We hope all readers will find value in the volume given their particular interests.

## FINAL REMARKS

We hope this book spurs ideas in readers related to how property surrounds them each day. We see it in what we know as our own—our house, car, office, clothes, food. We also see it in what is someone else's—their house, their car, their office, their clothes, their food. That is, personal possession and the right to exclude from one's "own" seem to be the most salient aspects of property in our daily lives. What is not so evident is the social acceptance of this definition, without which even "real" property would not exist. Common decency dictates what is socially acceptable to do related to property, but if common decency always prevailed we would not need this volume or the myriad others on the topic. To us, the many books about property from a variety of disciplinary lenses, including ours, are necessary given the ever-changing property landscape.

## REFERENCES

Alexander, G. S., & Penalver, E. M. (2010). *Property and community.* New York, NY: Oxford University Press.

———. (2012). *An introduction to property theory.* New York, NY: Cambridge University Press.

Andrèe, P. (2007). *Genetically modified diplomacy: The global politics of agricultural biotechnology.* Vancouver, BC: UBC Press.

Banner, S. (2011). *American property: A history of how, why, and what we own.* Cambridge, MA: Harvard University Press.

Bernstein, P. L. (1998). *Against the gods: The remarkable story of risk.* New York, NY: Wiley.

Bovaird, T., & Loffler, E. (2003). Evaluating the quality of public governance: Indicators, models, and methodologies. *International Review of Administrative Sciences, 69,* 313–328.

Broderick, J. J., & Kuschel, K. G. (2016). Sharing economy: Developments in collaborative workspaces. www.natlawreview.com/article/ sharing-economy-developments-collaborative-workspaces.

Crowley, M. (2016). Trump's overseas properties spark security fears. www.politico.com/story/2016/11/trump-overseas-security-231948.

Hardin, G. (1968). The tragedy of the commons. *Science* 162: 1243–48.

Koepsell, D. (2015). *Who owns you?: Science, innovation, and the gene patent wars.* 2nd ed. West Sussex, UK: Wiley-Blackwell.

Lessig, L. (2006). *Code: And other laws of cyberspace, version 2.0.* New York, NY: Basic Books.

Locke, J. (2003). *Two treatises of government and A letter concerning toleration.* New Haven, CT: Yale University Press.

Moore, A. D. (2001). *Intellectual property and information control: Philosophic foundations and contemporary issues.* New Brunswick, NJ: Transaction Publishers.

Nozick, R. (1974). *Anarchy, state, and utopia.* New York, NY: Basic Books.

Nussbaum, M. C. (2000). *Women and human development.* New York, NY: Cambridge University Press.

———. (2007). *Frontiers of justice: Disability, nationality, and species membership.* Cambridge, MA: Harvard University Press.

———. (2011). *Creating capabilities: The human development approach.* Cambridge, MA: Belknap Press.

Poovey, M. (2008). *Genres of the credit economy: Mediating value in eighteenth- and nineteenth-century Britain.* Chicago, IL: University of Chicago Press.

Rawls, J. (1971). *A theory of justice.* Cambridge, MA: Harvard University Press.

Sen, A. K. (1999). *Development as freedom.* New York, NY: Alfred A. Knopf.

———. (2009). *The idea of justice.* Cambridge, MA: Harvard University Press.

# SECTION ONE HISTORICAL ROOTS OF PROPERTY RIGHTS

The first section of this volume relies on historical accounts of property debates, discussions, and disputes as foundations for some of the same problems and concerns we see in contemporary governance spaces related to property. Corporations in the United States, for example, have the same rights as people when it comes to free speech thanks to the U.S. Supreme Court's *Citizens United* decision in 2010. Commons problems still manifest related to animals, land, and even other forms of property. For example, after hurricanes hit, debris usually falls everywhere. People get into disputes about whose tree fell where and onto what part of the property. The historical cases and examples presented in this section of the book shed light on the truism: history often repeats itself.

## HISTORICAL PROPERTY DEVELOPMENTS

As the title of the book indicates, the connections between the chapters are issues of governance at their cores. Above, we defined governance as idealized spaces for shared decision making as borrowed from the public administration literature. Within that discipline, governance in theory and practice is seen as almost an antidote to prescriptions for "running government like a business." Business-minded reforms changed the values of government agencies (Box, 2001), so governance is an attempt, at least linguistically, to move away from what some see as a redefinition of public values. In the 1990s, for example, governments around the world turned toward New Public Management (NPM), which focused on efficiencies and the infamous "doing more with less," with distinct and measurable outputs rather than outcomes (Hood, 1995). Managers relied upon corporations and private enterprises for guidance, which shifted attention from commons problems such as, for example, education provision to checking boxes for service delivery without measuring outcomes. This is what Box (2001) meant by changing the values of governing, leaving out the people behind the numbers.

Governance ideally requires a new way of thinking and operating, especially horizontally rather than vertically, as shown in the chapters in this section with necessary collaborations—or failures therefrom. Johnston (2010) argues for a governance infrastructure, "the collection of technologies and systems, people, policies, practices, and relationships that interact to support governing activities" (p. s122). Property relates directly to Johnston's dimensions of working within, across, and between boundaries that are every day becoming more permeable. For example, his "between dimension" (p. s123) includes natural resources, transportation, and land-use policies as examples of activities that naturally cross any formal boundaries. The Dakota Access Pipeline standoff in the United States, for example, centered upon a battle for natural resources, land, clean water, and even sovereignty. This is inherently a property issue and a governance one as well, given the many actors involved on both sides of the dispute, which eventually saw a positive resolution for the protestors trying to save their land and drinking water, and prevent the runoff of pollutants from the pipeline downstream. "As governance infrastructures allow for more direct and informed involvement in some government activities, power is returned to the people such that values are articulated through their actions rather than by a one-off vote of stated preferences" (ibid., p. s124).

Even with governance, traditional governing skills remain necessary: communication, collaboration, leadership, negotiation, facilitation, citizen participation, etc. (Bingham, Nabatchi, & O'Leary, 2005). Although spaces are opened for collaboration, citizens still might not want to participate (Box, 2001). We see this especially at the local government level when it comes to ideas of property. People often turn out to participate only when a government decision directly impacts them. NIMBY (Not In My Backyard) issues related to property or a perceived encroachment on it often increase citizen participation in government processes. As one practitioner notes, though, NIMBY "input adds little objective value to the substantive discussion" (Walker, 2014, p. 629). Often these issues are technical and cross boundaries, and stakeholders frequently do not have the technical expertise to contribute meaningfully to assessing the risk involved with the development projects (Eckerd, 2014). In his study, Eckerd even found that government officials and the public often framed environmental issues differently—were speaking different languages. Public comments tended to focus on human risk at the local level related to development projects, while government officials put attention on the natural environment. The focus is micro versus macro and is familiar to property and commons disputes nationally and internationally.

Again, we do not want readers to think this section is exhaustive. Law classes on property last an entire semester and schooling in the subject lasts years for a reason. Instead, we offer a short history of property changes largely from a U.S. perspective. Authors included in this section of the book borrow on international examples to broaden that perspective. Field (1989) articulates that property often is seen as a dichotomy: individual versus collective. For Field, these categories often prove too inflexible given the myriad elements involved in property rights. When does something stop being "yours" alone and the community's?

In a perfect world, Field contends, the resources available would equal the community needs, but this is not always the case. He frames this exclusivity problem, then, as a governance decision between two alternative stakeholders: those using the resource in a commons and those excluded from using the commons resources. Each property relationship has a transaction cost (Coase, 1960) for the involved parties, especially monetary costs and even social costs. We can think about gated communities meant to purposefully exclude certain rent seekers. Governance interventions in terms of policies can help or inhibit commons problems. Essentially, property rights have evolved, and continue to evolve, between these two poles with no one (individual or collective) becoming dominant.

Let us take, for example, the lobster fishing industry to give an example of this historical evolution. McMullan and Perrier (2002) take as their case Canadian laws put in place to prevent lobster poaching. As they detail, when the industry began to take off in Canada there were few formal regulations in place and instead "community customs structured the rights of access, management, and stock protection" (p. 684). To Field's (1989) point about inclusivity and exclusivity, not everyone was allowed to fish for lobsters (exclusivity) but those who did followed the unspoken rules to maintain the commons. With the rise of technology, Canadian government officials inserted themselves more directly into the industry, becoming the sole regulators and taking away community control (McMullan & Perrier, 2002). An unintended consequence of the policies was reduced fisher incomes, making them more reliant on government programs rather than their own businesses. "By creating a system of selective licensing and establishing a *privilege* to fish, the right to the commons was transformed into the private property of the fisher, albeit a highly restricted right to access and harvest the resources" (ibid., p. 686; emphasis in original).

As can be seen in the chapters in this section, we can learn from the past. The evolution of property rights and responsibilities follows this individual versus collective pattern that still remains today. The more things change, the more they stay the same.

## REFERENCES

Bingham, L. B., Nabatchi, T., & O'Leary, R. (2005). The new governance: Practices and processes for stakeholder and citizen participation in the work of Government. *Public Administration Review*, 65(5), 547–558.

Coase, R. H. (1960). The problem of social cost. *The Journal of Law and Economics* 3, 1–44.

Eckerd, A. (2014). Risk management and risk avoidance in agency decision making. *Public Administration Review*, 74(5), 616–629.

Field, B. C. (1989). The evolution of property rights. *Kyklos*, 42(3), 319–345.

Hood, C. (1995). The "new public management" in the 1980s: Variations on a theme. *Accounting, Organizations & Society*, 20(2/3), 93–109.

Johnston, E. (2010). Governance infrastructures in 2020. *Public Administration Review*, 70(1), 122–128.

McMullan, J. T., & Perrier, D. C. (2002). Lobster poaching and the ironies of law enforcement. *Law & Society Review*, 36(4), 679–718.

Walker, M. J. (2014). "Worth the effort? NIMBY public comments add little value. *Public Administration Review*, 74(5), 629.

# 1 Is There a History of Property?

## Periodization of Property Regimes and Paradigms

ANN E. DAVIS

## PROPERTY AS INDICATOR OF STAGES OF CIVILIZATION

Property has been a founding concept in various forms of government for centuries. Forms of property have been considered as an accurate indicator of levels of development or stages of civilization (Barkan, 2013; Cheney, 2010; Hont, 1990; Jameson, 1998; Pocock, 1983; Smith, 1994). Hints at the ambiguity in the definition of protection of property are present, nonetheless, even in the work of leading scholars (Acemoglu, Johnson, & Robinson, 2005). In the context of the French Revolution, for example, protection of property was a means to enforce the political clout of the emerging bourgeoisie against the monarch and the nobility (Cheney, 2010).

In developing a historical institutional approach to property, the question addressed below is whether the various forms of property are a resource for periodization. Given its persistence and apparent constancy, is the variation in property forms important for delineating different eras of political economy? For example, was land the prototypical form of property in the feudal period, whereas labor was more salient with the development of market economies? Is there a tendency toward increasing levels of abstraction over time, from tangible to intangible forms? Is intellectual property a more advanced form? This chapter will use the concept of the corporation as a form of property to trace the evolution of property forms, from the medieval to the modern period.

While referring to the rhetorical role of land as the image of property, Underkuffler notes that property plays the role of bulwark for the individual against the collective, providing a *"sphere of individual autonomy and control"* (Underkuffler, 2003, pp. 40–41; emphasis in original) in the modern liberal state. Yet whatever the concrete and material properties that the metaphor of land conveys, "property is, under *any* conception, quintessentially and absolutely a social institution" (ibid., p. 54; emphasis in original). The particular definition of property in any period also structures social relationships (Singer, 2000). In this sense, the concept of absolute individual private property would be particularly appropriate in the modern liberal state, where the individual is the fundamental unit of analysis (Davis, 2011; England, 1993; McKeon, 2005). In this sense, the various forms of property can reflect the norms and culture of a given period, as well as personality and the form of the state (Brewer & Staves, 1996).

## DEFINITION OF ABSTRACTION

Before addressing the periodization of property using the corporate form, there is an important definition of the methodological approach proposed for this exploration. First, when using the term *property* in reference to nonmaterial aspects, such as intellectual property or financial assets, reification is required, or the treatment of a relationship or a privilege as a thing (Brewer and Staves 1996; Jameson 1998). Further, the term *abstraction* is used to refer not to generalizations and definitions of categories but to a social process (Davis, 2017; Moore, 2015; Marx, 1967, I, 71–83; Poovey, 2007; Sewell, 2014). The social process of abstraction operates to make a designated object amenable to the commodity form, whether land, labor, or capital. The process of abstraction operates on the form and shape of the object itself as well as the knowledge and linguistic reference to it. That is, to make land into a commodity, certain historical processes were required (Marglin, 2008; McKeon, 2005; Van Bavel, 2010), such as renunciation of feudal rights, the marking of boundaries, and the enforcement of legal contracts. Further, the development of a labor market is described (Bellofiore, 2004; Polanyi, 1944) as both a legal and social process. The term *abstract labor* requires the separation of work from the home, the necessity of wage labor for subsistence, and the discipline of the factory (Clegg, 2015; Maifreda, 2012). The development of a capital market also required certain prior conditions (Sylla, 2009). Ultimately, the formation and extension of the market required the conception of the market as a system (Poovey, 1998), as well as the reduction of transaction costs by establishing infrastructures to support commerce, such as roads and canals (Smith, 1994).

The market "system" is itself one such reifying abstraction (Poovey, 2002), to which reference is made as if it had a separate, self-regulating material existence. At the same time, market processes, although social, also have implications for material production and organization of ecologies, as well as scientific paradigms. The view from nowhere of objective science sees nature as separate from humankind and as an object for study and potential transformation (Latour, 2013; Moore, 2015). The market system itself may provide such a distant view of nature from on high (Maifreda, 2012). According to a social theory of value proposed by Davanzati, a late-sixteenth- century Florentine merchant and translator of Tacitus,

Economic knowledge should place itself, like a panoptical eye, in the sky, or gaze from some "very high peak". It would require an immense concave mirror on which to register its markets, thanks to which it would bring forth the truth of value with immediate and undeniable self-evidence. (Maifreda, 2012, p. 94)

In Davanzati's "grandiose metaphor ... [his] Platonic inspiration is evident," where "reciprocal conditioning of two worlds ... become mirrors of each other" (Maifreda, 2012, p. 94). In this period in the Florentine Renaissance, the art of representation was appreciated, in painting and sculpture, as well as in money and objects, as well as political process (Najemy, 1982).

Often these preconditions were legal, while others were social, such as an acceptance of the operation of the market, which was beyond personal control, subject to "fortuna" (Pocock, 1975). The limits of the market were constituted by competing territorial states, as well as customs and values that were contrary to the market, such as the prohibition on usury (Sandel, 2012).

## THE "CORPORATION" AS PROPERTY

One particular long-standing form of property is the corporation. The conception of the corporation in the early modern period was a Leviathan, and it was visualized as a monster in the early-nineteenth- century United States (Barkan, 2013). Adam Smith was famously critical of joint stock companies for managing "other people's money ... [and are likely to do] more harm than good" (Smith 1994, 800). Marx echoes Smith's criticism of "other people's capital" and sees the joint stock company as a form of the "social means of production [which] appear[s] as private property" (Marx, 1967, III, pp. 436–441).

Institutional economists find the corporation to be a persistent organizational form from the medieval to the contemporary period (Greif, 2006), defined as a voluntary association with consistent rules for membership and decision making, which persists beyond the life of any individual member. For Searle, the unique aspect of the corporation is the type of property, which does not have a material referent (Searle, 2010). This type of property is created by a form of linguistic statement called a status function declaration. These statements commit the speaker and specific individuals to concrete actions, as part of the meaning of the statements (Searle, 2010). These actions are extralinguistic but are considered part of the meaning of the linguistic utterance and are enacted in the associated institutions (Najemy, 1982). Actions such as the creation of a corporation involve specific authorities whose designation can be described as part of a given institutional setting or background (Searle, 2010). That is, language constitutes this form of property, where a group of people is allowed by law to form a single entity that has certain powers and privileges. There are formal membership criteria, and decision-making processes, which allow the group to be represented by a single individual or symbol. The status function declaration both describes and prescribes certain behaviors and roles that call the corporation into existence. The corporate charter is like a social contract, similar to all language statements, which involve commitment to the truth of these statements by the speaker (Searle, 2010, pp. 62, 165). Because these enactments are contingent and in the moment, a representation of the corporation is necessary in written documents. These language statements or other symbolic representations permit the corporation to continue in existence in perpetuity, beyond the lives of the specific individuals who perform these roles and functions in a particular moment. Where Searle emphasizes representation in formal language statements, Poovey (1998) stresses the role of numbers in providing credibility and support, and special types of writing such as double-entry bookkeeping. Visual representations by means of cartography as well as paintings and woodcuts are important for cultural transmission and familiarity for such concepts as the republic and commerce (Hale, 1994).

The centrality of language statements to all social institutions, in Searle's analysis, offers a useful method for historical institutionalism. With common use, the definition of a term conveys its meaning, along with the obligation to use the term consistently, or risk social opprobrium. In this sense, power is bottom-up and is reinforced by the requirements of meaningful communication and social norms (Searle, 2010). For the theorist, the specific terminology, *corporation* in this case, can provide a template for tracing its shift in meaning historically, along with the associated institutional forms in each period. For example, the corporation was at one time the church and represented the body of Christ, the "*corpus mysticum*" (Barkan, 2013), but in contemporary usage it is a private business corporation. This historical approach is complementary with legal institutionalism (Deakin et al., forthcoming; Hodgson, 2015), which stresses the role of law, itself a specific form of language statement with institutional interpretive and enforcement mechanisms that evolve historically. The use of the same term *corporation* over time may aid in habituation and legitimation, conferring a type of customary authority, in spite of the gradual shifts in meaning.

## CORPORATION AS BOTH COLLECTIVE AND INDIVIDUAL

Corporations are flexible, responsive to individual and small group initiatives. Corporate charters are a form of privilege, meaning private law, which are a form of exceptional recognition by a public authority (Barkan, 2013). Even without royal charters, the early medieval communes were formed for mutual defense by swearing an oath to the other members (Wickham, 2015). The privilege of the corporation provides a vehicle of capital accumulation, a function even Smith understood (Smith, 1994). The perpetual existence of the corporation as a separate entity and the protection of its assets from claims of creditors (Dari-Mattiacci, Gelderblom, Jonker, & Perotti, 2013), facilitates accumulation of capital in financial resources, if not also in physical plant, technological capacity, and innovation (Perez, 2002). The strength of protection of the outside investor is a common criterion for the protection of property rights in the legal origins literature and is considered a significant characteristic of financial institutions (Guinnane, Harris, Lamoreaux, & Rosenthal, 2007).

The corporation is consistent with liberal governmentality, which focuses on the representative individual with specific predictable needs and desires (Poovey, 1998). The corporation is a permissible collective that is treated as an individual in the context of the liberal state. This corporate individual acts in a manner consistent with the rational economic man, which seeks to maximize profit in a competitive context, and whose survival is determined by meeting the bottom line in every time period. The context of the liberal state grants the corporation specific rights and privileges not available to single human persons. The corporation is disciplined by financial flows and is also empowered by access to credit. The private business corporation is a strategic agent in a modern industrial economy, while also serving as a form of individual private property.

## LONG-TERM HISTORY OF CORPORATION

Although the corporate form has existed for centuries in a wide variety of settings (Greif, 2006; Hodgson, 2015a), it is possible to identify key turning points. After the decline of the Roman Empire, the commune and the church were types of local corporations, with governance rather than commercial function. The guild was part governance and part provision for subsistence, whose members were free (Smith, 1994, III, pp. 426–438), while long-distance trade was conducted by a separate organization of merchants. Merchant organizations began with partnerships and later developed into groups of merchants representing a certain city-state in foreign ports, the merchant nation (Trivellato, 2009). The formation of merchant monopoly corporations designated by the crown was also a matter of political controversy (Acemoglu et al., 2005). The North American colonies were governed by merchant corporations until the American Revolution. The corporation continued to evolve in the United States, from public municipal corporations to private business corporations. The private business corporation expanded in scale with waves of merger movements, and development of new technologies for production and new products. The development of information technology enabled global systems of production, and was itself the first product to be produced in this manner (Grunwald & Flamm, 1985). Opening national borders to capital flows after the 1980s enabled a wider reach and increased capacity of the corporate form, with global supply chains that were more flexible and porous than prior iterations (Gereffi, 2014; Milberg & Winkler, 2013).

The corporate form was the foundation for the first public debt (Stasavage, 2003). The first experiments with public debt were in communes and city-states in early modern Italy (Gelderbom & Jonker, 2004). In Italy and the Low Countries, there was considerable experience with debt instruments from the early sixteenth century (Gelderblom & Jonker, 2004). The formation of the Dutch East India Company in 1602 (VOC) was required to raise capital for longer voyages, permanent outposts, and military armaments, as well as to consolidate competing shipping companies. The VOC became permanent in 1612 and was authorized to use military power, with the Estates General retaining a role in its decision making (Gelderblom, De Jong, & Jonker, 2013). With limited liability and transferable shares, the VOC stocks gave rise to a secondary market in Amsterdam in the early decades of the seventeenth century (Gelderblom & Jonker, 2004). VOC stocks and public debt IOUs were traded on the same exchanges, which improved liquidity for both types of financial assets. The declining interest rates and increasing capital raised attracted imitators in the English financial markets. The combination of capital commitment and liquid secondary markets provided a vehicle for accumulating savings from a wider variety of households (Dari-Mattiacci, Gelderblom, Jonker, & Perotti, 2013). The corporation was differentiated from the state, although clearly under its auspices, in seventeenth-century Dutch and English forms, and later became protected from the state as private property, in the United States in the early nineteenth century (Wright, 2014).

The establishment of a secure public financial system in the late-eighteenth-century United States under Hamilton's leadership, along with the chartering of increasing numbers of corporations, led to the development of the U.S. financial markets (Sylla, 2002, 2009). The growth of securities markets in Boston, New York, and Philadelphia, which traded both public and private financial assets, mobilized savings to finance increasing levels of investment (Rousseau & Sylla, 2005). The rise of the securities markets, in turn, provided the opportunity to promote shareholder democracy and to extend ownership of financial assets to the general public. The increase in ownership of corporate stocks, in turn, provided the greater legitimacy of financial markets, especially in political debates in the late nineteenth century (Ott, 2011). With general incorporation laws in the early nineteenth century, the corporation became a "legal embodiment of capital separate from the state and the stockholders" (Barkan, 2013, p. 57).

The existence of property in financial assets, protected from the state and by the state, and permitted to accumulate in perpetuity, helped provide the foundation for the public sphere. Beginning in coffee shops patronized by stock traders in London, the relevance of information and its provision by the press created the space for deliberation and debate for the abstract bourgeois individual. This civil sphere for the critical public provided scrutiny and facilitated legitimacy for the state, now differentiated from the private sphere, via the press and voluntary associations (Habermas, 1991; McKeon, 2005; Sewell, 2014).

## CORPORATE GOVERNANCE

As a key institution in industrial capitalism, corporate governancehas been the focus of considerable comparative study. The history of a particular country can help trace the customary style of corporate governance (Harris, 2010) and in turn affects the direction and dynamism of the economy (Lazonick & O'Sullivan, 2002), like Searle's systematic fallouts (Searle, 2010). Because of these different institutional settings, there are a variety of capitalisms (Hodgson, 2016) and varieties of financial/nonfinancial institutional relationships.

### Corporation as Part of Financial Circuit (Circular Flow)

The financial circuit is constituted by financial flows among these specialized institutions, such as the corporation, households, and the state. Historically, the distinction between personal and business financial circuits was inscribed in the practice of double-entry accounting (Goldthwaite, 2015; Maifreda, 2012; Padgett, 2012; Poovey, 1998). The business firm was originally a family partnership, with no distinction between personal and business accounts (Trivellato, 2009). As the business firm expanded to include other members from the same city-state, and eventually became an impersonal corporation, with abstract bureaucratic processes (North, Wallis, & Weingast, 2009), the accounting distinctions between personal and firm became more strictly enforced. Ultimately, the merging of personal and business accounts became a form of corruption. At the same time, financial institutions gradually became impersonal, rather than familial (Pak, 2013), and women were no longer considered property of their fathers and husbands (Brewer & Staves, 1996).

There is a dialectical institutional development: the first corporations in the medieval period were communes, formed for self-defense. The early modern city-states were corporations, which enabled the formal public commitment for public debt, or bonds. With secure public debt, financial institutions and capital markets developed, then allowing the creation of a business corporation, a capital-raising institution. With capital markets and corporations, the investment function became a strategic driver of economic development. Such a dynamic has led some scholars to suggest a finance-led theory of growth (Rousseau & Sylla, 2005). Examples of the synergy include the early merchant corporations, VOC and the EIC, and the rise of the capital markets (Murphy, 2014), as well as the railroads in the United States and the growth of the investment banker (Carosso, 1987). Financiers then play a key role in the turn of the century merger wave in the United States and the formation of the first large industrial enterprises (Chandler, 1977). The visible hand may apply to the banker as well as to the manager. "The turn-of-the-century merger movement in effect created a market in industrial securities, particularly for the issues of dominant corporations that were listed on, and hence endorsed by, the New York Stock Exchange" (Lazonick, 1991, p. 30).

Then, business corporations divide again into production and finance. The Medici bank did both production for the market, as well as trade and finance, for example, but later institutions specialized and then divided by types of market segments even within finance.

## Corporation as Agent of Abstraction and Integration

The corporation is an intermediate organization between the individual and the state, and so is an exception for the liberal state. This exception is rationalized by the treatment of the corporation as an individual person with rights of political representation and speech. Although a single entity, the corporation has many aspects. The corporation is an agent with rights to certain actions in certain contexts. The corporation is both a creator of markets and an integrator of markets (Lazonick, 1991). For example, the corporation is a privileged agent in capital and labor markets, as well as intellectual property, production, and trade. The role of the corporation in labor markets has been characterized as a form of public power, yet the corporation itself is considered as private (Commons, 1995). The corporation operates in many separate markets, yet provides for integration within its treatment as a separate entity in legal terms.

## Corporation as Economic Agent

In most economic models, the strategic agent is the firm or corporation. That is, the corporation has access to its own retained earnings and to credit. This capacity to borrow enables the firm to innovate and to expand, and is typically considered the source of growth by means of its investment function, for entrepreneurs to develop new products (Schumpeter, 1983). Unlike the model of the perfectly competitive firm, the corporation can choose prices and products, in contrast to Sen's blind follower of price signals (Sen, 1977). The mechanism of competition spurs increasing productivity and the associated treadmill (Postone, 1993) of continuing innovation. For Schumpeter (1983), the capital market exists to finance entrepreneurship, and so is the "headquarters of the capitalist system" (p. 126). Keynes was critical of the capacity of investors to make rational decisions on the financial markets, or casinos, and reasoned that the state had a broader perspective and more concern with the public interest (Keynes, 1964). The capacity for rentiers to absorb the surplus and reduce the rate of growth has been noted historically (Adams, 2005) and in the current period (Sawyer & Passarella, 2015). In fact the term *financialization* has been given to the recent period (Epstein, 2005, 2013; Lapavitsas, 2014), when the primary goal is to expand money, represented as M – M' in financial circuit literature, rather than invest in production and innovation.

## Corporate Evolution as Political

The strategic actions of the corporation are political, in the sense of affecting the foundation of the state, and affected by the form of the state, in turn. The major transitions in corporate form have been the subject of political controversy historically. For example, the guild community was able to discipline the warrior magnate class, and helped to form the first guild republic in thirteenth- and fourteenth-century Florence (Najemy, 1982, 2006). Further, the formation of the business partnership system in 1382 in Florence was a response to the rebellion of the woolworkers, the Ciompi Rebellion of 1378 (Padgett, 2012). The increasing political power of merchants had an important impact on the formation of the modern liberal state (Acemoglu, Johnson, & Robinson, 2005). The modern liberal state was itself an evolution of the corporate form, from the Third Estate in the French Revolution, based on the system of corporate representation in the French Parliament. Learning from the evolving model from the Italian city-states, the Dutch republic, and the king in parliament model in England after 1688, the liberal state spread throughout Europe, especially after the revolutions of 1848. The liberal model consisted of a unified tax system, parliamentary veto, and stable annual budget processes (Dincecco, 2009). These fiscal procedures improved the tax capacity of the state, and the ability to make war, to provide public goods, and to support commerce. In the successive leading merchant-based city-states, a form of economic citizenship emerged, by which the duty of the citizen to pay taxes was rewarded with the provision of public goods. These public goods in turn improved commerce for the benefit of both the citizen and the state (Van Zanden & Prak, 2006). This liberal nation-state model mirrored the corporate form, with its impersonal rules of membership, regular decision-making procedures, and representation of a single whole composed of many individuals (Davis, 2015). "The State is itself a kind of corporate entity" (Turner, 2014, 169).

### Corporation as Agent of the State

The reorganization of state finance was necessary with the increasing cost of war (Schumpeter, 1991). The corporation also served the state by improving commerce and expanding production, a form of power among competing nation-states in a commercial period (Hont, 1990). Commerce itself became part of the "reason of state" (Hont, 1990, p. 45) and merchant monopoly corporations were part of the competitive arsenal (Harris, 2010). Corporate privileges also challenged the state (Barkan, 2013).

## CORPORATION AND REIFICATION

### Importance of "Representation"

Searle stresses the importance of representation for the durability and recognition of institutions. A status function declaration must be capable of being represented in documents or symbols, but there are important double meanings of the term *representation*. On the one hand, representation can refer to political and legal processes by which governance institutions can articulate the needs and interests of their constituents. On the other hand, representation is a linguistic term, referring to the correspondence between words and things. Metaphors such as the "body" and "land" provide a semblance of materiality for such mental concepts as corporation and property (Underkuffler, 2003, pp. 16–17). There can be a problematic of representation, nonetheless, by which the assumed correspondence can be challenged and questioned (Poovey, 2008). This *double entendre* of the term *representation* has special resonance in the history of money and credit, institutional forms that were first developed by communes and city-states. The legitimate political processes by which early modern states were capable of decision making provided the credibility by which such institutions were able to issue debt (Stasavage, 2015). That is, political representation in parliaments facilitated the issue of debt, a symbolic form of representing the solemn commitment of the entire community, a bond.

The corporation itself is characterized by dualities and divisions; it is at once public and private, financial and real, personal and impersonal, as well as abstract and concrete. These diverse aspects are relatively invisible due to its specific representation in each context. On the other hand, the unity of the corporation, as a single body, facilitates the integration of each aspect, primarily in the context of the financial circuit. The corporation can integrate across space and time as a single privileged agent.

Functions of Reification

In such situations, the process of reification can be important. If the word is taken as the thing itself, such as the term *property* standing for the object, such as land, then the questioning of this representation is less likely. As the word *becomes* the thing, in normal parlance, its meaning becomes etched in an enhanced institutional reality that exists in everyone's mind as shared background (Searle, 2010). No one questions the existence of money with a U.S. dollar bill in hand, with its authoritative text, symbols, and signatures, as well as its purchasing power. Yet money, even U.S. dollars, is like a modern metaphysical being with preternatural powers, which is presumed to exist, and so guides daily behavior in the moment. All contingency based on human institutions becomes irrelevant to the reality of the financial instrument. A currency with global recognition, favorable terms of trade, strict enforcement, and demonstrable purchasing power becomes a hard currency, as if it were actually made of precious metal. There is a hierarchy of currencies, reflecting the degree of confidence in the nation that is represented, as well as its economic, political, and military power. The nation with a credible currency can then issue debt in its own currency, and achieve access to credit more easily (Eichengreen, 2011; Terzi, 2006).

Perpetuity

With the existence of perpetual institutions, such as the corporation and the state, there can be an infinite money market that is constructed on that institutional scaffolding. The money market, or finance, stretches into the future with no limit, its existence a daily reality. Governments can issue perpetual bonds and so raise money in the present. Corporations with perpetual lives can issue stock and become a vehicle for entrepreneurship, investment, and accumulation. Money is a symbol of the infinite state and the perpetual corporation. The corporation and the state cooperate in the management of the financial circuit, which maintains flows of real goods and labor, production and consumption. The central bank manages the value of the purchasing power of money in the present and future. "Interest is a premium on present over future purchasing power ... regarded as a means of control over production goods" (Schumpeter, 1983, p. 157), which embody innovation permitting increasing productivity of labor.

This tripartite system, consisting of private business corporations, central banks, and the state, originates and manages financial assets, and allocates investment, by means of the financial markets. The direction of the economy is the outcome of the competition for surplus between corporations and the state, while they also collaborate in maintaining the stability and integrity of the financial system. The state, a corporate form defined by territory, becomes mobile by means of its private business corporations, which organize investment and reap surplus on a global scale. Together these interlocking corporate forms manage space and time.

This representation of money enables the *trading in time,* such as saving now for the future, and taking future returns and calculating present discounted value in the moment. With the deregulation of finance in the United States beginning in the 1980s, after the end of Bretton Woods, the trading of financial assets expanded to arbitrage the differences in present value, with the financial assets taken as valuable in themselves (Poovey, 2008). The function of intertemporal intermediation, whereby banks acquire short-term liabilities and manage long-term assets, resolves increasingly to reliance on short-term arbitrage, and the rise of the counterparty to manage risk in the present. Further, high frequency trading developed with advancing information technology, which allowed trading in the instant on differences in expected present discounted value among alternative financial assets. Finally, the reification of money cements its claim to the first share of the surplus, in the settlement of debt contracts and bankruptcies.

## Modernity

In this context, the definition of modernity is the foundation based on this tripartite system of power, involving the corporation, the state, and the central bank. This interlocking complex of institutions issues currencies and debt, and uses and manages the financial markets in a complementary fashion. This modern institutional complex contrasts with the medieval constellation of town, guild, and church. This medieval complex is evident in the European architecture of every urban center. In the medieval context, the foundation was land and its management, along with production and distribution of the surplus.

In the modern complex, the foundation is finance, a fluid, fictional entity, liquid, subject to flows, which are more contingent and more challenging to manage. The corporate form of the guild was repurposed to operate in a new commercial context, with the emergence of long-distance trade, and provided a transitional institutional mechanism or homology (Padgett & Powell, 2012). In this context, reification of money and property served the purpose of promoting the image of permanence, in spite of the ubiquity of an intangible medium of money and credit based on public confidence and belief. In this context, orthodoxies become important (Poovey, 2008), and such mantras as "there is no alternative." The modern individual is abstract (Davis, 2011), along with property. The individual's right to his own property, emphasized by Locke and Smith, becomes compromised with the separation of the individual from his property with the introduction of money and the division of labor. Property and its increase, nonetheless, remain the rationale of the system (the wealth of nations) over abstract space and continuous time.

The status and character of the individual are nonetheless reflected in their own property, a mirroring relationship. This reflection is especially important with the separation of ownership of the worker and their product, a form of reintegration in the private sphere, for the purposes of display in the public sphere, via an equalizing conspicuous consumption (Sewell, 2014).

## A SYSTEM OF LINKED INSTITUTIONS: CAPITALISM

There is a growing literature on the history of capitalism. It is important to define capitalism to establish it as a set of institutions that has a history, and to distinguish from the view that capitalism is merely human nature. A definition is required to specify its historical emergence (Clegg, 2015). In this context, the definition of capitalism is a system of modern institutions, whose goal is to expand money. These criteria include the dependence on market, the agency of corporation in the entrepreneurial role, and the goal of expansion of value, M – M.' Credit is a key institution, a capability that is a function of the operation of the entire system, which can enable innovation and growth, and debt can serve a disciplinary function within the context of competition.

### Method of Historical Institutionalism

Based on the institutions of the corporation, the state, and money, the definition of capitalism is possible. The money market, whose goal is to expand, is a dominant institution of capitalism, composed of the competing agents of corporations and states, cooperating to complete financial circuits on a global scale. The purpose of continual expansion can represent the ultimate value, but value itself becomes divided into intrinsic, nonmarket virtues and market-oriented commercial transactions, reinforced by the disciplinary separation of art and literature versus market information and investment strategies (Poovey, 2008). That is, the infinite expansion of money for its own sake can become purposeless and tautological, the very absence of value and meaning.

Further, the era of modernity can be defined as the society with a perpetual financial market, a society that is capable of organizing its own time. Such a perpetual financial market empowers the state to borrow, tax, and spend, and allows individuals to have social power and mobility, women to have freedom of action beyond the need for assured inheritance, competition among workers for employment and among firms for revenue and profit, access to resources defined as parcels of the planet Earth, and competition among countries for access to the sovereign debt market. The social construction of money organizes lives, nations, and worlds in this period of history. Yet money organizes modern society in a distinctive way, with its ubiquity, reification, and conventional acceptance preventing even the envisioning of alternatives.

REFERENCES

Acemoglu, D., Johnson, S., & Robinson, J. (2005). The rise of Europe: Atlantic trade, institutional change, and economic growth. *The American Economic Review, 95(3)*, 546–579.

Adams, J. P. (2005). *The familial state: Ruling families and merchant capitalism in early modern Europe.* Ithaca, NY: Cornell University Press.

Banner, S. (1998). *Anglo-American securities regulation: Cultural and political roots, 1690–1860.* New York, NY: Cambridge University Press.

———. (2000). *Legal systems in conflict: Property and sovereignty in Missouri, 1750–1860.* Norman, OK: University of Oklahoma Press.

———. (2005). *How the Indians lost their land: Law and power on the frontier.* Cambridge, MA: Harvard University Press.

———. (2007). *Possessing the Pacific: Land, settlers, and indigenous people from Australia to Alaska.* Cambridge, MA: Harvard University Press.

———. (2011). *American property: A history of how, why, and what we own.* Cambridge, MA: Harvard University Press.

Barkan, J. (2013). *Corporate sovereignty: Law and government under capitalism.* Minneapolis, MN: University of Minnesota Press.

Bellofiore, R. (2004). "As if its body were by love possessed:" Abstract labour and the monetary circuit: A macro-social reading of Marx's labour theory of value. In

R. Arena and N. Salvadori (Eds.), *Money, credit, and the role of the state: Essays in honour of Augusto Graziani* (pp. 89–114). Burlington, VT: Ashgate.

Brewer, J., & Staves, S. (1996). Introduction. In *Early modern conceptions of property* (pp. 1–18). New York, NY: Routledge.

———. (1996). *Early modern conceptions of property*. New York, NY: Routledge.

Carosso, V. P. (1987). *The Morgans: Private international bankers 1854–1913*. Cambridge, MA: Harvard University Press.

Chandler, A. D. (1977). *The visible hand: The managerial revolution in American business*. Cambridge, MA: Harvard University Press.

Cheney, P. (2010). *Revolutionary commerce: Globalization and the French monarchy*. Cambridge, MA: Harvard University Press.

Clegg, J. J. (2015). Capitalism and slavery. *Critical Historical Studies, 2(2)*, 281–304.

Commons, J. R. (1995). *The legal foundations of capitalism*. New Brunswick, NJ: Transaction.

Cott, N. (2000). *Public vows: A history of marriage and the nation*. Cambridge, MA: Harvard University Press.

Davis, A. E. (2015). *The evolution of the property relation: Understanding paradigms, debates, prospects*. New York, NY: Palgrave MacMillan.

Davis, J. B. (2011). *Individuals and identity in economics*. New York, NY: Cambridge University Press.

Dari-Mattiacci, G., Gelderblom, O., Jonker, J., & Perotti, E. (2013). The emergence of the corporate "form." Amsterdam Law School Legal Studies Research Paper No. 2013-11; Amsterdam Center for law & Economics Working Paper No. 2013-02. University of Amsterdam.

Deakin, S., et al. (Forthcoming). Legal institutionalism: Capitalism and the constitute role of law." *Journal of Comparative Economics*.

Dincecco, M. (2009). Fiscal centralization, limited government, and public revenues in Europe, 1650–1913. *The Journal of Economic History, 69(1)*, 48–103.

Eichengreen, B. (2011). *Exorbitant privilege: The rise and fall of the dollar and the future of the international monetary system*. New York, NY: Oxford University Press.

England, P. (1993). The separative self: Androcentric bias in neoclassical assumptions. In M. A. Ferber and J. A. Nelson (Eds.), *Beyond Economic Man: Feminist Theory and Economics* (pp. 37–53). Chicago, IL: University of Chicago Press.

Epstein, G. A. (2005). *Financialization and the world economy*. Cheltenham, UK: Edward Elgar.

——. (2013). *The handbook of the political economy of financial crises*. New York, NY: Oxford University Press.

Fisk, C. L. (2009). *Working knowledge: Employee innovation and the rise of corporate intellectual property, 1800–1930*. Chapel Hill, NC: University of North Carolina Press.

Freeman, C., & Louca, F. (2001). *As time goes by: From the industrial revolution to the information revolution*. New York, NY: Oxford University Press.

Fried, B. H. (1998). *The progressive assault on laissez faire: Robert Hale and the first law and economics movement*. Cambridge, MA: Harvard University Press.

Gelderblom, O. (2009). The organization of long-distance trade in England and the Dutch Republic, 1550–1650. In O. Gelderblom (Ed.), *The Political Economy of the Dutch Republic* (pp. 223–254). Burlington, VT: Ashgate.

Gelderblom, O., & Jonker, J. (2004). Completing a financial revolution: The finance of the Dutch East India Trade and the rise of the Amsterdam capital market, 1595–1612. *Journal of Economic History, 64(3)*, 641–672.

Gelderblom, O., De Jong, A., & Jonker, J. (2013). The formative years of the modern corporation: The Dutch East India Company VOC, 1602–1623. *Journal of Economic History, 73(4)*, 1050–1076.

Gereffi, G. (2014). A global value chain perspective on industrial policy and development in emerging markets. *Duke Journal of Comparative and International Law, 24*, 433–458.

Godley, W. (2004). Weaving cloth from Graziani's thread: Endogenous money in a simple (but complete) Keynesian model. In R. Arena & N. Salvadori (Eds.) *Money, credit, and the role of the state: Essays in honour of Augusto Graziani* (pp. 127–135) Burlington, VT: Ashgate.

Goldthwaite, R. (2015). The practice and culture of accounting in Renaissance Florence. *Enterprise and Society, 16(3)*, 611–647.

Grunwald, J., & Flamm, K. E. (1985). *The global factory: Foreign assembly in international trade*. Washington, DC: Brookings.

Guinnane, T., Harris, R., Lamoreaux, N. R., & Rosenthal, J. (2007). Putting the corporation in its place. *Enterprise and Society, 8(3)*, 687–729.

Hale, J. R. (1994). *The civilization of Europe in the Renaissance*. New York, NY: Atheneum.

Habermas, J. (1991). *The structural transformation of the public sphere: An inquiry into a category of bourgeois society*. Cambridge, MA: MIT Press.

Harris, R. (2010). Law, finance, and the first corporations. In J. J. Heckman, R. L. Nelson, & L. Cabatingan (Eds.), *Global perspectives on the rule of law*. New York, NY: Routledge.

Hartog, H. (2000). *Man and wife in America: A history.* Cambridge, MA: Harvard University Press.

Hodgson, G. M. (2013). *From pleasure machines to moral communities: An evolutionary economics without homo economicus.* Chicago, IL: University of Chicago Press.

———. (2014). What is capital? Economists and sociologists have changed its meaning: Should it be changed back? *Cambridge Journal of Economics, 38(5),* 1063–1086.

———. (2015a). *Conceptualizing capitalism: Institutions, evolution, future.* Chicago, IL: University of Chicago.

———. (2015b). Much of the "economics of property rights" devalues property and legal rights. *Journal of Institutional Economics, 11(4),* 683–709.

———. (2016). Varieties of capitalism: Some philosophical and historical considerations. *Cambridge Journal of Economics, 40(3),* 941–960.

Hont, I. (1990). Free trade and the economic limits to national politics: Neo-Machiavellian political economy reconsidered. In J. Dunn (Ed.), *The Economic Limits to Modern Politics* (pp. 41–120). New York, NY: Cambridge University Press.

Jameson, F. (1998). *The cultural turn: Selected writings on the postmodern, 1983–1998.* New York, NY: Verso.

Keynes, J. M. (1964). *The general theory of employment, interest, and money.* New York, NY: Harcourt, Brace, and World.

Lapavitsas, C. (2013). *Profiting without producing: How finance exploits us all.* London, UK: Verso.

Latour, B. (2013). *An inquiry into modes of existence: An anthropology of the moderns.* Cambridge, MA: Harvard University Press.

Lavoie, M. (2004). Circuit and coherent stock-flow accounting. In R. Arena & N. Salvadori (Eds.), *Money, credit, and the role of the state: Essays in honour of Augusto Graziani* (pp. 136–151). Burlington, VT: Ashgate.

Lazonick, W. (1991). *Business organization and the myth of the market economy.* New York, NY: Cambridge University Press.

———, & O'Sullivan, M. (2002). *Corporate governance and sustainability prosperity.* New York, NY: Palgrave Macmillan.

Maifreda, G. (2012). *From Oikonomia to political economy: Constructing economic knowledge from the Renaissance to the Scientific Revolution.* Burlington, VT: Ashgate.

Marglin, S. A. (2008). *The dismal science: How thinking like an economist undermines community.* Cambridge, MA: Harvard University Press.

Marx, K. (1967). *Capital, Vol. I–III.* New York, NY: International Publishers.

McKeon, M. (2005). *The secret history of domesticity: Public, private, and the division of knowledge.* Baltimore, MD: Johns Hopkins University Press.

Milberg, W. & Winkler, D. (2013). *Outsourcing economics: Global value chains in capitalist development.* New York, NY: Cambridge University Press.

Monson, A., & Scheidel, W. (2015). *Fiscal regimes and the political economy of premodern states.* New York, NY: Cambridge University Press.

Moore, J. W. (2015). *Capitalism in the web of life: Ecology and the accumulation of capital.* New York, NY: Verso.

Murphy, A. L. (2014). Financial markets: The limits of economic regulation in early modern England. In P. J. Stern & C. Wennerlind (Eds.), *Mercantilism reimagined: Political economy in early modern Britain and its empire* (pp. 263–281). New York, NY: Oxford University Press.

Najemy, J. M. (1982). *Corporatism and consensus in Florentine electoral politics, 1280–1400.* Chapel Hill, NC: University of North Carolina Press.

———. (2006). *A history of Florence 1200–1575.* Oxford, UK: Blackwell.

North, D. C., Wallis, J. J., & Weingast, B. R. (2009). *Violence and social orders: Conceptual framework for interpreting recorded human history.* Cambridge, MA: Harvard University Press.

Ott, J. (2011). *When Wall Street met Main Street: The quest for an investors' democracy.* Cambridge, MA: Harvard University Press.

Padgett, J. F. (2012). Transposition and refunctionality: The birth of the partnership system in Renaissance Florence. In J. Padgett and W. W. Powell (Eds), *The emergence of organizations and markets* (pp. 168–207). Princeton, NJ: Princeton University Press.

Padgett, J. F., & W. W. Powell. (2012). The problem of emergence. In J. Padgett and W. W. Powell (Eds.), *The emergence of organizations and markets* (pp. 1–29). Princeton, NJ: Princeton University Press.

Pak, S. J. (2013). *Gentleman bankers: The world of J. P. Morgan.* Cambridge, MA: Harvard University Press.

Perez, C. (2002). *Technological revolutions and financial capital: The dynamics of bubbles and golden ages.* Cheltenham, UK: Edward Elgar.

Pocock, J. G. A. (1983). Cambridge paradigms and Scotch philosophers: A study of the relations between the civic humanist and the civil jurisprudential interpretation of eighteenth-century social thought. In I. Hont & M. Ignatieff (Eds.), *Wealth and virtue: The shaping of political economy in the Scottish Enlightenment* (pp. 235–252). New York, NY: Cambridge University Press.

Poovey, M. (1998). *A history of the modern fact: Problems of knowledge in the sciences of wealth and society.* Chicago, IL: University of Chicago Press.

———. (2002). The liberal civil subject and the social in eighteenth century British moral philosophy. *Public Culture, 14(1)*, 125–145.

———. (2008). *Genres of the credit economy: Mediating value in the eighteenth- and nineteenth-century Britain*. Chicago, IL: Chicago University Press.

Postone, M. (1993). *Time, labor, and social domination: A reinterpretation of Marx's critical theory*. New York, NY: Cambridge University Press.

Rousseau, P. L., & Sylla, R. (2005). Emerging financial markets and early U.S. growth. *Explorations in Economic History, 42(1)*, 1–26.

Samuel, W. J. (2013). Kenneth Boulding's *The Image* and contemporary discourse analysis. In W. Dolfsma & S. Kesting (Eds.), *Interdisciplinary economics: Kenneth E. Boulding's engagement in the sciences* (pp. 126–152). New York, NY: Routledge.

Sandel, M. J. (2012). *What money can't buy: The moral limits of markets*. New York, NY: Farrar, Straus, and Giroux.

Sawyer, M., & Passarella, M. V. (2015). The monetary circuit in the age of financialisation: A stock-flow consistent model with a twofold banking sector. *Metroeconomica*, DOI: 10.1111/meca.12103.

Schumpeter, J. A. (1983). *The theory of economic development: An inquiry into profits, capital, credit, interest, and the business cycle*. London, UK: Transaction Books.

———. (1991). The crisis of the tax state. In R. Swedberg (Ed.), *Joseph A. Schumpeter: The economics and sociology of capitalism* (pp. 99–140). Princeton, NJ: Princeton University Press.

Searle, J. R. (2010) *Making the social world: The structure of human civilization*. New York, NY: Oxford University Press.

Sen, A. K. (1997). Rational fools: A critique of the behavioral foundations of economic theory. *Philosophy and Public Affairs, 6(4)*, 317–344.

Sewell, W. H., Jr. (2014). Connecting capitalism to the French Revolution: The Parisian Promenade and the origins of civic equality in eighteenth-century France. *Critical Historical Studies, 1(1)*, 5–46.

Stasavage, D. (2003). *Public debt and the birth of the democratic state: France and Great Britain, 1688–1789*. New York, NY: Cambridge University Press.

———. (2007a). Cities, constitutions, and sovereign borrowing in Europe, 1274–1785. *International Organization, 61(3)*, 489–525.

———. (2007b). Polarization and publicity: Rethinking the benefits of deliberative democracy. *The Journal of Politics, 69(1)*, 59–72.

———. (2011). *States of credit: Size, power, and the development of European polities*. Princeton, NJ: Princeton University Press.

———. (2012). Democracy, war, and wealth: Lessons from two centuries of inheritance taxation. *American Political Science Review, 106(1)*, 81–102.

———. (2014). Was Weber right? The Role of urban autonomy in Europe's rise. *American Political Science Review, 108(2)*, 1–18.

———. (2015). Why did public debt originate in Europe? In A. Monson & W. Scheidel (Eds.), *Fiscal regimes and the political economy of premodern states* (pp. 523–533).New York, NY: Cambridge University Press.

Smith, A. (1994). *An inquiry into the nature and causes of the wealth of nations*. New York, NY: Modern Library Edition.

Swedberg, R. (1991). *Joseph A. Schumpeter: The economics and sociology of capitalism*. Princeton, NJ: Princeton University Press.

Sylla, R. (2002). Financial systems and economic modernization. *Journal of Economic History, 62(2)*, 277–292.

———. (2009). Comparing the UK and US Financial systems, 1790–1830. In J. Atack & L. Neal (Eds.) *The origins and development of financial markets and institutions: From the seventeenth century to the present* (pp. 209–240). New York, NY: Cambridge University Press.

Taylor, C. (2004). *Modern social imaginaries*. Durham, NC: Duke University Press.

Terzi, A. (2006). International financial instability in a world of currencies hierarchy. In P. Louis-Rochon & S. Rossi (Eds.), *Monetary and exchange rate systems* (pp. 3–21). Cheltenham, UK: Edward Elgar.

Trivellato, F. (2009). *The familiarity of strangers: The Sephardic diaspora, Livorno, and cross-cultural trade in the early modern period*. New Haven, CT: Yale University Press.

Turner, H. S. (2014). Corporations: Humanism and Elizabethan political economy. In P. J. Stern and C. Wennerlind (Eds.), *Mercantilism reimagined: Political economy in early modern Britain and its empire* (pp. 153–176). New York, NY: Oxford University Press.

Underkuffler, L. S. (2003). *The idea of property: Its meaning and power*. New York, NY: Oxford University Press.

Van Baval, B. (2010). *Manors and markets: Economy and society in the Low Countries, 500–1600*. New York, NY: Oxford University Press.

Van Zanden, J. L., Luiten, J. & Prak, M. (2006). Towards an economic interpretation of citizenship: The Dutch Republic between medieval communes and modern nation-states. *European Review of Economic History, 10(2)*, 111–145.

Wickham, C. (2015). *Sleepwalking into a new world: The emergence of Italian city communes in the twelfth century*. Princeton, NJ: Princeton University Press.

Wright, R. E. (2014). *Corporation nation*. Philadelphia PA: University of Pennsylvania Press.

Yalom, M. (2001). *A history of the wife*. New York, NY: HarperCollins.

## 2    Law versus Democracy
## Rewriting the History of Property Law in the Early Twentieth Century

R. BEN BROWN

Literary theorists have argued that genre rules that describe and limit literary forms have the power to create reality. Mary Poovey illustrated this power in her study of the genre rules that created money in eighteenth-century England. The genre rules that circulating banknotes followed gave those notes the power to become bearers of value (Poovey, 2008). In a similar way, the American legal system developed genre rules that described appropriate judicial opinions. Opinions that followed the genre rules were then accepted by lawyers, judges, and legal commentators as the reality of American law. These opinions often created a new legal reality rather than accurately reporting the law. This chapter examines a particular issue in American property law, the question of whether animal owners or landowners had to build fences to control livestock. In the early nineteenth century, local customs, town ordinances, and state statutes balanced the rights and duties of animal owners and landowners to build fences (Brown, 1993; Edwards, 2009). However, by the turn of the twentieth century legal scholars had identified one leading American case, *Rust v. Low*, as establishing the dominant American rule. In *Rust*, the judge opined that the English common law rule, which required animal owners to fence in their animals, applied in Massachusetts. Because *Rust* followed the genre rules that legal scholars had identified as the correct statement of American law, this case replaced the reality of the local democratic control of property law. By the turn of the twentieth century, this "leading case" with its adherence to a genre formula, a formula that emerged after the case was written, created the reality of American property law and gave Law the power to overcome Democracy (Horwitz, 1977; Simpson, 1979).

Morton Horwitz's path-breaking work connecting the private law of the antebellum period to the economic expansion of those years made one significant mistake. He read the cases that were reported as if they had been issued by justices who had hierarchical power over lower courts and as if the lower courts had easy access to the controlling cases and acknowledged these cases as precedent and followed the higher-court rulings (Horwitz, 1977). In making these assumptions, Horwitz was following the lead of the early-twentieth-century treatise writers who made the same assumptions and very aggressively argued that American laws have been crafted by American judges. This judge-centered history of antebellum private law misrepresents the variety of legal arguments that were made in the early nineteenth century and privileges the limited role of written judicial opinions over the role of local ordinances, statutes, and custom.

This chapter proceeds in three parts. Part one examines the genre rules of judicial opinion writing that legal scholars, judges, and lawyers adopted and how *Rust* conformed to those rules. Part two documents the rejection of *Rust* by most jurisdictions in the antebellum period, its contemporary time. Part three describes the process by which *Rust* came to be accepted as the "leading case" that states the "American rule" despite its rejection by the antebellum courts.

## PART ONE: *RUST* AND GENRE RULES

If the majority of contemporary judges and legislatures that considered *Rust* rejected it, then why did commentators, academics, and judges maintain decades later that *Rust* was the controlling precedent on the fencing question in nineteenth-century United States? What were the properties of the *Rust* opinion that appealed to later legal writers? The answer is that *Rust* successfully resisted democratic control over this issue by presenting the question as one that should be decided by sources of law that predated the founding of the country. *Rust* severely limited the power of the legislature and presented law as a body of judge-made rules that preexisted the creation of the state. Judges, not legislatures or city commissions, were the guardians and interpreters of law. Judicial opinions that based their rulings on this theory and, by means of their literary structure, obscured the power claims of the judiciary were the ones that later commentators would celebrate.

What were these genre rules that the legal commentators adopted as appropriate for important decisions, and that later judges and lawyers came to view as "correct" expressions of American law? The first was the source of law: judges must base their decisions on judicial opinions, not legislation, customs, or local ordinances. Second, judges must use legal logic to analyze cases and discover the preexisting rule of law. Third, this "discovered" rule should be applied to the facts of this case by analogizing facts, although only "appropriate" facts should be considered. And fourth, the result should be presented as the inexorable working out of legal logic, not the whim of either the judge or the electorate.

Any second-year law student would recognize these genre rules as the basis for a well-reasoned case. However, early American judges did not follow these rules and, as we will see by the judges who rejected *Rust v. Low* as precedent, these judges were not heavily influenced by precedents just because they followed these rules. Such cases could be cited, but opinions that did not conform to this genre and other sources of law such as customs and ordinances were just as influential. During the course of the nineteenth century, lawyers, judges, and legal commentators elevated this genre of judicial opinion writing into the only appropriate form for legal opinions and gave opinions that followed this genre the power to state the "rule of law" that governed. By the twentieth century, legal commentators, ignorant of the earlier legal reality, anointed *Rust* as a correct statement of Law because it conformed to their genre rules.

*Rust* itself conformed to all the genre rules. In the case, some cattle had wandered from Mr. Rust's land, through the lands of his neighbor onto the defendant's land (Rust, 1809). The defendant's agents impounded Rust's cattle, demanding Rust pay compensation for the damages the cows had done. Rust sued for the return of the cattle, but the defense claimed that under common law they could hold the cattle until the cows' owner paid. Chief Justice Theophilus Parsons ruled that the English common law controlled the obligations of the parties, despite Massachusetts statutes that seemed to require the landowner to build a fence against the wandering animals or forfeit the right to damages. Justice Parsons severely limited the effect of the statute, ignored the realities of Massachusetts' agricultural practices and imposed the common law obligations on the plaintiff. In doing so, Justice Parsons wrote an opinion that admirably embodied the genre rules that would come to be expected of leading legal opinions.

Justice Parsons got the ammunition he needed to fulfill the first of the genre rules from the landowner's attorneys, Nathan Dane and Joseph Story. Dane and Story were committed to a vision of the common law that preexisted the foundation of the state (Dane, 1823; Newmeyer, 1985). Lawyers with this commitment would work diligently throughout the antebellum period to create law's edifice and use it to battle democratic claims to create the law. Story provided the scholarship necessary to make *Rust* a fine example of the common law genre. As the variety of sources that Story cited shows, Boston had the necessary legal resources to allow this type of argument. Story took full advantage of the resources and Justice Parsons took full advantage of Story's detailed work. In his later summary on Story's brief in *Rust*, Dane recorded that Story "very ably and largely cited and examined the year and other ancient books" (Dane, 1823). The yearbooks were reports of English cases from 1268 to 1535 written in Latin or Law French. Story translated and cited these old English cases for the rule that only special circumstances required landowners to fence against roaming animals. Story's pedanticism extended to translating more than thirty cases from the yearbooks to prove that in the early seventeenth century an English judge, Lord Hale, had mistranslated some year book cases. Since Lord Hale's opinion was the only English opinion that contradicted Story's version of the common law, Story detailed Lord Hale's mistake. While correcting Lord Hale's error might seem a minor matter, the importance of this kind of erudite case analysis was crucial to the genre of legal opinions that would come to dominate. Justice Parsons took insufficient notes of Story's discussion of Lord Hale's mistake in the first hearing of the *Rust*, so Parsons required a rehearing so that he could take accurate notes of Story's discovery of Lord Hale's error. Parsons then corrected Lord Hale, writing as if he had unearthed the error. Story later claimed that Justice Parsons had ordered this rehearing to satisfy an immodest desire to correct Lord Hale (W. Story, 1851). Genre rules gave greater weight to opinions that corrected the mistakes of long-dead English judges in their legal logic than to the reality of Massachusetts' farm life.

Story also had to convince Justice Parsons that the common law, not Massachusetts statutes, controlled his decision. As early as 1642, Massachusetts law had protected livestock owners if their animals did damage in insufficiently fenced fields (Koenig, 1979; Rose, 1986). This statute protecting livestock owners had been updated in 1789 after Massachusetts became a state (Dane, 1823). The statute allowed landowners with good fences to sue stock owners for damages. Story argued that the Massachusetts statute applied between adjoining landowners and then only if the neighbors had agreed to build fences and one of them had built an insufficient fence. In the absence of an agreement between adjacent landowners, the common law controlled and stock owners were liable. Since Rust's animals had already trespassed, the defendant had no duty to fence against them.

The problem with Story's interpretation is that it thwarted the will of the legislature. The legislation was not dealing with the narrow issue of duties between neighbors but with addressing the larger issue of the landowner's duty to fence stock out. The legislation required landowners to build fences before they could recover for damages from free-roaming animals. The statutes also dealt with the reciprocal duties of adjoining landowners to build fences. The statutes, however, did not include a connection between the reciprocal duties of adjoining landowners and the limitation on recovering damages for unfenced fields. Only Story's claim that the statute had to be interpreted against the background of the common law rule could make this connection. In much of early-nineteenth-century Massachusetts the law and the custom was that landowners had to build fences or stock owners would not be liable for damages caused by free-roaming stock. By persuading Justice Parsons that the legislation had to be interpreted as a narrow exception to a general common law rule, Story was using the "year and other ancient books" to impose a legal order at the expense of democratic will.

Not only did Story's argument negate the Massachusetts legislature's will, but it also ignored prior Massachusetts precedent. While working on his *Abridgment* of American law, Dane discovered at least four cases decided between the Revolution and 1806 that had ruled on the issues raised by *Rust* (Dane, 1823). In three of these cases the livestock owners had won and the court had validated the open range. Yet the stock owner's attorneys in *Rust* did not cite these Massachusetts cases. It is quite possible that these cases were not readily available to Massachusetts lawyers. It was not until much later in the antebellum period that regular printed reports of state cases became available (Hoeflich, 2010; Cook, 1981). Yet Story could readily find centuries-old precedents in the more readily available English lawbooks (Newmyer, 1985).

This examination of the decision in *Rust* shows how this case fit the genre rules that twentieth-century commentators came to be prefer. Justice Parsons used ancient cases as the source of law. He used esoteric legal logic in interpreting these cases—even criticizing poor dead Lord Hale. His analysis limited the "appropriate" facts—since the statutory duties only applied to adjoining landowners, they did not apply in *Rust* since the cattle belonged to a non-neighbor. And finally, this result was the inexorable working-out of a centuries-old principle that existed independently of the sovereignty in which it was applied. Law came from English cases. Legal rules arose from logical inferences from those cases. Statutes were minimized and customs were ignored. And the resulting logic should be rigorously imposed without any attention being paid to agricultural realities.

This type of opinion writing did not dominate in the antebellum period. In fact, as the next section shows, legal commentators had to cherry-pick cases to find those that met the genre rules, and then elevate them above the clear majority of cases that were less rigorous in their attention to case law and case logic and paid more attention to the statutes, customs, and facts on the ground.

## PART TWO—REJECTING *RUST* IN THE ANTEBELLUM YEARS

The case that more accurately stated the antebellum duty to fence animals came from North Carolina in 1843. In *Hellen v. Noe*, the Beaufort town constable seized a pig owned by Isaac Hellen because the pig was roaming free within the township. The town commissioners had passed an ordinance declaring free-roaming pigs a nuisance and authorized the constable to seize and sell them. Hellen sued when the constable enforced the ordinance.

The trial judge ruled that Hellen had had the right to range his pigs and the town could not infringe on that right. The town appealed this ruling to the North Carolina Supreme Court. The town's attorney submitted a substantial brief, citing numerous English precedents that justified towns in regulating nuisances. He discussed the specific facts of several English cases on abating nuisances and engaged in an analysis of these precedents. The town's counsel argued that since common law precedents allowed towns to abate the nuisance of free-roaming pigs, the Supreme Court should allow this constable to take up Hellen's hog.

The North Carolina Supreme Court ruled for the town, but rejected the common law argument. The court also ignored English common law cases. Instead, Judge Joseph Daniel relied on the political power of the township commissioners to pass those laws that were necessary for the health and welfare of the town's inhabitants. In the case report, the summary of the town's brief exceeds three pages of careful legal reasoning based on precedents. Judge Daniel ignored these precedents. Judge Daniel relied instead on the democratic procedures the commissioners used to pass the ordinance. He recited the state statute that authorized the commissioners to pass such an ordinance. He then continued:

> The commissioners are to be annually elected by the free white men of the town, who are of the age of 21. Their rules or ordinances are subject to be repealed or amended at the pleasure of a majority of the Commissioners.... If a majority of the citizens of the town deemed the ordinance impolitic or injurious to the people of the Corporation, they have the power in their own hands to remedy the evil. (p. 372)

Although the city attorney had provided the judge with all the ammunition necessary to render a sound common law opinion, Judge Daniel instead relied upon the people's right to provide for their own welfare.

This opinion lays bare the political power of the voters and the town commission and elevates that power above the common law. In doing so, it rejects the idea that property rules existed before the creation of the state, which rules common law judges could "discover." This rejection fails to conform with the genre rules governing appropriate opinion writing, which had emerged by the end of the nineteenth century. In the late nineteenth and early twentieth century judicial opinions that carried weight were those that obscured the role of politics and power and instead presented the law as originating from rules that existed before the creation of the political realm, which rules judges deduced from prior opinions.

Other courts that were well aware of the common law rule also refused to impose the English rule and treated this issue as one that should be decided by the will of the local populace. In *Seeley v. Peters*, an 1848 Illinois case, the majority opinion analyzed the legislative history of the state statutes. The trial court had instructed the jury that the common law required animal owners to fence in their animals. The majority ruled that statutes, not the common law, set forth the binding legal standard. Under the statute the failure of a landowner to build a fence that complied with the statutory requirements meant that the stock owner was not responsible for the damage his hogs did to crops.

The attorneys for both parties extensively briefed the issues. William Herndon, Abraham Lincoln's law partner, argued for the landowner. He cited *Rust* and used its logic: Illinois statutes only supplemented the common law, and should be interpreted narrowly to apply only to adjoining landowners. Herndon conducted a section-by-section analysis of the fencing statute arguing that the statute had not preempted the common law. However, the very thoroughness of his analysis contradicted the argument by emphasizing the comprehensiveness of the statutory scheme.

The majority opinion took Herndon's argument seriously, but they took the legislature's power more seriously. Illinois had a reception statute. Reception statutes adopted the common law but with limitations. Judge Lyman Trumbull ruled that Illinois had only adopted the common law "so far as the same is applicable" (p. 141). The statutory regime proved that the common law was not applicable to semi-frontier conditions of Illinois agriculture. Moreover, Judge Trumbull took notice of the customs that had developed among and between Illinois farmers and stock owners. These customs required farmers to build strong fences and the custom was further evidence that the English common law was not applicable. As Judge Trumbull said, "[I]t has been the custom in Illinois so long, that the memory of man runneth not to the contrary, for the owners of stock to suffer them to run at large" (p. 142). Judge Trumbull's analysis rejected the English rule and adopted an American rule based upon statutes and custom. Judge Trumbull was well aware of *Rust* and specifically rejected it as a binding precedent.

Judge John Caton wrote a strong dissent in *Seeley* arguing vigorously for a property right that preceded the formation of the state. He argued, "the common law is most unquestionably the law of natural justice" (p.151). The property rights embedded in the common law protected against the popular will of the people who in their fickleness might invade legal rights. The common law limited statutes and customary practices:

> Who does not see, if we start out with the principle of making our decisions conform to public opinion . . . we shall soon end in making our notion of their wants and interests rather than the common law or the express statute, the rule of determination. . . . We shall be left to our own arbitrary notions of what is best adapted to the public good. (p. 154)

The whole purpose of the common law from Judge Caton's point of view was to limit the power of the people. Judge Caton relied heavily on *Rust* and its logic for the principle that statutory fencing laws did not abrogate the common law, but he failed to convince a majority.

The battling opinions in *Seeley* illustrate the conflict between judicial opinions that rely on common law precedents and close precedential analysis and judicial opinions that broadly interpret statutes and even use custom to enforce the perceived will of the people. The common law was premised on the idea that the state should protect property rights, which rights preceded the creation of the polity. The vast majority of antebellum courts ruled that the people should have the right and power to create a fencing law that best fit their needs. The conflict between the natural rights of property owners and the judgment of the citizens was exactly the conflict that the late-nineteenth- and early-twentieth-century legal educators, commentators and judges wanted to obscure. Therefore, cases such as *Seeley* and *Hellen* had to be subordinated and *Rust* proclaimed the "leading case." Twentieth-century academics knew of these other cases, but rejected them as unimportant because their rhetoric was not persuasive to twentieth-century legal readers.

Even jurisdictions that were closer geographically to Massachusetts and had similar agricultural histories rejected *Rust*. In 1841, in *Studwell v. Ritch*, two neighbors were fighting over the damage that some wandering cows had done to a farmer's crops. The neighbors had never fenced between their lands. Under Connecticut statutes, just as in Massachusetts, the neighbors had the right to require each other to contribute to the building of a fence. According to the statute, if they did not build the fence, then the cattle could run free and the neighbor could not complain about the damages. At the trial court, the judge enforced this statute and ruled in favor of the cow owner. On appeal, the crop owner's attorney used *Rust* to argue that in the absence of a request to build a dividing fence between the lands, the common law should apply. The cow owner argued that the statute had completely preempted the common law and that Connecticut law required that a landowner fence his land before he complained of a trespassing cow.

The majority of the *Studwell* court ruled that the will of the legislature, not the common law, should apply. The majority acknowledged the *Rust* case and acknowledged that the Massachusetts and Connecticut statutes were quite similar. However, the Connecticut court ruled that they were not bound to follow Massachusetts in their interpretation of the statute. The majority found that the legislature had rejected the common law since colonial days and that the statute completely superseded the common law. The crop owner had a duty to build a fence that complied with Connecticut statutes before he could recover damages. The Connecticut court preferred the specifics of nineteenth-century custom and statues to timeless common law principles and logic.

In 1820, the state of Maine was carved out of Massachusetts. When the fencing question was first raised, Maine judges felt compelled to follow the Massachusetts precedent in *Rust* and ruled that the common law controlled with minor statutory exceptions (*Little*, 1828). However, conditions in Maine were much more frontier-like than in Massachusetts and the legislature reacted to the Maine court's decision by passing new fencing legislation, which required farmers to fence animals out of their fields. In 1836, the Maine court revisited this issue and ruled that the statute aimed explicitly at rejecting the *Rust* precedent was a valid exercise of legislative power and preempted the common law (*Gooch*, 1836). Vermont also rejected *Rust* (*Mooney*, 1829).

## PART THREE—ELEVATING *RUST*

So how did *Rust* survive as the appropriate statement of American law even though it had little contemporary impact? Legal analysts kept the logic of *Rust* alive even when courts and legislators were rejecting it. Nathan Dane and Joseph Story were important legal commentators in the antebellum period. Dane published his eight volume *A General Abridgment and Digest of American Law* in 1823. He devoted twenty-seven pages to a description of *Rust* and claimed, incorrectly, that *Rust* stated the American rule on the issue of fences. In his Commentaries, James Kent picked up on Dane's claims and cited *Rust* as the New York rule (Kent, 1832).

New York provides a wonderful example of how legal commentators spread the doctrine of *Rust* even when judges and legislatures were less enthusiastic. In *Bush v. Brainard*, an 1823 New York case, the fencing issue presented itself in the case of a cow with a fatal sweet tooth. A man named Bush owned an unenclosed maple forest where he made maple syrup. Bush left buckets of syrup in an open shed on his property. Brainard's cow found the shed and, acting in a manner more swinish than bovine, drank to such an excess that it died. Brainard sued for the value of the animal; Bush defended that the cow was wrongfully on his property. The New York Court in a very short opinion analogized these facts to an English case where a horse fell into a pit and killed itself but the horse's owner could not recover since the horse was trespassing. The court then asserted that the common law prevailed in New York and therefore Bush was not liable for his negligence in leaving the syrup where the cow could get to it.

The opinion takes up just two pages of the New York reports; the discussion of *Rust* and its protection of the common law is relegated to a footnote. But the footnote discussing *Rust* and arguing that the common law prevailed in New York flows on for thirteen pages. The footnote examines *Rust* at length and adopts its reasoning that only animals that are rightfully on adjoining land need be fenced against. The footnote even quotes Parsons's discussion of Lord Hale's factual mistake. The footnote then adopts the *Rust* holding and reasons, "[T]his case settles directly the doctrine before advanced, that one is not bound to fence, except against such cattle only as are lawfully in the adjoining close" (p. 85).

The problem with this adoption of *Rust* as precedent is that the court did not pen this footnote. The footnote was added by the case reporter, Esek Cowen. When later cases followed this precedent, they assumed that the judge had adopted the *Rust* doctrine and that the footnote was part of his decision. This footnote seemed to state New York law, but in 1855, a New York court rejected the footnote's reasoning and defended this rejection by pointing out that a reporter and not a judge had written the footnote (*Corwin*, 1855). The judge knew of this author-ship because in 1844 in the third edition of Esek Cowen's *A Treatise on the Civil Jurisdiction of Justices of the Peace in the State of New York*, Esek's son, Sidney, who edited the third edition, claimed that *Rust* was the correct statement of New York law and cited to a note of the reporter. The *Corwin* judge reasoned that New York courts were not bound by a reporter's interpolation.

Earlier, the New York legislature also resisted *Rust*'s use of the common law to take away the legislature's power to control the range. The legislature passed a law in 1830 that allowed town councils to determine the sufficiency of fences and specifically authorized the town to regulate the times and manners of allowing animals to run at large on the highways. By adding that phrase "at large on the highways," the legislature changed the status of free-roaming stock from tres-passers to legitimate users of the highways. Since the animals were roaming the highway legally, if they entered a field through an insufficient highway fence the landowner could not sue. The legislature protected the town's democratic power to decide how it wanted to deal with animals and fences from the mischievous court reporter (*Griffin*, 1849).

Sidney Cowen, the son of the case reporter who added *Rust* to the *Bush* precedent, did not lightly accept the state legislature's usurpation of the common law's prerogative to void land-use statutes violating preexisting notions of prop-erty rights (Cowen, 1844). Sidney Cowen attempted to thwart the legislature by convincing local justices of the peace that the New York statute was void and the *Rust* doctrine should prevail. Cowen's tactic with a sound one. Controversies over free-roaming animals usually were decided at the local level and were not appealed. If Cowen could convince local JPs that the ordinances were invalid, then their rulings would decide the majority of these lawsuits. In his treatise, Cowen rehashed at length the *Rust* decision, treating it as if it were binding New York precedent and citing it fifteen times in seven pages. Cowen acknowledged that the New York legislature had attempted to overturn *Rust* and claimed that the New York legislature's amendment was "a radical change in the provisions of the statute" (p. 430). The Legislature probably just thought they were saving the original meaning from an aggressive court reporter. Cowen also raised a constitutional argument. He claimed that the New York legislature did not have the power to authorize towns to allow animals on the roads because stock grazing along the roadway were taking the landowner's property without compensation; that is, they were eating the landowner's grass.

However, the New York legislature prevailed in the end. In 1849, Justice John Willard ruled that the legislature had specifically amended the law to allow towns to choose whether or not animals could roam at large (*Griffin*, 1849). Justice Willard rejected all the arguments based upon *Rust* and reasserted the democratic right of towns to control this essentially local issue. Instead of examining the common law, Willard examined legislative history and ruled that the purchase of rights of passage for roadway included any incidental herbage that animals might chomp as they passed. Although Sidney Cowen and the courts he influenced made it difficult, in the end New York gave townships the same power that North Carolina had in *Hellen*. Despite the expansive judicial discussion of *Rust*, in the end *Rust* did not create law in antebellum New York. Stock and fences were a political issue for local townships to control. The best summary of the effect of *Rust* before the Civil War is that *Rust* was often discussed by legal commentators, but was seldom followed.

When we jump across the divide of the Civil War, we see that a legal scholar had converted the minority position that *Rust* had held in the antebellum period into the statement of American law. In his 1874 book, *A Treatise on the Law of Boundaries and Fences*, Ransom Tyler begins his discussion of the fence law controversy by discussing English precedents. He then presents these precedents as the basis for the American law on this issue. "It is perfectly well-settled and understood that by common law no man was bound to fence against the cattle of others" (Tyler, p. 342). The first case he cites in support of this understanding of the law is *Rust*. Tyler then presents a long quote from *Rust* where Justice Parsons "laid down the rule" (p. 342). *Rust* is the binding precedent because it conforms with the genre requirement by relying upon ancient cases and logically deriving legal rules from those cases. Tyler himself quotes from a "very ancient English author" (p. 342) to support the strictness of the requirement that stock owners fence in their cattle. Tyler then begins a multipage exploration of when adjoining landowners have a right to insist that their neighbors fence their land. He ends the first section of his discussion of the law of fences by proclaiming that his discussion of English and American cases set forth the true law: "The foregoing are principles of universal application, and are recognized both where the subject of fences is regulated by statute, and where it is not. It is pertinent, therefore, that they be distinctly referred to in this place" (p. 360).

Why is it necessary for Tyler to make this proclamation of universal application? Because the next 173 pages of his discussion of the rights and duties of landowners and stock owners are all about the statutes that various states have passed. The subsequent chapters can best be interpreted as completely undermining his claim that the foregoing principles are of universal application. Instead, he finds it necessary to proceed jurisdiction by jurisdiction and discuss the statutes that have been passed and the individual state courts' interpretations of those statutes. For instance, in discussing New York he is forced to admit that the state legislature rejected the initial adoption of *Rust* in *Bush*. Tyler has to acknowledge that a New York court found the legislation constitutional, but he then spends more than a page rehashing Esek Cowen's treatise and Cowen's claim that the statute should be ignored. Tyler prefers Cowen's analysis to that of the New York courts. Only at the end of his discussion does Tyler finally admit that local authorities could indeed allow animals to roam at large, but he softens this blow by noting, "[V]ery many of the towns have no rules permitting cattle and other beast to go at large" (p. 380).

Reading Tyler's treatise with a knowledge of the antebellum statutes and cases is a bewildering experience. Tyler is a good enough legal scholar to accurately report on the myriad statutes and the general failure of the courts to reject the statutes in favor of the "first principles" with which he began his discussion. Yet his commitment to the common law as the appropriate protection of property rights requires him to constantly resist the legislature's power. So as he ends his discussion of New York law, he cannot resist quoting Stanley Cowen's treatise for a nonbinding, but from a common law view persuasive, refutation of legislative power.

The same bias exists in Tyler's discussion of other jurisdictions. In his discussion of Maine's law, he notes the acceptance of the *Rust* precedent in *Little* (1828), but fails to note the subsequent statute that overturned that adoption and the subsequent Maine case that accepted the statute as valid (*Gooch*, 1836). This leaves the false impression that Maine followed *Rust*'s "first principles." Similarly, in discussing Connecticut's laws, he briefly mentions *Studwell* but fails to note that the Connecticut court rejected the reasoning of *Rust* in favor of enforcing the Connecticut statutes.

Commentators such as Dane, Cowen, and Tyler successfully obscured the failure of *Rust* to actually control the substance of the fence law. By the early twentieth century, John Henry Wigmore relied upon those commentators, and the power of genre rules that make *Rust* persuasive to twentieth-century lawyers, to present *Rust* as the leading case on this issue, with the implication that *Rust* had correctly stated the law for more than a century (Wigmore, 1912). Wigmore begins his discussion under the subtopic "Keeping Animals" by excerpting five-plus pages of the *Rust* opinion. The excerpt includes a summary of Dane and Story's brief. The excerpt includes Justice Parsons's claim that a landowner is not required to fence by common law and that the statute only applies to a limited number of adjoining landowners. The excerpt includes more than a page of Justice Parsons's detailed investigation of early English common law cases, as well as Parsons's correction of Lord Hale. Wigmore's chosen digest of Parsons's opinion does not include any statutory references. Wigmore thus presents *Rust* as the American authority on the issue of the respective duties of landowners and stock owners and completely obscures the power of statutes, custom, and local ordinances. A twentieth-century lawyer researching the respective duties of landowner and stock owners by turning to Wigmore would be confronted by a leading case heavily based on early English common law cases protecting landowner's property rights and using deductive legal reasoning to conclude that the stock owners were liable.

## CONCLUSION

Mary Poovey warns us to beware the power of literary form. By the early twentieth century, common law cases that portrayed the law as a stable edifice that stretched back through the centuries became the reality of Law. Despite the exhaustive democratic power struggles over the respective rights and duties of landowners and stock owners, Wigmore could present the "American Rule" as embodied by one case, even though that case had been rejected as authority by most antebellum courts. *Hellen* more accurately reflected the contingency of the battle over fences—legislatures could either require fencing or delegate power to the local citizens to decide who had to fence. But Wigmore chose to present the Law embodied by *Rust* and obscure the democratic control that *Hellen* laid bare. Wigmore could perpetuate this misunderstanding because *Rust* conformed to the rules of judicial opinions that had been adopted by those who preferred Law over Democracy. *Rust* attempted to create a legal regime stretching back through the centuries. It detailed this regime with discussions of obscure English opinions: "year and other ancient books." It followed the logic of the law: Ah ha! Lord Hale made a mistake; let us correct him and get credit for doing so. And it limited the power of democratic institutions: statutes are merely supplementary to the preexisting and all-encompassing truth of a preexisting Law, and so statutes must be interpreted to apply as narrowly as possible. Customs had not power to stand before Law. And for the next one hundred years, lawyers could comfortably read the truth in Wigmore and inform their clients that the law was well settled, in happy ignorance of the myriad political battles that this "history" obscured.

## REFERENCES

### Cases

*Bush v. Brainard*, 1 Cowen 78 (N.Y. 1823).
*Corwin v. New York & Erie R.R. Co.*, 13 N.Y. 42 (1855).
*Gooch v. Stephenson*, 13 Me. 371 (1836).
*Griffin v. Martin*, 7 Barb. 297 (N.Y. 1849).
*Hellen v. Noe*, 25 N.C. (3 Ird.) (1843).
*Little v. Lathrop*, 5 Greenl. 356 (Me. 1828).
*Mooney v. Maynard*, 1 Ver. 470 (1829).
*Rust v. Low*, 6 Mass. 90 (1809).
*Seeley v. Peters*, 10 Ill. 130 (1848).
*Studwell v. Ritch*, 14 Conn. 292 (1841).

### Books and Law Review Articles

Cook, C. M. (1981). *The American codification movement: A study of antebellum legal reform.* Westport, CT: Greenwood Press.

Brown, R. B. (1993). The Southern Range: A study in nineteenth century law and society (unpublished doctoral dissertation). University of Michigan, Ann Arbor, MI.

Cowen, E., Barbour, O. L., & Cowen, S. J. (1844). *A treatise on the civil jurisdiction of justices of the peace in the state of New York* (3rd ed., Vol. 2). Albany, NY: W. & A. Gould.

Dane, N. (1823). *A general abridgement and digest of American law with occasional notes and comments* (Vol. 2). Boston, MA: Cummings, Hilliard.

Edwards, L. F. (2009). *The people and their peace: Legal culture and the transformation of inequality in the post-revolutionary south.* Chapel Hill, NC: University of North Carolina Press.

Hoeflich, M. H. (2010). *Legal publishing in antebellum America.* New York, NY: Cambridge University Press.

Horwitz, M. J. (1977). *Transformation of American Law, 1780–1860.* Cambridge, MA: Harvard University Press.

Kent, J. (1832). *Commentaries on American law* (Vol. 3). New York, NY: O. Halsted.

Konig, D. T. (1979). *Law and society in Puritan Massachusetts: Essex County, 1629–1692.* Chapel Hill, NC: University of North Carolina Press.

Newmyer, R. K. (1985). *Supreme Court Justice Joseph Story: Statesman of the Old Republic*. Chapel Hill, NC: University of North Carolina Press.

Poovey, M. (2008). *Genres of the credit economy: Mediating value in eighteenth- and nineteenth-century Britain*. Chicago, IL: University of Chicago Press.

Rose, C. (1986). The comedy of the commons: Custom, commerce, and inherently public property. *The University of Chicago Law Review, 53(3)*, 711.

Simpson, A. W. (1979). The Horwitz Thesis and the history of contracts. *The University of Chicago Law Review, 46(3)*, 533. doi:10.2307/1599448.

Story, W. W. (1851). *Life and letters of Joseph Story, associate justice of the Supreme Court of the United States, and Dane professor of law at Harvard University*. Boston, MA: C. C. Little and J. Brown.

Tyler, R. H. (1874). *A treatise on the law of boundaries and fences including the rights of property on the sea-shore and in the lands of public rivers and other streams, and the law of window lights*. Albany, NY: W. Gould.

Wigmore, J. H. (1912). *Select cases on the law of torts, with notes, and a summary of principles* (2nd ed., Vol. 1). Boston, MA: Little, Brown.

# 3 Early Roadway Construction and Establishing the Norm of Just Compensation for Takings

JILL FRALEY

Within the common law tradition, the requirement of compensation for the taking of private property dates at least to the Magna Carta (1215, pp. 16–17). American law review articles tend to cite the Magna Carta norm, note limited application during the colonial period, and then skip forward to Supreme Court jurisprudence. American scholars who study takings in more depth tend to focus on the periods following the American Civil War (Skouras, 2000) with the greatest emphasis on the modern development of regulatory takings (Epstein, 1985). Only a few scholars have dedicated pages to the earlier history of takings (Reynolds, 2010).

In America as in England, roadway construction provides some of the earliest public projects on record. Scholars who have written about early roadway takings in America have tended not to see much in the way of the development of takings norms. Indeed, William Treanor concluded that "[e]ighteenth-century colonial legislatures regularly took private property without compensating the owner" (Treanor, 1985, p. 695).[1] Treanor's account is particularly meaningful because of the way that it frames takings norms as more modern, more a product of the new republic than a feature of the common law tradition more generally. Such modern framing positions takings more as a product of industrialization and development—something much closer to the eventual move to compensating for regulatory takings—as opposed to a common law norm dating to the Magna Carta.

With such framing in mind, then, it is important to inquire specifically of the evidence supporting Treanor's account. One explanation for the phenomenon of non-compensation that Treanor explains has been that states did not yet incorporate clear requirements for just compensation (Treanor, 1985, p. 695). This explanation has, however, been disputed. Bernard Siegan argues that no explicit formulation of a takings rule was necessary in early America, due to the incorporation of takings norms into due process requirements (Siegan, 2001, pp. 108–112). Siegan's explanation addresses the lack of specific statutes, but it does not address another important argument raised by Treanor. Treanor cites specific examples of non-compensation for takings—in particular, examples that relate to the construction of roadways (Treanor, 1985, pp. 695–697). Siegan's explanation does not account for these; under Siegan's explanation, takings should be compensation—and he cites many examples in which takings were compensation—just via the due process mechanism rather than a specific takings prohibition. Thus, Treanor's history of non-compensation remains unexplained.

If one were seeking evidence to support a more robust theory of just compensation during the colonial and early republic eras, one could simply look to the conflicting evidence signed by Siegan. One might then simply attempt to argue that the larger body of evidence supports the position that Siegan has taken of an existing, well-used mechanism for takings compensation in the colonial and early republic eras—just a mechanism that hides well under due process rather than specific requirements for just compensation for property. Such an approach, however, would too neatly avoid a more fundamental oddity in the historical record. Roadway takings were compensated within Great Britain; there is no obvious reason for the same types of takings to suddenly not be compensated in America unless there were a definite shift in the understanding of property rights or the nature of sovereignty.

This chapter focuses on the oddity of noncompensated takings in early America and compensated takings within Great Britain. In an effort to understand how the takings norm developed in Great Britain and whether there are consistent explanations for the examples that Treanor cites, this chapter begins by elaborating the early history of roadway development in Great Britain, focusing on the ownership of lands used for roadways and the ownership of materials used for repairing roadways.

This chapter demonstrates that initial construction projects displayed a significant respect for private property. Every effort was made to situate roads on commonly held lands such as commons and wastes rather than on privately allocated property. Indeed, often the roadway fell on the edge of the waste or commons and formed the boundary between a waste and other parcels of privately held property. Crossing privately owned property occurred only when other, commonly held lands were not available.

Additionally, the process of sourcing materials for building and repairing roads lends other support to the clear prioritization of public sourcing over private sourcing. Statutes and other historical sources demonstrate that those tasked with building and maintaining roadways first sought their materials within the commonly held lands. Provided that the material could be acquired there, no compensation was paid. If, however, materials were not available within the commonly held lands, commissioners sought necessary materials on private lands, paying both for the materials and for any consequential damage made to the private property due to the movement of such materials.

In both positioning the roads and sourcing materials for the roads, the government displayed a significant respect for private property. This was despite a still-existent feudal system that ultimately placed the title of lands in the hands of the Crown. This chapter argues that the level of respect granted to private property in these early takings established a precedent for how takings law would evolve in the future.

Having established the history of road takings in Great Britain, this chapter looks to how that history explains Treanor's evidence of non-compensation within early North America. Ultimately, this chapter argues that a full understanding of the nature of common and private property in Great Britain, combined with an understanding of the perfection of title in colonial property, explains in full the instances of non-compensation that Treanor discussed. Rather than representing a history of regular taking without compensation to the private owners, these examples demonstrate fidelity to other core concepts in property law, particularly norms related to the full establishment of title to private property. As a result, the instances of non-compensation are better understood as instances in which the private party was not property situated to make a claim for takings compensation due to the lack of a fully established private right to the land.

## A HISTORY OF ROAD TAKINGS IN GREAT BRITAIN: AVOIDING PRIVATE PROPERTY

The earliest roadway constructions in Great Britain favored crossing the commons, and particularly the wastes, rather than private property. Wastelands encompassed diverse landscapes, united primarily by a simple lack of economic utility. Wastes included those areas where the soils starved or rejected plants. Such areas provided little in the way of opportunities even for underclasses known for creatively pressing out a living from the most inhospitable of landscapes. Little could be had from land described as "naturally barren" (Hutchinson, 1794, V. 2, pp. 547–548). The unifying characteristic of the wastelands was "barren ground . . . of which no profit ariseth or groweth" (Gwillim, 1801, p. 1645).

As a result of the lack of economic viability, the ownership of wastes was historically rather cloudy. Simply put, there was no real incentive for anyone to claim it. Somner declared that in the earliest "days the whole weald appertained to none but the King, acknowledging no private lord or proprietor" (Somner & Kennet, 1693, p. 107). Somner concluded that some particular extensive wastes were "not parcelled, carved, or canton'd out into manors" (p. 110). Private claims to waste generally appear rarely and later in the eighteenth or nineteenth century, when the pressures of population and the development of agricultural improvement techniques gave rise to new valuations of land. During the earlier periods, there is a strong history of a tradition of public use and ownership (Fraley, forthcoming). Wastes were used as dumping grounds and burial places for strangers. Additionally, wastes allowed towns a type of ad hoc zoning, allowing them to ostracize the more unpleasant occupations and their wares.

Wastes made excellent places to position new roadways. First, wastes were unlikely to be needed for cultivation. A waste was generally without "the slightest vestige of cultivation," and more commonly the land was full of "stunted heath, rushes and bent," along with "granite, whinstone, and innumerable smaller stones," which were "everywhere visible" (Blaikie, 1837, pp. 97–98). Second, wastes were unclaimed or of common ownership. Third, wastes were not enclosed and thus road construction did not involve the removal or relocation of walls and fences. Even the more useful of the common areas would "generally lie open, without hedge or fence to divide and distinguish them from their adjoining and continuous neighbors" (Molesworth, 1723, p. 5). For all of these reasons, the wastes formed the perfect place to set about road construction in Great Britain.

It was not unusual for a road to "pass through a moss or muir nearly the whole way" (Fourth Report of the Commissioners, 1809, V. 4, p. 35). Such a tract might be "the most dreary and waste of any in the highlands." The waste of Drumforskie, for example, was rarely seen before the creation of a roadway through the waste connecting Aberdeen with Stonehaven. James Blaikie, Provost of Aberdeen, found that, "[p]revious to the formation of this turnpike in 1799, this tract of land was literally inaccessible, indeed almost unknown, and a more comfortless and desolate waste could scarcely be fancied" (1837, p. 98). Such roads often were not well kept. The roads through open, common lands were "generally very bad . . . being but slightly mended, and seldom half the work done thereon, that is required by statute" (Molesworth, 1723, p. 44). The use of wastes to construct roads was so standard that by 1731 a table of acres of land in England grouped by usage placed together the "roads and waste-land" (Hatton, 1731, p. 246).

Commonly, roadways formed the boundaries between larger parcels of land. One of the most common examples is of roadways being created on the edge of wastelands, such that the road formed the boundary between the waste and the adjoining private parcels. For example, the muir of Drumquhyle, near Aberdeen, Scotland, lay "wholly on the west side" of the roadway, "by which it is bounded for nearly half a mile" (Blaikie, 1837, p. 97). Similarly, the boundaries of Fornett were "wastercourses, roads, or lines dividing ancient waste" (Davenport, 1967, p. 2).

Daniel Defoe wrote of one such road following the edge of a waste for miles. He explains, "On the road to Manchester, we passed the great bog or waste, called Chat-moss. . . . It extends on the left side of the road for five or six miles east and waste, and they told us it was in some places, seven or eight miles from north to south." Defoe (1761) was not particularly impressed, telling his reader, "there are many of these mosses in this country: take this for a description of all the rest" (p. 248).

By the end of the eighteenth century, statutes explicitly stated the norms for building roads on the properties known as commonly held. Thus, for example, a statute in 1788 provided for trustees to "divert, turn or alter the course of any part or parts of the said road, over or through any down, common, moor or waste ground, without making any satisfaction for the same" (Parliament of Great Britain, 1788).

Of course, building on waste roads had drawbacks. With no private ownership, the wastes provided an area of respite for those who wished to remain outside the law. For example, the parish of Caldback was said to be largely "forest and waste." Within this area "an highway, or main road, from Westmoreland and the eastern parts of Cumberland, to the western coasts of this country . . . lay long under the imputation of being the resort of such free-booters, and dangerous outlaws, as we suppose Robin Hood and his fellows to have been" (Hutchinson, 1794, V. 2, p. 376). Even without robbers, the roads through wastes lacked the security of nearby human habitation, which left travelers without the availability of emergency assistance or the possibility of asking for directions. As a result, "the traveler, worn out with fatigue is frequently lost" (Commissioners for Road and Bridges in the Highlands of Scotland, 1809, V. 4, p. 35)

Still, with all these drawbacks, the government focused road building on the wastes and common areas, directing such projects away from private lands when at all possible. When building on the wastes was not possible, laws demanded just compensation. Statutes explicitly required and authorized payment to individuals when a roadway was constructed or diverted through private land. The road could go "upon, over, or through any private lands or hereditaments," so long as the trustees tasked with building the road began by "first making satisfaction to the owners thereof" (Parliament of Great Britain, 1788).

## A HISTORY OF ROAD TAKINGS IN GREAT BRITAIN:
## CREATING PRIVATE PROPERTY IN THE WASTES

Moving into the later eighteenth and nineteenth century, the push to create private property in wastes gained steam. The enclosure movement, which first separated the open, common fields into private property, eventually made its way down the land hierarchy to the wastes. As a result, some wastes were allotted to particular individuals or manors and ultimately the proprietor made a private claim to the waste. In such cases, the courts had to address how to deal with the construction of new roads and the maintenance of existing roads through what would now become private property.

In those circumstances, if a road already existed, there was some doubt as to how to address the situation. In 1634, Duncomb's Case addressed the problem of a road across land that the owner wished to enclose. The court found that the owner could enclose the land, but "he must leave a sufficient way, and repair it at his own charge." Where private parties set out to ask Parliament to divide the commonly held wastes into private parcels, they would first set about establishing the portion from which road repair supplies would be taken. Thus, they would ask Parliament to appoint commissions who would "in the first place . . . set out and appoint such place or places as they shall think convenient and proper, such parcels of the said commons and waste grounds . . . for the purpose of furnishing gravel, stone and sand . . . for the repair of the several roads and highways within the said township or hamlet" (Powell, 1802, V. 1, p. 425). The second task of the commissioners would be to "mark and set out all the proper public or private roads over or across the said commons, and waste lands, of such breadth and in such directions as to them shall seem most proper." Private claims to wastelands were only established after these public claims to benefits were already established.

## A HISTORY OF ROAD TAKINGS IN GREAT BRITAIN: BUILDING AND REPAIRING ROADS

The building and repair of roads also speaks to the tradition of just compensation for takings in Great Britain because building and repair required raw materials, preferably from nearby areas. Road repair depended, initially, on whether roads were considered public or private ways. According to Austin's Case from 1672, a road that led "only to a church, to a private house or village, or to fields" was a private way. On the other hand, if a road led "to a market, and were a way for all travelers, and did communicate with a great road," then it would be a public way. In general, the courts found that determining public or private status was a matter of common custom. Where the way was public, then the parish was responsible for repairs. On the other hand, private ways were "to be repaired by the village, or hamlet, or sometimes by a particular person." Public repairs then depended on a source of resources that could be made available.

Parliament appointed commissioners and surveyors to care for the road-ways. Statutes enabled those parties to remove the materials they needed from nearby wastes and commons. A statute in 1771 thoroughly explained that the commissioners and surveyor were entitled to "cut, dig, gather, take, and carry away, any furze, heath, stones, gravel, sand, or other materials proper for the raising and repairing of said streets, and for making and repairing said roads, out of and from any waste ground or common, river or brook, in any Parish, town, or place" (Statutes at Large, 1774, V. 11, p. 87). Moreover, the commissioners and surveyors were not limited to the adjoining parcels of land. In fact, the statute authorized the taking of needed materials "in or within three miles of which any Port of the said road or streets do lie, without paying any thing for the same." With that said, the commissioners and surveyors had to take care when transporting these materials. If they made any damage to private lands while conveying the materials from public lands, the landowner would receive compensation.

Statutes first demanded that supplies for road repair be taken from the commons and wastes nearby. When such supplies were unavailable, the commissioners and surveyors could take supplies from private lands. First, supplies could not be taken from "a yard, garden, park, paddock, planted walk, or avenue to any house, or any enclosed ground planted and set apart as a nursery for trees" (Statutes at Large, 1774, V. 11, p. 87). With those areas exempted, the commissioners and surveyors could "search for, dig, gather, take and carry away" such materials as they needed "upon or out of, from and over the lands of any person or persons." In summary, if there were not freely available "sufficient materials for the repair of the highways" within the same parish or township, then "the surveyor of the highway may be forced to buy such materials" (Hawkins & Leach, 1777, V. 1, p. 379). The statute seems to have required, however, good notice to the landowner before his stones were carried away.

## A HISTORY OF ROAD TAKINGS IN GREAT BRITAIN:
## REFLECTIONS ON THE TRADITION OF JUST COMPENSATION

The British history of takings and road construction offers a number of insights into how the norms of just compensation were developing through the seventeenth and eighteenth centuries. The tendency to place roads across wastes represents a notable bow to the importance of not the right to just compensation, but more definitely, the right of private property owners to exclude others. By placing roads across waste lands before other areas, the government demonstrated a respect for private property that, in fact, goes a bit beyond the modern just compensation requirement. By requiring that wastes were used first, the government made a specific effort to avoid making takings of private property. Just compensation for private property, then, was a secondary measure—one that was sought only in the true instances of necessity.

In addition, indicators suggest that the norm of just compensation is quite robust. The requirement of proper compensation was written; it was not simply drawn from the Magna Carta, but repeatedly reemphasized and mechanized through particular statutes addressing road construction. Moreover, the right to compensation was a robust one—a right that authorized not only compensation for land, but also compensation for the removal of building materials such as stones and gravel. Finally, the right to compensation was substantial enough to even carry over to consequential damages—the right to compensation for damage caused by the removal of materials or the carrying of materials across one's property. Overall, the British projects of road construction demonstrate a strong set of property norms surrounding the idea of just compensation.

## ROAD CONSTRUCTION IN AMERICA

This strong tradition of just compensation norms within the British road history—a tradition that goes so far as to privilege avoiding a taking when possible—brings us full circle to the problem of explaining the odd contradiction between these norms and what Treanor describes as a norm of non-compensation in early American roadworks. Looking at this trend of non-compensation in more detail, Treanor (1985) cites two particular types of evidence. First, he notes that there are cases where when the "owner had failed to develop his property," then the government "simply transferred [ownership] to another person" (p. 695). Second, he finds that "[e]xcept for Massachusetts, no colony appears to have paid compensation when it built a state owned road across unimproved land. Legislatures provided compensation only for enclosed or improved land." In the following two sections, this chapter addresses each of these two strands of evidence, arguing that both strands are understandable in the context of British property norms more generally.

The British tradition included a strong preference for arable land (Fraley, 2016a). As Lord Coke explained, "It is true that agriculture and tillage is greatly respected and favoured as well by the common law, as by the common assent of the king, lords spiritual and temporal, and all the commons, in many Parliaments." The clear rule was that "The common law prefers arable land before all other" (Coke on Littleton, §85b).

This preference became a key part of the British approach to colonization, and most importantly, a key part of the process of articulating land claims against Native Americans and other Europeans who also sought territorial control (Fraley, 2016a). Improvable land invited settlement. Proponents of colonization argued, "It is the jus gentium, or law of nations, whatever waste or uncultured country is the discovery of any price, it is the right of that prince who was at the charge of that discovery ... to preserve and improve" (Crouch, 1735, p. 100). Under this international norm, British colonization focused on the creation of fenced and planted fields that would solidify claims to territory. Colonization, therefore, focused on "the enclosure and improvement of all the open grounds and waste land of the whole country" (O'Pheilly, 1767, p. 41). Such work of planting and fencing then justified British land claims to other European powers (Tomlins, 2003, p. 481). The English concepts of planting and fencing were crucial to their territorial claims (Arneil, 1996, p. 18) and drew on a long history of English attitudes to proper land use and fencing (Cronon, 1983). This strategy effectively rebutted both native claims to possession[2] and the less settled claims of other groups, such as the French, who built lines of forts instead of planning "to plant and settle" (Wynne, 1770, V. 2, p. 11).[3]

British possession of North America depended highly on this set of norms: undeveloped land was either common or unowned. Property claims required the investment of labor articulated by Locke to be perfected. Relying on this theory of perfecting possession to land, early colonial laws essentially created a multistep process for the establishment of individual property grants. The first step was the formal grant of the territory from the king or his designee in North America. This, however, created only an unperfected claim. Perfecting title to such grants generally required some type of visible improvement to the land—generally cultivation, fencing, or draining. For example, patentees could settle their lands (thereby vesting their property rights) either by planting three of every fifty acres granted, or alternatively, by clearing and draining three acres of wetlands (Price, 1995, p. 115). Such restrictions on the process of perfecting grants appeared in local laws as well as on the face of patents themselves.

Taking into account this history of how the idea of possession and private property claims evolved in the colonial realm, one can reexamine Treanor's approach. Treanor found a history of non-compensation for the taking of property because he saw state governments removing property from owners who had failed to develop and then transferring that property to other parties. Viewed in light of the colonial process of establishing land rights, both at the national and local level, such evidence reads a bit differently.

Treanor speaks of an "owner" who had failed to develop his property. In fact, there is every reason to believe that the colonial legislatures would not have viewed such persons as owners of the land. Rather, such persons were patentees who failed to fully vest their property claims. Such lands, then, were not properly understood as being private property. Establishing property claims in full required adhering to certain conditions of development after a grant was made. Without meeting those conditions, the patentee failed to fully create a claim to the land.

## ROAD CONSTRUCTION IN AMERICA: CROSSING UNIMPROVED LANDS

Treanor's second piece of evidence supporting his assertion that colonial legis-latures regularly took private property without compensation focuses on roads crossing unimproved lands. Specifically, Treanor (1985) states that "[e]xcept for Massachusetts, no colony appears to have paid compensation when it built a state owned road across unimproved land. Legislatures provided compensation only for enclosed or improved land" (p. 695).

One might argue that this type of taking fits with the previous type of taking of undeveloped land. The problem, however, is that statutes specifically governed the process of vesting patents to land. Those statutes, as the example above shows, demonstrate that it was possible to perfect claims to land without developing anywhere near all of the land. Thus, under the typical statute or grant restriction, the full parcel would be vested even if only three of fifty acres were cultivated and fenced. Thus, while the overall idea of undeveloped lands being less secure in title may have been relevant to the thinking of legislatures at the time, the particular problem of a lack of a fully vested title does not really explain the lack of compensation for a taking.

On the other hand, the British tradition of taking roads through common or waste lands may well be relevant to understanding the choice of non-compensation. Traditionally, undeveloped lands such as wastes were not fully and properly claimed as private property; claims that were made to such lands were tenuous and unclear. And even when wastes were being claimed as private property, as demonstrated above, the roadways could be taken out first for public benefit. This was, in fact, the only category of non-compensation related to roadworks within the British tradition.

The justification for such non-compensation was twofold. The first justifica-tion for this approach was the general concept of waste lands being public property due to their lack of development. Additional justification came from the benefits received from road construction. The surrounding properties generally increased in value due to the availability of transportation routes that could move goods and resources. Thus, it could be said that there were, in fact, no damages to the parcel as a whole, because although slightly smaller, the parcel would be of greater value.

Notably, there are many reasons to see the attitudes toward waste lands as comparable in Great Britain and colonial America. British settlements in North America specifically incorporated the concept of waste lands within their laws. Moreover, colonists continued the use of such lands for public purposes such as noxious uses (Fraley, forthcoming). In particular, the tradition of using wastes for roads continued in early North America. Colonial records in North Carolina, for example, disclose numerous bills allocating money for the construction of public roads across swamps and other such low-lying areas (Saunders, 1888, V. 6, pp. 874, 923). The tradition is also made clear in the literature of surveying. A surveyor's guide for "how to lay out new lands in America" made specific provisions for setting out roads that would travel through waste lands in the new country (Love, 1704).

There is, however, a much more important reason that compensation was not particularly fair, necessary, or reasonable when a road crossed the unimproved portions of a parcel. In the process of surveying lands in North America, surveyors did not count the areas that were viewed as nonarable. Such lands were simply excluded from the count—the grantee did not pay for them. Notably, some such grants even specifically noted that the included amount of extra for waste also included lands for "highways." For example, one grant read from, "Aaron Blackley's line, in length twenty chains, bounded east by Samuel Potter, north by Aaron Blackley and John Johnson, west by the swamp, south by Eliezer Lampson and unsurveyed land; containing in all the above and tracts of upland and meadow, after allowances for barrens, highways, etc., two hundred acres, being allotted for the parsonage" (Kavenagh, 1983, p. 1493). In short, surveyors simply estimated the content of wasteland and then subtracted that from the intended grant. If the king said to award two hundred acres, then the grant was actually for 250 acres, if that region contained a one-fifth portion of waste per arable acre.

If such allowances for barren and unused ground, which would later make nice spaces for roadways, was initially included within the grants, and, in fact, not paid for by the owner, then there would be very little reason to believe that compensation was necessary for the later construction of roadways.

## CONCLUSION: BRITISH AND AMERICAN LAW AND THE TRADITIONS OF TAKINGS LAW

The history of takings appears episodic in the scholarly literature—with points of emphasis, valleys too deep to discern much content, along with sudden shifts and contradictions. It is a rather odd life history of a concept that dates back to the Magna Carta. Admittedly, not all histories, intellectual or otherwise, are smooth. On the other hand, law does have more mechanisms built in to ensure fidelity—particularly within the common law, precedent-based tradition (Fraley, 2016b). For this reason, it is logical to seek greater continuities within the law of takings. Such continuities not only may more accurately render the history of the law, but also provide additional theoretical insights. Additionally, aligning the American norms with their British counterparts also pushes back against the continual push toward viewing everything through the lens of American exceptionalism and brings American legal scholarship more into the tradition of Atlantic inquiry.

Here, the point of inquiry was an oddity in the historical record—a tradition of compensated roadway takings in Great Britain and a scholarly account denying the same in America. Such conflicts in the historical record are more than aberrations in the scholarship. Given the degree to which British law was imported into America, there is every reason to look for explanations when traditions do not align. In particular, within the context of property law, it is critical to look at precisely those points to inquire as to whether there was a definite shift in the understanding of property rights or a shift in other core concepts such as property and possession.

Working out this particular conflict in the record demonstrates a few key points. First, Treanor is likely mistaken when he says that colonial legislatures regularly took private property without compensating the owner. At least in the two types of situations Treanor examined, there is reason to believe that compensation was not in fact due because either (1) the party did not have a vested right in the property, or (2) the party had been given a grant that already excluded nonarable lands, which would be precisely the lands used for road building.

Second, while we may tend to see the long view of takings in American history as a tradition of growing rights—particularly in light of the development of regulatory takings compensation—American takings likely initially fell short of the more clear British preference for avoiding takings by using property that was already public.

## NOTES

1. Not everyone agrees with Treanor's assessment. For example, Bernard Siegan much more favorably relates instances of colonial compensation (Siegan, 2001, pp. 108–114).

2. The argument followed along these lines for native peoples:

> For they account it a very just cause of war, if any nation will hinder others to come and possess a part of their soil, of which they make no use, but let it lie idle and uncultivated; since every man has by the law of nature a right to such a waste portion of the earth as is necessary for his subsistence. (More, 1743, p. 61)

3. In the British view only "barbarous nations ... abolished improved agriculture," instead "possessing, without labor or trouble, the vast deserts which their arms had made, and cultivated, very superficially, only a small spot near their habitations" (Mills, 1762, V. 1, p. v).

# REFERENCES

Arneil, B. (1996). *John Locke and America: The defence of English colonialism.* Oxford, UK: Clarendon Press.

Austin's Case, 1 Vent. 189 (1672).

Blaikie, J. (1837). Report of the system of improvement followed on the muirs of Drumforskie and Drumquhyle. In *Prize-essays and transactions of the Highland and Agricultural Society of Scotland.* Edinburgh, Scotland: Blackwood & Sons, pp. 97–120.

Coke on Littleton §85b.

Cronon, W. (1983). *Changes in the land: Indians, colonists, and the ecology of New England.* New York, NY: Macmillan.

Crouch, N. (1735). *The English Empire in America.* Dublin, Ireland: S. Fuller.

Davenport, F. G. (1967). *The economic development of a Norfolk manor: 1086–1565.* New York, NY: A. M. Kelley.

Defoe, D. (1761). *A tour thro' the whole island of Great Britain.* London, UK: D. Browne.

Dumcomb's Case, 1 Roll. Abr. 390 (1634).

Epstein, R. (1985). *Takings: Private property and the power of eminent domain.* Cambridge, MA: Harvard University Press.

*Fourth report of the commissioners for road and bridges in the highlands of Scotland.* (1809). London, UK: House of Commons.

Fraley, J. M. (2016a). The anti-wilderness bias in American law. In *Modern studies in property law* (forthcoming).

———. (2016b). A new history of waste law. *Marquette Law Review, 100,* forthcoming.

———. (forthcoming). *Property law, Wastelands and international boundaries.*

Gwillim, H. (1801). *A collection of acts and records of Parliament: With reports of cases, argued and determined in the courts of law and equity, respecting tithes.* London, UK: Early English Books.

Hatton, E. (1731). *An intire system of arithmetic.* London, UK: G. Strahan.

Hawkins, W., & Leach, T. (1777). *A treatise of the pleas of the crown.* London, UK: His Majesty's Law-Printers.

Hutchinson, W. (1794). *The history of the county of Cumberland.* Carlisle, UK: F. Jollie.

Kavenagh, W. Keith. (Ed.). (1983). *Foundations of colonial America: A documentary history.* Vol. 3. Philadelphia, PA: Chelsea House.

Love, John. (1688). *Geodaesia.* London, UK: J. Rivington.

Magna Carta. (1215). In R. Perry & J. Cooper (Eds.), *Sources of our liberties: Documentary origins of individual liberties in the United States Constitution and Bill of Rights* (pp. 1–22). Chicago, IL: American Bar Foundation, 1959.

Mills, J. (1762). *A new and complete system of practical husbandry.* London, UK: R. Baldwin.

Molesworth, R. (1723). *Proposals for the improvement of common and waste-lands.* London, UK: James Roberts.

More, T. (1743). *Utopia, or the happy republic.* Glasgow, Scotland: R. Foulis.

O'Pheilly, D. (1767). *The ants: A rhapsody.* London, UK: L. Davis.

Parliament of Great Britain. *An act for amending, widening, and keeping in repair, the road from the bottom of Whitesheet Hill, through Hurdcot, to the Wilton Turnpike Road* (1788).

Powell, J. J. (1802). *Original precedents in conveyancing.* London, UK: W. Clarke & Sons.

Price, E. T. (1995). *Dividing the land: Early American beginnings of our private property mosaic.* Chicago, IL: University of Chicago Press.

Reynolds, S. (2010). *Before eminent domain: Toward a history of expropriation of land for the common good.* Chapel Hill, NC: University of North Carolina Press.

Saunders, W. L. (Ed.). (1888). *The colonial records of North Carolina.* Raleigh, NC: P. M. Hale.

Siegan, B. H. (2001). *Property rights: From Magna Carta to the Fourteenth Amendment.* New Brunswick, NJ: Transaction.

Skouras, G. (2000). *Takings law and the Supreme Court.* Bern, Switzerland: Peter Lang.

Somner, W., & Kennett, W. (1693). *A treatise of the Roman ports and forts in Kent.* London, UK: Early English Books.

*Statutes at large, from the tenth year of the reign of King George the Third to the thirteenth year of the reign of King George the Third inclusive.* (1774). London, UK: C. Eyre.

Tomlins, C. (2003). In a wilderness of tigers: Violence, the discourse of English colonizing, and the refusals of American history, *Theoretical Inquiries in Law, 4,* 451–489.

Treanor, W. M. (1985). The origins and original significance of the just compensation clause of the Fifth Amendment. *Yale Law Journal, 94,* 694–716.

Wynne, J. H. (1770). *A general history of the British empire in America.* London, UK: W. Richardson.

# 4 The Honest Speculator

## Property, State, and Financial Regulation in Restoration France

TYSON LEUCHTER

"Sir, the law cannot obstruct me on this point, regarding my property, regarding my will; it cannot prevent me from purchasing or selling, if it pleases me to do so" (Perdonnet, 1823, p. 52). Forceful words, but the man speaking them did not exist. He was an invention, a rhetorical device created by Paris stockbroker Vincent Perdonnet as part of his legal defense in a landmark series of trials spanning 1823–24, which saw him facing off against the aristocrat Charles-Théodore-Palamède-Antoine-Félix de Tertulis, Comte de Forbin-Janson. The fictional speaker represented an average investor seeking to obtain substantial profits through risky speculative ventures at the Paris Stock Exchange. As scripted by Perdonnet, this hypothetical investor held no doubts that financial speculation was permitted by laws and sanctioned by society. After all, public debt futures contracts—the primary speculative vehicle—remained the investor's property and therefore under his dominion. Were it otherwise, the investor suggested, then France's system of law would fall into disorder, with individual will and the circulation of property unjustly restricted.

This imaginary investor's faith would promptly be shaken to its core. Perdonnet confronted him with an imaginary stockbroker, tasked with disabusing the deluded investor of his too-rosy picture of France's economic order. The stockbroker agreed that laws should step out of the way of the individual, permitting him to transact as he saw fit. But Perdonnet argued through his fictive mouthpiece, a malign new legal interpretation of financial speculation had arisen. The investor, Perdonnet argued, would be able to speculate at the Paris Stock Exchange; the risks, however, would be borne entirely by the intermediary party—the stockbroker—as courts had recently held that the futures contract was an illicit financial form, stripping it of many legal protections. A crafty investor could therefore speculate in risky gambits, then repudiate his debts if the venture turned out poorly; the corresponding stockbroker would be left footing the bill. Upon hearing this news, the imaginary investor was thunderstruck. "Thus the public would have the privilege of speculating on the credulity or the imprudent temerity of stockbrokers, and of exploiting, to its profit (without any other danger than that of seeing its *bad faith* recorded in a holding), the confidence that they are obliged to grant to their clients, because it would be impossible to comply with the law!!!" To such a sorry state of affairs, the imaginary stockbroker could only soberly respond, "Yes, sir" (Perdonnet, 1823, pp. 52–53).

This trial marked an important development in the concept of property in postrevolutionary France. At stake was the nation's position on the relations between the legitimate boundaries of property and financial risk. How might or might not a discursive universe that typically valorized land over moveable property and liquid assets be reconciled with financial speculation? How might one promote an affirmative defense of financial speculation, inherently risky, that figured it not only as a regrettably ineradicable element of the modern economy, but as a valuable tool for states and citizens alike? As I will argue, the course and results of the Perdonnet and Forbin-Janson trial highlight the contested nature of France's jurisprudential approach to the appropriate balance between risk, property, and the ambiguous moral character of speculation.

## PROPERTY AND FINANCIALIZED PROPERTY
## IN EUROPEAN HISTORIOGRAPHY

Debates over the meaning of property had a long history in Europe (Blaufarb, 2016; Brewer & Staves, 1995; Pocock, 1985; Pocock, 2003; Ryan, 1984; Shovlin, 2006; Young & Smith, 1984). The conversation ranged across a number of conceptual areas, including political theory, contract law, agriculture and land use, economic domains, and phenomena relating to various forms of domination and human bondage, among others. Debates about property in specifically financialized form—notably, public and private debts, negotiable instruments, stocks, and futures contracts—encompassed concerns over the moral character of the supposedly "fictional" character of this property, its connection to the nature of state formation and the threatening specter of violent interstate competition, as well as how moveable property might or might not provide solid grounds for virtuous action (Carruthers, 2009; Darnton, 2003; Dickson, 1967; Gontard, 2003; Hissung-Convert, 2009; Hoffman, Postel-Vinay, & Rosenthal, 2003; Hont, 1993; Kaiser, 1991; Kessler, 2007; Lagneau-Ymonet & Riva, 2012; Leuchter, 2016; Michie, 2009; Poovey, 2007; Preda, 2001; Sonenscher, 2007; Stanziani, 2011; Stasavage, 2003; Thompson, 2000; Vause, 2012). This concern with the nature of property, both at the broader conceptual level and in financialized form, carried through to the French Revolution of 1789. Indeed, as Rafe Blaufarb has argued, the concept of property was of central importance to the revolutionaries, prompting a rethinking of the conceptual and legal categories of property (Blaufarb, 2016, p. 21). And as Rebecca Spang notes, a desire to protect the sanctity of property translated into intense revolutionary attention to the stability and consolidation of the public debt (Spang, 2015, pp. 58–72).

After the upheaval of the revolution, stabilizing property was, along with anchoring patriarchal power, one of the key means of reestablishing a certain form of social stability during the Napoleonic era (1799–1815) (Desan, 2004). Specifically, Article 544 of the 1804 Civil Code—the main document defining the landscape of France's civil law system—gave wide expanse to the uses of property: "Property is the right to enjoy and dispose of things in the most absolute manner, provided one does not make a usage prohibited by laws or regulations" (Civil Code, 1804).

This definition would be circumscribed by other domains of law. Articles 421 and 422 of the 1810 Penal Code ruled certain forms of speculation illegal, including those involving public debt. However, just what counted as legal or illegal speculation in the public debt remained ambiguous. In the absence of definitive statutory guidance, the decision was largely left to the courts. This hesitation between the push for substantively expansive property rights and the desire to restrict what were deemed illicit or immoral uses of property would continue into the Restoration regime (1815–1830). This regime at once promoted an individualized view of property rights, in which many barriers to the free circulation of property were abolished; at the same time, the Restoration state also sought to stamp out illicit uses of property (Girard, 1985; Steiner, 2012; Whatmore, 2012). As Francis Démier has argued, "Thus the idea emerges, in the experience of the Restoration, that in order to take root durably, the 'market' must be mastered, its practice regulated, the risks it represents attenuated" (Démier, 1993, p. 137).

The confrontation between Perdonnet and Forbin-Janson represents a particularly heightened example of such "risks." The burden of this confrontation revolved around the validity of the circulation of public debt futures at the Paris Stock Exchange, mixing concerns over private financial speculation and the robustness of indebted states. The Restoration state had turned to public debt to finance payment on a substantial war indemnity after the fall of Napoléon in 1815 (White, 2001, pp. 339–341). That debt now circulated at the Exchange, where speculators could bet on a rise or decline in prices. But the ways in which financial speculation at the Exchange appeared to dissolve the links between property, materiality, and time would prove both troubling and troublingly difficult to control.

The course and outcome of the Perdonnet–Forbin-Janson trial thus revealed the moral fault lines over financial regulation and the acceptable uses of property in a regime seeking to stabilize itself after war, revolution, and social upheaval.

## PERDONNET, FORBIN-JANSON, AND THE LEGITIMACY OF SPECULATION

Articles 421 and 422 of the 1810 Penal Code had proscribed illicit speculation on the public debt. But sanction generally fell down upon only those contracts in which prices were netted without securities exchanging hands; the vast majority of futures contracts were seen as legally valid. This interpretation was confirmed by court decisions in 1810, 1812, and 1814 (Hissung-Convert, 2008, pp. 64–65). Perdonnet himself had fought, and won, an earlier case that upheld futures contracts as valid forms of commerce in 1806 (Journal du Palais, 1838, p. 195).

He must therefore have felt quite secure in his legal footing when Forbin-Janson first requested his services on November 25, 1822. Initially, Perdonnet refused to sign on as Forbin-Janson's broker—nearing the end of a lengthy career, Perdonnet had his eyes set on his approaching retirement and was reluctant to take on any major new business, particularly ones involving immense sums ordered by an individual. But Forbin-Janson was persistent. The next day, Forbin-Janson returned and, as Perdonnet would later recount, regaled him with tales of "his long habitude in affairs of this genre, of the constant prudence with which he has guided these affairs, of the success he has obtained, of the advantages offered by his name, his rank, and his illustrious relations, in order to be promptly informed of circumstances likely to influence public credit." In addition, Forbin-Janson proudly highlighted his own personal, as well as familial, wealth, which, he stressed, should allay any fears Perdonnet might have had about potential defaults. Finally, Forbin-Janson promised to deposit a substantial amount of securities with Perdonnet, to be liquidated if needed to cover any debts incurred. This fusillade of assurances finally won Perdonnet over. As he wrote, "The totality of this language, the consideration of the distinguished rank that the Forbin-Janson family occupied in society, and the fear of offending monsieur le comte determined me not to persevere in my refusal" (Perdonnet, "Historique rapide," p. 1).

Flattery and personal fortune had not quite worn away all of Perdonnet's reserve, however, as he stipulated a number of conditions before agreeing to do business. First, his orders for Forbin-Janson were not to exceed inscriptions above 150,000 francs of public debt. Second, as guarantee, Forbin-Janson was to deposit stock in the company managing the Canal de Bourgogne, amounting to 150,000 francs valued at par. And third, he was to augment this deposit according to the market fluctuations in the above stock, maintaining a steady buffer of 150,000 francs (Perdonnet, "Historique rapide," p.2).

In what would prove to be an ill omen, Forbin-Janson was only too pleased to cooperate—to a degree. He transferred to Perdonnet stock in the Canal de Bourgogne, but not quite in the amount Perdonnet had requested: the total par value of the inscriptions amounted to 120,000 francs, falling 30,000 francs short of the agreed-upon amount (Perdonnet, "Historiqe rapide," p. 2). Perdonnet was distressed, but, his concerns perhaps assuaged by his client's high social status and repeated protestations of honor and probity, he did finally agree to serve as Forbin-Janson's agent.

The pair initially experienced some success. Through a series of purchases and resales over the course of November and December 1822, all utilizing the futures contract form, Forbin-Janson gained a net profit of 22,395 francs. Forbin-Janson promptly reinvested the initial capital—150,000 francs—back into public debt futures. It was at this point that the trouble began.

In this specific futures contract form, the price and quantity of the inscriptions of public debt to be bought or sold were locked in at the time the contract was drawn up. Forbin-Janson was, moreover, an *haussier,* that is, a speculator betting on a rise in prices. At the end of December 1822 and beginning of January 1823, he ordered Perdonnet to repurchase 150,000 francs of public debt, with the price locked in at 89 francs per inscription; the final settlement date was to be the end of January, or earlier at Forbin-Janson's will (Perdonnet, "Historique rapide," pp. 2–3). In that month-long interval, Forbin-Janson was hoping that the price of the public debt would climb, meaning that he could purchase debt at the contractually stipulated below-market rates; in turn, he would then be able to resell his holdings on the spot market—that is, immediately—to great profit. This financial maneuver was not without risks. If prices moved in the contrary direction—fell instead of rose—then the purchaser would not be able to resell at a profit. Instead, the purchaser would have to cover the spread between the contractually stipulated higher price and the lower market rate out of his or her own personal funds, a potentially daunting risk given the vast sums involved.

To Perdonnet's and Forbin-Janson's presumed horror, this potential risk quickly became actual. The public debt markets witnessed a sudden and substantial downturn, prompting Perdonnet to urge Forbin-Janson to withdraw his investment as soon as possible, in order to minimize losses (Perdonnet, "Historique rapide," p. 3). But Forbin-Janson was troublingly quiet. He would not respond until January 19, 1823. Tragedies, he plaintively recounted, were beginning to pile up around his person; his uncle, the illustrious Victurnien-Bonaventure-Victor de

Rochechouart, marquis de Mortemart, had died suddenly, diverting his attention from the turbulent Parisian financial markets for several unfortunate days. But he urged Perdonnet to remain in "perfect security," since he would certainly be able to cover any forthcoming losses out of his personal fortune. He wrote, "[T]he faithfulness to fulfill my commitments is not something that may depend on the rise or fall [of public debt prices]" (as cited in Duprat, 1823, p. 7). He also promised to come visit Perdonnet to confirm his upcoming transactions on January 21, 1823.

Forbin-Janson's attestation of faith was not quite enough to soothe Perdonnet's worries, particularly given the ongoing downward trend in the price of the public debt. Moreover, Forbin-Janson's communication and presence had become increasingly erratic. He delayed the January 21 meeting until January 24, at a time during which days mattered. In this visit, he further swore that he would be able to meet his obligations, promising a payment of 250,000 francs in specie to Perdonnet by February 4, 1823, with more income to arrive from the mortgage of a piece of land valued at 1 million francs (as cited in Duprat, 1823, p. 7).

Several more days of silence followed, with multiple letters from Perdonnet going worryingly unanswered. Finally, on January 30, 1823, the day before the trade was to be executed, Perdonnet finally heard back from his erstwhile client. "I was not able to respond quickly to the letter I received from you yesterday morning," Forbin-Janson wrote, "an urgent affair forced me to leave." Declining to specify just what this "urgent affair" might have been, Forbin-Janson continued: "Everything that this letter includes is *perfectly just, reasonable, conforming to that which we had agreed upon*" (as cited in Duprat, 1823, pp. 9–10; all italics in original). Perdonnet was to complete the futures contract, purchasing 150,000 francs of public debt at a preestablished rate of 89 francs, then reselling those debt inscriptions at the going market rate.

Perdonnet did just that. The result, communicated to Forbin-Janson in a letter of February 1, 1823, was a substantial debit to the Comte's account: 341,325 francs, to be exact. Acting with uncharacteristic celerity, Forbin-Janson wrote back that same day, confirming that Perdonnet's account of the trade was "*perfectly exact*" (as cited in Duprat, 1823, p. 11). Forbin-Janson had been searching long and hard for ways to borrow against his property; in the meantime, he authorized Perdonnet to sell the stock in the Canal de Bourgogne, as a way to raise some much-needed cash (Duprat, 1823, p. 11). The proceeds from the sale, unfortunately, were disappointing, resulting in Forbin-Janson's outstanding debt still amounting to 281,385 francs. Perdonnet expected to receive Forbin-Janson in his office on February 3, 1823, to settle up payment and close out the contract (Duprat, 1823, pp. 11–12).

Perdonnet would not see him that day. Instead, Perdonnet welcomed Forbin-Janson's lawyer, Luxeuil, into his office, who delivered the following sobering news. Unable to borrow against his land, Forbin-Janson had vanished. Moreover, Perdonnet was not the only stockbroker embroiled in Forbin-Janson's financial woes; in fact, he had contracted with six other stockbrokers, with debts impressively totaling more than 1,120,00 francs. Substantial though Forbin-Janson's assets may have been, they were not sufficient to cover this entire sum. His total outstanding debt thus remained at 281,325 francs, as Forbin-Janson's other creditors would be paid out first.

Perdonnet and Forbin-Janson's lawyer attempted to find some kind of equitable agreement, in which Forbin-Janson would pay a reduced portion of his debts. But these negotiations quickly deteriorated and, on May 20, 1823, the case of Perdonnet versus Forbin-Janson made its first appearance in the courts, at the Tribunal de commerce de la Seine (Duprat, 1823, pp. 12–13).

Forbin-Janson's legal strategy involved two primary claims. First, he argued that the case was not justiciable before the Tribunal de commerce, since his transactions with Perdonnet did not constitute a legitimate business deal; since the Tribunal de commerce was habitually more favorable to stockbrokers and the world of finance generally, Forbin-Janson wanted jurisdiction shifted to the civil courts (Duprat, 1823, p. 13). His second gambit was to invoke the "*exception du jeu.*" This was the principle that illicit gambling debts could not create legally binding obligations, since the initial transaction was itself not permitted by law. One could not, in other words, take a rival to court to collect on debts from a card game. And because, according to Forbin-Janson, futures contracts were exactly just such gambling debts, he could not be forced to pay his debts to Perdonnet. Futures contracts in the public debt, in other words, did not constitute a valid form of property.

Perdonnet, unsurprisingly, disagreed, maintaining that the matter under review was a commercial transaction, and that futures contracts were legitimate forms of financial property. True to its character, the Tribunal de commerce found in favor of Perdonnet, ordering Forbin-Janson to pay up or face debt imprisonment (Duprat, 1823, p. 13).

Through a series of appeals, the case eventually reached the Cour royale de Paris, with oral argument taking place on June 28, 1823. Forbin-Janson abandoned his claim that the case should not have been justiciable before the Tribunal de commerce (Duprat, 1823, p. 14). But he fiercely maintained that futures contracts were illegitimate. The thrust of his claims was that futures contracts by nature involved transacting with fictive property. At the time the contract was drawn up, the seller did not necessarily possess the actual securities, nor the purchaser sufficient funds. As his lawyers opined in a legal brief, "The law does not at all recognize these monstrous contracts of sale, in which the one who sells does not have the merchandise, the one who purchases does not have the money, and neither one nor the other has the intention of ever realizing the transaction" (Berryer fils, Berryer père, Bonnet, Coffinières, & Hennequin, 1823, p. 4). In this view, the futures contract truly was nothing other than a bet on price fluctuations in the public debt, with no underlying materiality in the form of real property. Since his debts thus stemmed from morally proscribed gambling—futures contracts here reduced to a game of differences—Forbin-Janson and his legal team held that he could not be legally forced to pay them.

Pleading for himself, Perdonnet mounted a thoroughgoing defense of financial speculation through futures contracts as not just legally valid but morally acceptable as well. In terms of futures contracts' legality, he argued first that this kind of financial speculation did eventually take material form as property, since, at the termination of the contract, money and securities did indeed change hands. Moreover, the legislation defining illegal financial speculation only required that the inscriptions of public debt be available at Paris Stock Exchange at the time of contract, not that they had to actually be possessed by the stockbroker, as ordered by his client, at that point; so long as the required amount of debt existed at the Exchange, rather than in the hands of the seller, the contract could legitimately be created. Thus, Perdonnet observed, the standard financial practice of drawing up a futures contract first and only obtaining the inscriptions of public debt once the contract was closed out was wholly in line with the law's commands. As Perdonnet himself had experienced, previous jurisprudence had upheld the futures contract on just these grounds (Perdonnet, 1823, pp. 22–36).

Most crucially, Perdonnet observed that the definitive statement on the legality of public debt futures had not yet been made. Article 90 of the 1807 Commercial Code, which was the legal institution governing transactions at the Stock Exchange, literally used the future tense, stating that there will be "rules of public administration regarding all that is related to the negotiation and transmission of the property of public funds" (as cited in Fournel, 1807, p. 68). These rules, however, had not yet been issued, remaining to be drafted by some future legislature. As Perdonnet exclaimed, "A promise in a code! This perhaps has never been seen before" (Perdonnet, 1823, p. 36).

The question of futurity weighed heavily on Perdonnet's mind. He wrote, "The legislator governs neither for the past, nor even for the present; —he governs for the future, and for the *future solely*" (Perdonnet, 1823, p. 58). The legislative authority, in this view, must take an *ex ante* perspective, seeking to adopt the optimal rules for society going forward, rather than retroactively assigning culpability, which would be the province of the courts. Thus, for Perdonnet, whenever the state did decide to fulfill the promise of Article 90 of the Commercial Code, it should do so in a way to produce good social outcomes; in the meantime, without clear guidance according to the law, the judge should follow prior jurisprudence and longstanding usage, which had established that public debt futures were indeed valid forms of property (Perdonnet, 1823, p. 54). To do otherwise would be to leave law in a disordered state, as Perdonnet's imaginary and bewildered interlocutor remarked in this very defense.

All this argumentation ultimately relied upon an affirmative defense of financial speculation. Perdonnet was only too happy to provide one. He baldly stated, "Speculation on public debt, through futures contracts . . . is not only useful, but necessary to government, to commerce, and to society, of which all branches have a right to equal protection" (Perdonnet, 1823, p. 64). Public debt, Perdonnet observed, had become the "thermometer" of a state's credit and of the "confidence that individuals placed in it" (Perdonnet, 1823, p. 64). Futures contracts served to calm fluctuations in the price of the public debt because they responded to speculators' future expectations rather than daily rumors or bad tidings that might precipitate a sudden drop in price. Financial speculation, even when it bet on a decline in the price of the debt, therefore served the state's advantage (Perdonnet, 1823, pp. 66–67).

This form of speculation also redounded to the individual's benefit. Through a combination of futures contracts and spot transactions, individuals could effectively borrow money at a comparatively low rate of interest, with few tedious obstacles to surmount. These individuals could, in turn, reinvest this sudden influx of money back into productive enterprise, or perhaps purchase land, converting moveable property into real estate (Perdonnet, 1823, pp. 69–70). Public debt futures were therefore not parasitic on the notionally "real" forms of property but rather an integral part of acceptable commerce.

Financial speculation, according to Perdonnet, helped states and individuals flourish. It was thus a valid part of France's moral universe and economic landscape. Naturally, some untrustworthy souls would maliciously choose to abuse the chances for speculation. As Perdonnet observed, "In fact, experience has told us that the honest speculator, who sees himself ruined by the unfortunate results of his operations, does not behave as did m. de Forbin-Janson. —he abandons the field and retreats from the Stock Exchange, informing the stockbroker of his deplorable situation and, in authorizing him to act as he believes appropriate to his own interest, approves in advance what he will have felt obliged to do" (Perdonnet, 1823, p. 40). Forbin-Janson, according to Perdonnet, had done none of these things. Forbin-Janson had instead acted as a dishonest speculator. And therefore, according to Perdonnet, the Cour royale must uphold the lower court's opinion and find in his favor.

The Cour royale disagreed. Though it did chide Forbin-Janson for his "bad faith" in repudiating his losses after having accepted the benefits of earlier speculations, the court found that Perdonnet had never made a "real offer" to deliver the inscriptions of public debt in question (as cited in Duprat, 1823, p. 19). Since Perdonnet did not materially possess those inscriptions at the time the contract was drawn up, the court found that these futures contracts were indeed a form of illicit gambling, legally null and incapable of serving as the basis for debt recovery litigation (Duprat, 1823, pp. 18–19). This judgment was a reversal of previous jurisprudence, but, in the court's view, the stakes were grave. The decision stated that, considering "that the strict execution of laws and regulations in this matter can alone arrest the immoderate ardor to enrich oneself, which has seized the fathers of families, who, in place of engaging in honest and useful professions, throw themselves into transactions disavowed by morality, and are always followed by complete ruin or scandalous fortune" (as cited in Duprat, 1823, p. 10). The court overturned the decision of the Tribunal de commerce, finding against Perdonnet and liberating Forbin-Janson from his debts.

Perdonnet had one chance remaining. In fact, both he and Forbin-Janson had appealed the Cour royale decision to France's high court, the Cour de cassation. Though he had won the decision, Forbin-Janson had reacted apoplectically to the Cour royale's statement that he had acted duplicitously; as an illustrious aristocrat, to see his honor tarnished in the verdict had wounded him deeply. In a series of public legal briefs, he vigorously defended himself against such judicial contumely. "Honor," he asked, "this first of all goods, must it not be the most inviolable of all properties?" (Forbin-Janson, 1824, pp. 3–4) And yet, he lamented, the Cour royale had failed in its duty to protect property, one of the key obligations of justice in a postrevolutionary moral universe. Worse still, given the spectacular nature of the trial—its coverage in newspapers, its public appeal—this "injurious epithet" that the court's decision had tarred him with had itself circulated around Paris and, indeed, beyond: "Every journal printed in the capital repeated this outrageous denomination and made it circulate in the whole world. The general interest of the trial, its solemnity, had attracted a most extraordinary attention. How many French, for whom my name was not wholly unfamiliar, must have felt the impression of a calumny that usurped the authority of a judicial sentence!" (Forbin-Janson, 1824, p. 6) The charge that he had acted in bad faith, the comte maintained, was plainly false; and yet, by being published in an official legal document, this odious falsehood would be taken as true. There must be, in his view, some legal recourse against such a scurrilous charge. For Forbin-Janson, to defend his personal honor was therefore to defend the sanctity of property, indeed of the entire justice system. He demanded that the Cour de cassation strip the offending phrase from the official decision.

The court declined, rejecting his appeal (Duprat, 1823, p. 19).

Perdonnet once again pled on his own account. And once again, he argued extensively that the futures contract was a legally valid form of property, rather than a kind of illegal gambling. But he also took the opportunity to expand his affirmative defense of financial speculation. Rhetorically addressing the Cour royale, he charged, "You have destroyed your own work; —you have recreated chaos. You have forbidden me from following decisions to which, for twenty-one years, you had commanded me to obey. You have condemned one of the necessities of society. You have killed moveable property, the most mobile after cash" (Perdonnet, 1824, p. 49). He fully acknowledged that the court had done so in the hopes of promoting the social good. But, in his view, the court had followed a superannuated vision of the good, one locked in an antiquated vision of the economic order. How could this antiquated vision still hold sway, Perdonnet inquired, "when time, the form of government, the ever-increasing movement of credit and industry, has created new needs, new relations, and system of finances completely different from the former; —when the government of today encourages and protects that which the government of the past believed must be condemned and forbidden; —when, at last, that which formerly could have born harm, is now useful, necessary, I almost said indispensable?" (Perdonnet, 1824, p. 24). The twinned change in the form of government and the implantation of a form of financial capitalism had altered the moral logic by which the magistrate should judge. Credit had become a central aspect of the contemporary regime. And, as Perdonnet claimed, "one of the greatest means of credit is the active circulation of values, —it is the facility of speculation" (Perdonnet, 1824, p. 81). Moveable property—public debt futures, in this case—was necessary to postrevolutionary society.

This then was the "chaos" that the Cour royale's decision threatened to unleash, if it were allowed to stand. Too firmly entrenched in the contemporary financial landscape, public debt futures would not vanish from the Paris Stock Exchange. But now the stockbroker perpetually risked his client, like Forbin-Janson, invoking the *exception du jeu* and repudiating his debts; the stability of public credit, of the financialized form of moveable property, would therefore be buffeted by uncertainty. In turn, this uncertainty would force stockbrokers and clients into deceptive practices, so as to shield themselves from legal risk. As Perdonnet warned the judges of the court, "[Y]ou will constrain the agents of negotiations, the bondholders, the most circumspect, even the most honest

speculators to fool the magistrates, by adopting fictions destined to defend themselves against these *savage* laws" (Perdonnet, 1824, p. 88). The attempt to purge
immoral speculation from the Paris Stock Exchange had, in Perdonnet's view,
rendered it more, not less, deceptive.

Such was his apologia for financial speculation. "I have done my duty,"
Perdonnet concluded, "come what may" (Perdonnet, 1824, p. 88).

From the August 11, 1824, decision of the Cour de cassation: "Considering
... that a law that has the goal of regulating the negotiation of public funds and
of repressing maneuvers that it declares illicit, eminently uphold the public order,
and that the acts that it forbids and annuls cannot, according to the articles cited
above, be validated by any convention or ratification; The Court rejects the demand
in cassation ... " (Bulletin des arrêts de la Cour de cassation, 1825, pp. 303–304).

Perdonnet lost and would soon retire to his native Switzerland. Despite
the adverse outcome of the trial, he remained quite wealthy, wealthy enough to
leave a gift of 200,000 francs to his hometown of Vevey upon his death in 1850
(Perdonnet, 1839, p. 106). Forbin-Janson, his wounded honor notwithstanding,
won the case and would not have to pay his debts; thenceforward, he largely
shunned public life, founding a sugar factory in the Vaucluse before dying in
Paris in 1849 (Bourloton, Cougny, & Robert, 1891, p. 25).

## CONCLUSION

The Perdonnet ruling set the juridical standard for illicit speculation going forward.
Given the confidentiality of financial transactions at the Stock Exchange, enforcement of this standard was quite difficult. Public debt futures continued to be vigorously traded without possession of the relevant securities beforehand; but when
financial transaction eventuated in contentious litigation, the Cour de cassation's
standard came into effect. Several more stockbrokers received the same judgment
as did Perdonnet, failing to recover their debts in court (Hissung-Convert, 2008).
The financialized form of moveable property at the Stock Exchange thus had been
shorn of its previous legal protections by the state.

Despite this increased legal suspicion, the Perdonnet standard was nonetheless constantly subverted at the practical level at the Paris Stock Exchange,
with public debt futures continuing to circulate in great quantities; the standard
would face criticism at the juridical level too. No less an authority than Raymond-
Théodore Troplong—a renowned expert on property law and soon to be president
of the Cour de cassation—wrote of the Perdonnet decision in 1845: "What would
become of our credit if we were to restrict transactions at the Exchange to the
spot market, and if we drove speculation, which must not be confounded with

gambling, from it?" (Troplong, 1845, p. 452). The Cour de cassation's 1824 decision would be challenged during the 1830s and 1840s and substantially walked back in 1857 (Hissung-Convert, 2008, p. 349). But without commanding statutory law in place, financial speculation through public debt futures still ran the risk of a sudden shift in jurisprudence.

The Perdonnet case dramatized the contentious, and sometimes uncertain, implantation of financial capitalism in postrevolutionary France on two stages: interpersonal and governmental. On both these stages, the evaluation of the concept of property was of central concern. During the seventeenth and eighteenth centuries, there was a distinct aristocratic ethos holding that debts of honor were between equals, while commercial debts, contracted with commoners, were "mere inconveniences" and repaid only with extreme indolence, if at all. Moreover, honor was key to private credit, to the ability to borrow depending on the value of one's name (Crowston, 2013, pp. 10, 179, 168, 196). The pretrial wrangling between Perdonnet and Forbin-Janson suggests the afterlife, but also the slackening, of this form of credit. Despite Forbin-Janson's high rank, Perdonnet expected all debts to be paid quite nearly in full, and promptly. Despite Forbin-Janson's illustrious name and family connections, he was not able to borrow against his land. Debts stemming from moveable property were thus, gradually, becoming commensurate with interpersonal debts based on rank and reputation.

At the same time, the Perdonnet case also displays a state regime highly ambivalent regarding the risks presented by financialized moveable property. In attempting to suppress public debt futures, the decisions of the Cour royale and Cour de cassation clearly viewed windfall profits and catastrophic losses stemming from risky price fluctuations at the Stock Exchange as immoderate, immoral, unacceptable. On the other hand, Tribunal de commerce was quite a bit more sanguine about these same risks. And other branches of the state also engaged in this same form of financial speculation through the state's attempt to amortize the debt, as Perdonnet had observed during his trial (Perdonnet, 1823, pp. 49–50). Indeed, finance minister Villèle, arch conservative and no friend to liquid wealth and moveable property, orated before the Chamber of Deputies on April 30, 1824: "No doubt that speculation [agiotage] bears its harms and dangers. But how, with the necessity imposed on us by our financial system, to support public credit in order to retain the capability of borrowing in extraordinary circumstances? How, I say, is it possible to conceive of a form of public funds that does not give rise to speculation? What produces speculation? The two chances of rising and falling. If you kill these chances, you kill credit" (as cited in Troplong, 1845, p. 452).

Through the Perdonnet case, France's high court had tried to restrict the financialized circulation of moveable property at the Paris Stock Exchange. But, as Perdonnet had argued, financial speculation was now an ineradicable aspect of contemporary states. The Perdonnet standard increased the risks involved, but without definitive statutory law on the flow of financialized property, the courts could not once and for all prohibit speculators—honest and dishonest alike—from engaging in financial speculation through public debt futures; and France's jurisprudence would soon retreat from the strictures of the Perdonnet decision. Finally, on March 28, 1885, the legislative promise contained in Article 90 of the Commercial Code would be fulfilled by a law specifically regarding futures contracts. The first article of the law stated, "All futures contracts on public funds and others . . . are recognized as legal. No one may, in order to escape the obligations arising therefrom, invoke article 1965 of the Civil Code, even if these obligations are resolved by the payment of a simple difference" (Law of March 28, 1885, 1885). The risks of financial speculation had been legitimated by the state. The chances for complete ruin still existed. But at the legal and juridical level, "scandalous fortune" had by now been converted into fortune alone. Despite concerted efforts by the state to root it out, financial speculation could not be disentangled from the concept of property.

## REFERENCES

Article 1, Law of March 28, 1885. (1885).

Berryer, Berryer, Bonnet, Coffinières, & Hennequin. (1823). *Consultation pour M. le Comte de Forbin-Janson*. Paris, France: J. Didot.

Blaufarb, R. (2016). *The great demarcation: The French Revolution and the invention of modern property*. New York, NY: Oxford University Press.

Brewer, J., and Staves, S. (Eds.). (1995). *Early modern conceptions of property*. New York, NY: Routledge.

Bulletin des arrêts de la Cour de cassation, rendus en matière civile. (1824). Paris, France: Imprimerie royale.

Carruthers, B. G. (2009). *City of capital: Politics and markets in the English financial revolution*. Princeton, NJ: Princeton University Press.

Code Civil, Livre II, Titre II, Article 544 (1804).

Crowston, C. H. (2013). *Credit, fashion, sex: Economies of regard in Old Regime France*. Durham, NC: Duke University Press.

Darnton, R. (2003). *George Washington's false teeth: An unconventional guide to the eighteenth century*. New York, NY: Norton.

Démier, F. (1993). L'impossible retour au régime des corporations dans la France de la Restauration, 1814–1830. In A. Plessis (Ed.), *Naissance des libertés économiques. Liberté du travail et liberté d'entreprendre: Le décret d'Allarde et la loi Le Chapelier, leurs conséquences, 1791 fin XIXe siècle* (pp. 117–142). Paris, France: Institut de l'histoire de l'industrie.

Desan, S. (2004). *The family on trial in revolutionary France.* Berkeley, CA: University of California Press.

Dickson, P. G. M. (1967). *The financial revolution in England: A study in the development of public credit, 1688–1756.* New York, NY: St. Martin's Press.

Duprat. (1823). *Mémoire pour m. Perdonnet, agent de change à Paris, demandeur en cassation de l'arrêt de la Cour royale de Paris, du 9 août 1823, contre m. de Tertulis, Comte de Forbin-Janson, défendeur.* Paris, France: Éverat.

Fournel. (1807). *Code de commerce, accompagné de notes et observations.* Paris, France: Dufresne.

Girard, L. (1985). *Les libéraux français, 1814–1875.* Paris, France: Aubier.

Gontard, M. (2000). *La Bourse de Paris: 1800–1830.* Aix-en-Provence, France: Édisud.

Hissung-Convert, N. (2009). *La spéculation boursière face au droit, 1799–1914.* Paris, France: L.G.D.J.

Hoffman, P. T., Postel-Vinay, G., and Rosenthal, J.-L. (2003). *Priceless markets: The political economy of credit in Paris, 1660–1870.* Chicago, IL: University of Chicago Press.

Hont, I. (1993). The rhapsody of public debt: David Hume and voluntary state bankruptcy. In N. Phillipson and Q. Skinner (Eds.), *Political discourse in early modern Britain* (pp. 302–320). New York, NY: Cambridge University Press.

Journal du Palais. *Récueil le plus ancien et le plus complet de la jurisprudence Française.* (1838). Paris, France: F-F Patris.

Kaiser, T. E. (1991). Money, despotism, and public opinion in early eighteenth-century France: John Law and the debate on royal credit. *The Journal of Modern History, 63,* 1–28.

Kessler, A. D. (2007). *A revolution in commerce: The Parisian Merchant Court and the rise of commercial society in eighteenth-century France.* New Haven, CT: Yale University Press.

Lagneau-Ymonet, P. and Riva, A. (2012). *Histoire de la Bourse.* Paris, France: Découverte.

Leuchter, T. (2016). The illimitable right: Debating the meaning of property and the *marché à terme* in Napoleonic France. *Modern Intellectual History.* Advance online publication. doi: 10.1017/S1479244316000081.

Michie, R. G. (2009). *The London Stock Exchange: A history.* New York, NY: Oxford University Press.

Perdonnet, V. Historique rapide de mes rapports avec monsieur le Comte de Forbin-Janson, et des opérations que j'ai fait pour son compte. Box

B-0068562/3. Centre des archives économiques et financières, Savigny-le-Temple, France.

———. (1823). *Plaidoyer de m. Perdonnet, agent de change; Contre m. le cte de Forbin-Janson*. Paris, France: Bailleul.

———. (1824). *Plaidoyer de m. Perdonnet, agent de change à Paris, demandeur en casssation de l'arrêt de la Cour royale de Paris, du 9 août 1823; Contre m. de Tertulis, comte de Forbin-Janson, défendeur*. Paris, France: David.

Pocock, J. G. A. (1985). The mobility of property and the rise of eighteenth-century sociology. In J. G. A. Pocock, *Virtue, commerce, and history: Essay on political though and history, chiefly in the eighteenth century* (pp. 103–124). New York, NY: Cambridge University Press.

———. (2003). *The Machiavellian moment: Florentine political thought and the Atlantic republican tradition* (2nd ed.). Princeton, NJ: Princeton University Press.

Poovey, M. (2008). *Genres of the credit economy: Mediating value in eighteenth- and nineteenth-century Britain*. Chicago, IL: University of Chicago Press.

Preda, A. (2001). The rise of the popular investor: Financial knowledge and investing in England and France, 1840–1880. *The Sociological Quarterly, 42*, 205–232.

Ryan, A. (1984). *Property and political theory*. New York, NY: Blackwell.

Shovlin, J. (2006). *The political economy of virtue: Luxury, patriotism, and the origins of the French Revolution*. Ithaca, NY: Cornell University Press.

Sonenscher, M. (2007). *Before the deluge: Public debt, inequality, and the intellectual origins of the French Revolution*. Princeton, NJ: Princeton University Press.

Spang, R. L. (2015). *Stuff and money in the time of the French Revolution*. Cambridge, MA: Harvard University Press.

Stanziani, A. (2011). Marchés à terme, accaparement et monopoles en France, fin XVIIIe–1914. In N. Levratto and A. Stanziani (Eds.), *Le capitalisme au futur antérieur: Crédit et spéculation en France, fin XVIIIe'début XXe siècles* (pp. 69–106). Brussels, Belgium: Bruylant.

Stasavage, D. (2003). *Public debt and the birth of the democratic state: France and Great Britain, 1688–1789*. New York, NY: Cambridge University Press.

Steiner, P. (2012). Competition and knowledge: French political economy as a science of government. In R. Geenens and H. Rosenblatt (Eds.), *French liberalism from Montesquieu to the present day* (pp. 192–207). New York, NY: Cambridge University Press.

Thompson, V. E. (2000). *The virtuous marketplace: Women and men, money and politics in Paris, 1830–1870*. Baltimore, MD: Johns Hopkins University Press.

Troplong, R-T. (1845). *Commentaire du prêt, du dépot, du séquestre et des contrats aléatoires*. Brussels, Belgium: Meline, Cans et Cie.

Vause, E. (2012). "He who rushes to riches will not be innocent": Commercial values and commercial failure in postrevolutionary France. *French Historical Studies*, 35, 321–349.

Whatmore, R. (2012). War, trade and empire: The dilemmas of French liberal political economy, 1780–1816. In R. Geenens and H. Rosenblatt (Eds.), *French liberalism from Montesquieu to the present day* (pp. 169–191). New York, NY: Cambridge University Press.

White, E. N. (2001). Making the French pay: The costs and consequences of the Napoleonic reparations. *European Review of Economic History*, 5, 337–365.

Young, D. R., and Smith, B. G. (1984). What was property? Legal dimensions of the social question in France (1789–1848). *Proceedings of the American Philosophical Society*, 28, 200–230.

# SECTION TWO CONTEMPORARY EXPLORATIONS OF PROPERTY RIGHTS AND INTERPRETATIONS

In this portion of the book, we shift our focus from historical conceptualizations of property rights in governance context to contemporary examples and case studies. Some of the chapters, readers will note, are theoretical in nature, while others rely on existing case law and policies to deeply explore issues such as environmental economics, water rights, coastal lands, drones, intellectual property, and even place branding. The variety of topics highlights how far-reaching conceptualizations of property run.

Turning toward popular news sources shows us disputes about real and imagined property. Take, for example, the highly contested "stand your ground" laws throughout the United States. Perhaps the highest-profile case resting on this law comes from Florida: Trayvon Martin. As Weaver (2008) explains, the foundation for the case comes from the stand your ground law, which then-governor Jeb Bush signed into law in 2005 in Florida. At its core, the new law replaced long-standing legal principle to retreat prior to using deadly force. This new interpretation was especially meant to give people the right to protect their personal property and immediately go into attack mode at the feeling of threat (ibid.). The assumption is that if someone intends to do harm to your property or your place, you therefore have the right to fight back immediately without consequence (ibid.).

Lawson (2012) notes that the case made international news from Sanford, Florida, given the historical context in the United States regarding black males, use of force, and implicit bias. As she details, the Trayvon Martin case began when the black teenager was walking home wearing a hooded sweatshirt and carrying iced tea and candy. George Zimmerman was on neighborhood watch when he felt threatened, called the police, explained he was going to handle the situation, then killed the teenager. After a long trial, massive public outcry, and even riots beyond Florida's borders, the stand your ground law provided a successful defense of Zimmerman. He faced not a single penalty for the killing (Lawson, 2012). As Lawson describes, "The Trayvon Martin killing felt like a sequel to those past tragedies and reminiscent of a time period where no one wants to return, a time period which some say we never really left" (p. 281).

The essence of the case, supposedly, was visible property rights, but it became clear that the case sparked a debate over invisible property rights (racial issues and the fear of black bodies). In another example, the newspaper *The Guardian* published an intriguing story about the decline of the animal population and used the lens of property rights to develop measures to save them (Hadley, 2016). In the story, the author explains that someone would essentially speak on behalf of animals to give them a voice in the wake of habitat destruction when development occurs (ibid.). Indeed, Hadley has written a book-length volume on this idea of giving animals rights via human surrogates (Hadley, 2015), in which he notes that his ideas apply to nondomesticated animals who have no choice but to live off the land. If builders come in and continually destroy that habitat, then they should think about the ethical obligations of protecting animals and not just their bottom lines (ibid.).

Schlager and Ostrom (1992) take a similar approach in applying property rights and rules to examine the Maine lobster industry. Ideally, they argue, owners—who no doubt have exclusive rights regarding what to do with what is caught and fished—should think about common resources before overfishing or overtrapping. In the case of Maine, while the government owns the property rights, most fishermen work to protect those rights themselves. If someone is violating the rules, they all act together to protect the common-pool resources (ibid.). When government does try to intervene, by imposing quotas for example, the measures do not often work well, the authors note. The problem results from trying to legislate ethical behavior when all parties involved might not have the same ethic, so many options are needed to protect the pool resources.

As we write this in 2017, the Sioux of Standing Rock Reservation still are fighting the government's placement of a pipeline through its land in North Dakota. Several property rights elements are at play in the case. Protestors from the tribe and environmental groups gathered on what government officials were calling private lands to show their displeasure regarding the pipeline (Silva, 2016). According to various news reports, protesters were cleared from the camp after using weapons to escalate tensions between themselves and authorities (ibid.). The protestors are against the pipeline, which will come within a half-mile of tribal lands. They also worry that runoff from the pipeline might poison local water systems (ibid.). In an interview with National Public Radio, tribe chairman Dave Archambault II noted that the dispute is over clean drinking water and further encroachment on tribal lands (NPR, 2016).

We could keep going with countless examples of how property rights undergird contemporary stories popular in our news. Who owns your social media posts when you die? What rights do you have when someone steals your ideas then claims them as their own? How can we reconcile our desire for owning real property with that of the commons? How do public-private partnerships blur the property lines? These questions, and many others, are why property rights are so important in contemporary governance.

With property rights, the idea of governance has rung through time. As the historical examples in Section 1 show, property rights involve people agreeing on a social contract regarding rights and responsibilities related to real and imagined property. Breakdowns and disputes occur when there is no agreement any more on what counts as property. Keeping ethical foundations at the center of property rights and rules requires networked actors working together for an ideal common good. This sounds nice, but, as we see, it is more complicated to apply in practice. For example, Sell and Prakash (2004) examine the role of networks in helping— or even harming—free-trade agreements. They explain how business interests in one network and nongovernment organizations in another succeeded in forming their agendas related to intellectual property rights. On one side, business interests claimed that poverty and government issues in developing nations prevent HIV/ AIDS drugs from reaching the market at a fair price, while the NGOs argued that intellectual property rights prevented duplication and cheap replication of the drugs (Sell & Prakash, 2004). Both networks had success in various policy arenas but hit a snag related to U.S. policies. The authors conclude that words and networks do indeed matter when it comes to the intellectual property rights arena, showing the power both of working together and of property as an idea.

According to a World Bank paper (Keefer, 2004), governance actions play a crucial role in determining economic growth via policies related to property rights. At its core, growth is related to economic security, which also rests on property rights protections (ibid.). Put simply: no one will invest or develop if they fear the state will seize their assets. This becomes a bit trickier in developing nations, where government institutions might be less stable and the population less trusting (ibid.). Regarding rights and responsibilities once property decisions are made, Smith (2002) views them as covering a range from exclusionary to governance. One can think of this as purely individual rights on one end to commons protection on the other. Within this section, readers can see this tension in the examples the authors use to show the variations in property rights and protections. In an ideal situation, we all should think about the commons even when buying property for individual use: houses, cars, etc. Solar panels on homes or electric vehicles can lessen burdens on the commons, but sometimes those rational aspects are not part of purchasing decisions, showing the application of Smith's spectrum.

This section delves further into discussions of property in contemporary governance issues. Readers will recognize some of the current events and concerns the authors have selected as case studies. The Consalo chapter on water rights, for example, ties into the Dakota Access Pipeline and the public battles for clean water in cities throughout the United States and globally. For example, Pacheco-Vega (2013) illustrates how polycentric governance models related to water management in Mexico transfer the obligation to take action from one actor's hands into many. This idea sees responsibility for water governance as shared—the people who might be helped or harmed by the decisions should have a voice. This is what we see in Flint, Michigan, and at Standing Rock. Ravich's chapter on drones taps into an ever-evolving discussion about private air space, privacy concerns in general—with drones snapping photos overhead—and technology transfer. The remaining chapters in the section, summarized in the book's introduction, offer additional insights into pressing social issues viewed through a property lens.

## REFERENCES

Hadley, J. (2015). Animal property rights: A theory of habitat rights for wild animals. London, UK: Lexington Books.
———. (2016). Could giving wild animals property rights help stop their decline? Retrieved from: www.theguardian.com/environment/2016/oct/27/could-giving-wild-animals-property-rights-help-stop-their-decline.
Keefer, P. (2004). A review of the political economy of governance: From property rights to voice. World Bank Policy Research Working Paper 3315.
NPR (2016). In fight over N.D. pipeline, tribe leader calls for peace and prayers. Retrieved from: www.npr.org/2016/10/27/499479185/in-fight-over-n-d-pipeline-tribe-leader-calls-for-peace-and-prayers.
Pacheco-Vega, R. (2013). Polycentric water governance in Mexico: Beyond the governing-by-river-basin council model. Paper presented at the 2013 Latin American Studies Association.
Schlager, E., & Ostrom, E. (1992). Property-rights regimes and natural resources: A conceptual analysis. *Land Economics*, 68(3), 249–262.
Sell, S. K., & Parakash, A. (2004). Using ideas strategically: The contest between business and NGO networks in intellectual property rights. *International Studies Quarterly*, 48(1), 143–175.
Silva, D. (2016). Dakota Access Pipeline: More than 100 arrested as protesters ousted from camp. Retrieved from: www.nbcnews.com/news/us-news/dakota-access-pipeline-authorities-start-arresting-protesters-new-camp-n674066.
Smith, H. E. (2004). Exclusion versus governance: Two strategies for delineating property rights. *The Journal of Legal Studies*, 32(S2), s453–s487.
Weaver, Z. L. (2008). Florida's "stand your ground" law: The actual effects and the need for clarification. *University of Miami Law Review*, 63(1), 395–430.

# 5 Ecological Economics, Property Rights, and the Environmental "Meta-commons"

DONALD G. RICHARDS

There are (at least) two approaches to economics that concern themselves with environmental issues, and each takes a very distinctive approach to the meaning of environmental values. I refer to these approaches as environmental economics and ecological economics, respectively. The differences in their approaches to environmental values imply corresponding differences in their respective understandings of important economic categories such as commodities, resources, costs, capital, consumption, investment, and other familiar members of the economic lexicon. These differences in turn reflect differences in the two outlooks in terms of ethical presuppositions including their assumptions regarding what they consider to be an effective regime of environmental property rights and obligations. I argue that the goal of long-term sustainability, a notion that is itself contested between the two perspectives, requires the ecological economics framework. I further argue that this goal will require particular policy measures and agreements that are both domestic and international in scope. Some of these policy measures will require a reconceptualization of the understanding of property from its more standard understanding(s).

## ENVIRONMENTAL ECONOMICS VERSUS ECOLOGICAL ECONOMICS

To those unfamiliar with the two approaches, environmental economics (EE) and ecological economics (EcE) would appear to refer to the same subdiscipline within the larger study of economics.[1] Certainly, EE and EcE have in common that each is concerned with the human-nature relationship. But the differences that separate their respective understandings of that relationship are at least as important as the differences in their respective modifiers, environmental and ecological. Whereas the natural *environment* refers to the flora and fauna and organic and inorganic entities that coexist in a prescribed geography, nature's *ecology* refers to these entities, to the web of relationships that link them, and their mutual, dynamic interactions.

From the EE perspective, nature is regarded as a storehouse of natural resources that are appropriated and combined with other factors of production such as labor and capital to produce final goods and services. The value of natural resources, and therefore the value of nature, according to the EE view, is determined in markets for natural resource commodities. These values embodied in final goods are aggregated into gross domestic product (GDP), which is the all-encompassing measure of a nation's economic welfare. Nature, then, via the market mechanism, adds its value to aggregate national welfare in a way that is indistinguishable from that of other productive factors. The EcE perspective, by contrast, begins by rejecting the notion that human beings stand outside of nature, from which position they simply appropriate its "gifts." Rather, EcE regards the human species as an integral part of nature and dependent on the functioning of nature as a system, and on the functioning of its various subsystems, as are other species with which it shares the global environmental system. While EcE shares with EE the idea that human beings appropriate entities from nature for the purposes of production and reproduction, it maintains that the *manner* of this appropriation has implications for the long term sustainability and flourishing of its own species and of other species with which it shares the environmental system. The concept of sustainability, in fact, is one on which the two approaches substantially diverge and is deserving of more detailed consideration.

## Weak versus Strong Sustainability

EE is associated with conventional neoclassical economics, and the latter outlook in turn is closely identified with Robert Solow (Solow, 1993), who sets out a clearly articulated definition of sustainability. This definition has been labeled as weak sustainability (WS) and includes the following precepts. First, WS defines sustainability in terms of a non-declining stock of capital over time, where *capital* is understood to include both produced and natural capital, sufficient to maintain a constant stream of consumption. Supporting this definition are several provocative assumptions. The first of these is that produced and natural capital are substitutable such that a drawing-down of the stock of natural capital presents no threat to sustainability as defined, as long as future generations are compensated with a sufficient addition to their stock of produced capital. Capital as a whole then is considered perfectly fungible, and no part of the stock of natural capital is considered critical in the sense that its loss cannot be compensated for by an adequate investment in other forms of capital. A second assumption is that market prices are adequate to the task of (1) providing clear signals of the growing scarcity of natural capital and (2) providing adequate incentives to the producers of substitutes so as to maintain the total capital stock at the required level to sustain intergenerational utility at a non-declining level. A third assumption is that technological progress may be relied on to provide an adequate flow of innovations to replace the world's diminishing stocks of nonrenewable resources, or that will extend those stocks into an indefinite future until such substitutes can be found or are no longer necessary. The latter task is accomplished by increasing the efficiency with which they are employed.

EcE takes exception to each of these assumptions. First, as suggested earlier, it rejects the characterization of nature as simply a bundle of commodities, or capital, to be combined into a production function, or process. The strong sustainability (SS) perspective aligned with EcE regards nonhuman nature's economic relationship to human society as providing essential, life-sustaining services, some of which have no potentially manufactured alternatives.[2] As an example, EcE might cite the earth's ozone layer, which prevents excessive amounts of ultraviolet rays from penetrating the atmosphere and causing damage to the life forms on earth, including human beings. To date, there has not been invented a synthetic substitute for the ozone layer. This would belie the WS contention of substitutability of manufactured for natural capital as well as its related contention that no natural capital is critical, since in the absence of the protection provided by the ozone shield human life might cease to exist in any currently recognizable form.

EcE would also certainly take exception to the assumption that market prices are adequate to the task of allocating natural capital to their highest-valued uses and of providing adequate incentives for the development of synthetic or manufactured alternatives to natural capital. Doubt on the adequacy of the market mechanism is compounded in the case of the intergenerational allocation of environmental values inasmuch as future generations themselves have no contemporary market power and, hence, no voice by which their own preferences might be registered. Solow himself warns us against making unfounded inferences about the preferences of future generations for the kinds of values many environmentalists advocate, for example, wilderness. Future generations may well feel adequately compensated for the loss of nature, he argues, by new technologies and life-saving medical procedures that result from the exploitation of the natural environment. The EcE has two responses to Solow's warning (Gardiner, 2004; Helm, 2008; Neumayer, 1999). First, it is not presumptuous to preserve for future generations a full menu of environmental values. It is, to the contrary, quite presumptuous to eliminate any such options, including wilderness, through the reckless management of nature leaving those future generations with a reduced set of choices. Second, it is not in the least bit presumptuous to believe that future generations will desire a full measure of the sort of critical services that only an intact global ecology can provide. A functioning ozone layer that prevents excessive UV light from reaching the earth's surface is just one of these services. An appropriate balance of atmospheric gases to sustain life is another. A hydrological cycle that provides adequate rain in needed places, at the appropriate times, and at an appropriate rate is still a third. It is also a good bet that future generations will desire air that is fit to breathe and reasonably free from the kinds of particulate matter and toxins that are known to induce various diseases and cancers. The EcE also notes that the bridge to future generations is likely to be far less violent and traumatic if the disruptions and dislocations of the anticipated global climate change can be avoided. Rising sea levels, coastal flooding, drought, and violent storms, all the alleged results of anthropogenic climate change, may have devastating consequences for hundreds of millions of people and create geopolitical instability with its own catastrophic consequences unless due recognition of the global ecological disruption is made and the appropriate corrective measures taken.

A third EE precept that EcE contests concerns the former's technological optimism. EE takes it for granted that there will always be a continuous flow of innovations that will enable humanity to overcome whatever resource-related challenges it happens to encounter. If, for example, there occurs a threat to our supplies of fresh water, it is assumed that some inexpensive means will be found to desalinate and transport sea water. Similarly, as fossils fuels are exhausted, non-fossil energy sources will be developed into viable economic alternatives. While in some cases such optimism would seem to be reasonable, in others, such as those involving cataclysmic atmospheric and climate change, there is no basis for believing that technological heroism will prevent wholesale species extinctions, including our own (Huesemann, 2003). Given the uncertainty and risk associated with the depletion and degradation of critical natural capital to levels below that necessary for long-term sustainability of human life, the EcE urges the precautionary principle in relation to the use of this natural capital. The precautionary principle states that "where the environmental consequences of regulatory inaction are (1) in some way uncertain/ambiguous but (2) nonnegligible, regulatory inaction is unjustified. Safe minimum standards are a closely related constraint approach to environmental policy, whereby in conditions of uncertainty cautious minimum levels are set" (Common & Stagl, 2005).

EcE also argues for an investment in natural capital given the low levels to which it has fallen relative to the economy's size and its stock of manufactured capital (Daley, 1996). The question arises, however, as to how we might *invest* in natural capital given that it is by its character not subject to deliberate expansion but rather an endowment subject to increase by a slow process of regeneration and natural growth. The only decision we can make as members of the global commonwealth is to use or preserve our endowment of natural capital. "Investment" in the context of natural capital then is understood to mean the preservation of the environment as opposed to its exploitation for other alternative uses.

## NATURAL CAPITAL AS PROPERTY

The exploit-versus-preserve choice is obviously conflictual since either option provides benefits to some while denying foregone benefits to others. This is just to observe that natural capital is a scarce good. Market capitalism solves the exploit-preserve dilemma by assigning property rights to capital allowing the owners to use and allocate according to their preferences, at least where these uses do not impose external costs on or otherwise abrogate the rights of others. While in some cases properly regulated private property rights can and do govern the sustainable allocation of natural capital, in other important cases they do not, and in still other important cases they are utterly inconceivable. These possibilities are related to the degree to which particular environmental resources reveal the properties of public goods, or not. A public good is said to be characterized by (1) nonexcludability and (2) nonrivalry or subtractability. A good is considered nonexcludable when it becomes impossible to prevent nonowners of the good from its exploitation. Neither can these nonowners be forced to pay for access to the good, that is, act as free riders. A good is nonrivalrous when one person's use of a good does not diminish another user's potential use of it. These characteristics as they apply to environmental goods have important implications for the type of property regime that might govern their access and use and will be explored in more detail below.

The EE approach to the question of environmental capital assignment is to rely on the market mechanism to allocate such values to their highest-valued uses. The market solution, however, presupposes a preexisting property rights regime that identifies the rights and obligations of that capital. The Coase Theorem argues that it is less relevant who controls property rights than that such rights are held by some individual, group, or entity concerned with the rational use of the natural capital (Common & Stagl, 2005). Absent these rights, the argument asserts, open access to natural resources, combined with prisoners' dilemma–type incentives, will result in their complete degradation and loss.[3] By creating property rights, however, the property owner has the authority and the incentive to build a fence around the resource, limit access to it, and exploit the resource in a way that is economically efficient. But this perspective raises some important questions. First, is it possible to build fences around those types of natural capital that are most likely to constitute the global environmental commons? A good example is the oceans and their contents. It is difficult enough to control access to territorial waters that are in close proximity to the shores of continental and national landmasses. It becomes even more difficult if they are located far from such boundaries. Second, it is difficult to imagine how such global natural capital would be allocated to private interests in a way that would not violate fundamental concepts of distributive justice (Risse, 2012). For this reason the typical assumption is that property rights to global environmental resources are appropriately assigned to the state, or some state-like institution, as the guarantor of the common (global) welfare.[4]

While some property theorists see the possibilities for property regimes as confined to the dyad of individual private ownership versus monolithic state control, others posit the possibility under some circumstances of a common property regime (CPR) (Ostrom, 1990). In a CPR an insider group establishes rules of access for a common resource for both insiders and outsiders, typically privileging the former group while excluding the latter. Ostrom's design principles for a successful CPR make clear that such a regime is appropriate to *local* resource management under defined circumstances and has no application where the resource in question has global reach (Rose, 1999).[5] The difficulties surrounding the application of workable environmental property rights are compounded in the case of certain critical components of natural capital. These concern those aspects of our environment wherein certain systems play vital and multiple roles in maintaining the earth's ability to sustain human life.[6] The earth's atmosphere is a case in point. On the one hand, the complex of atmospheric gases, temperature, wind currents, and water vapor play an essential role in sustaining multiple life forms, including our own. On the other hand, this balance is being changed over time as humans use the atmosphere as a sink in which to dispose of wastes, mostly the result of burning fossil fuels. One of the problems associated with such "meta-commons" resources is that many of the earth's population are entirely unaware of the critical role that atmospheric balance plays in sustaining life and enabling our other economic and noneconomic activities.[7] They are unaware, for example, that atmospheric dynamics play a crucial role in regulating climate and rainfall (Baskin, 1998). They may be painfully aware, however, that attempts to regulate activity that contribute to carbon dioxide and methane emissions, to take two of the most prominent greenhouse gasses, have disruptive consequences for the pursuit of their livelihoods. Property issues are further complicated because the protection of the meta-commons often requires restrictions on the use of other natural capital, such as rainforests, that may more easily and readily be assigned via market mechanisms to private interests, or managed by a system of common property rights, as Ostrom described. Hence, there emerges an antagonism between conflicting bundles of rights.

As Cole (2002) explains, the form of a workable property regime that limits access to environmental resources that have both public goods characteristics (e.g., nonexcludability) and private goods aspects (e.g., rivalry or substractability) depends on the technical and institutional circumstances that govern their access and use. The physical boundaries that define a rainforest, for example, render it more likely to be subject to regulation by a regime of common, or even private, property rights in which local residents themselves determine sustainable access and use rules. The existence of boundaries implies the physical possibility of fences, after all. No such possibility exists for the atmosphere, however, at least not with given technology. To return to our previous example, if we are to maintain a protective ozone layer for some inhabitants of the earth, we need to provide it for all inhabitants. It is then unavoidable that atmospheric property be regulated by the state, or some state-mediated institution.

While much important environmental capital is nonexcludable, in general, it is rivalrous. This is so in one of two, or both, senses. First, much environmental capital is rivalrous *among users*. Environmental resources are often more degraded the larger the number of users, or the more intensively they are exploited. Second, environmental resources may be rivalrous *in use*. Using the ozone shield or atmosphere again as an illustration, this is natural capital that is both nonexcludable and nonrivalrous among users, but it is rivalrous in use. To the extent that the atmosphere is used as a sink for certain emissions it becomes degraded for other essential services it provides. Hence, once again we have the imperative for a state, or state-mediated institution to govern access and use.

## THE MONTREAL AND KYOTO PROTOCOLS

There exists no global regulatory authority to set standards, identify violators, and impose sanctions for the damage done to the global atmospheric commons. There have, however, occurred attempts to arrive at international agreements to establish such regulation, that is to say, "soft state" solutions to the tragedy of the meta-commons. Two such attempts are the Montreal and Kyoto protocols on ozone protection and climate change, respectively. It may be instructive then to compare and contrast these agreements to see what they imply about the potential for, and limitations of, international negotiations surrounding threats to the environmental meta-commons.

The Montreal Protocol (MP) on Substances that Deplete the Ozone Layer is considered one of the most successful global environmental agreements ever struck. Negotiations on the MP began in 1977 with a conference convened by the United Nations Environmental Programme involving experts from thirty-two

nations who adopted an action plan and established a coordinating commit-
tee. Ten years later, the MP was opened for signatures, and in 1989 it entered
into force to ban the use of chlorofluorcarbons (CFCs), which have the effect of
destroying the ozone layer that shields the earth from excessive UV radiation.[8]
The MP established a list of banned chemicals; assessment, compliance, and
administrative infrastructures; a sanctioning mechanism; and procedures for the
evaluation of new science and substances. The United States ratified the MP in
1990 by making the necessary modifications of its Clean Air Act (Hans, 2013).
The MP has also been largely successful in meeting its environmental objectives
as, since its implementation, the emission of ozone-depleting chemicals has been
reduced by 95 percent while atmospheric concentrations of the chemicals have
been declining since 1994. It is anticipated that the ozone layer should be repaired
to its mid-1970s condition by 2050.

The Kyoto Protocol (KP) on climate change, by contrast, has not been nearly
as successful. The KP was preceded in 1988 by the Intergovernmental Panel on
Climate Change (IPCC), which issued a report on the impact of greenhouse gases
(GHGs) on climate and on what needed to be done. This was followed in 1992
by the Rio "Earth Summit" that established desirable targets for GHG emissions reductions, though no specific commitments from particular nations were
sought or given. Such commitments were sought by the KP in 1997, and by 1998
the agreement was signed by fifty-eight countries accounting for 39 percent of
CO2 emissions. President Clinton signed the agreement on behalf of the United
States, but the Senate withheld ratification. Without the full commitment of
the United States to the KP, few other nations were willing to meet their own
commitments, and the agreement remained largely ineffective. So, the obvious
and important question is, why was the United States willing to ratify the MP,
but not the KP, when the two agreements seemed on the face of things to have
so much in common?

Several commentators argue that the difference in the two protocols is a
matter of their comparative economic incentives. Benefit-cost analyses on the
MP conducted by the United States Environmental Protection Agency (Barrett,
1999) and the Council of Economic Advisors (Sunstein, 2007) show that the
agreement's benefits for the United States far exceed its costs. The benefits in this
case are largely a matter of the avoidance of loss of life and cost of treatment of
skin cancer due to exposure to excessive levels of UV rays. They also include the
avoided costs of environmental and agricultural damages. The costs of the MP
are those associated with the development and substitution of new materials for
the banned CFCs. These costs were not estimated to be particularly high. The fact

that a U.S. company, DuPont, had just such substitutes in development provided added incentive to embrace the accord. As Sunstein (2007) argues, the benefit-to-costs ratio of reducing emissions of CFCs was high enough that the United States had all the incentive it needed to *unilaterally* undertake such action. In the case of the MP, then, there never was any prisoners' dilemma to contend with.

The case for the KP is much different. A number of studies indicate that the marginal benefits of GHG abatement are modest in comparison with the marginal cost of stabilizing atmospheric concentrations, or reductions in such concentrations, for the United States (Barrett, 1999). The benefits are limited by several factors (Sunstein, 2007). First, their realization requires a far greater reduction in global temperatures than is likely to occur from U.S. mitigation efforts alone. They require, for example, strong commitments on the part of GHG emitters in poorer, developing countries, particularly India and China, who did not sign, and are not bound by, the KP. Second, global climate change is tied not merely to current or future *flows* of GHGs, but also to the *stock* of these substances already existing in the atmosphere. The KP assigns obligations to some of its signatories to reduce flows, but not to undertake the effort to reduce overall atmospheric concentrations of them in any absolute sense. Thus, we can anticipate rising temperatures for the foreseeable future even with full compliance to the terms of the KP. Third, the KP does not actually commit nations to cut emissions *substantially below* the levels prevailing in 1990, but merely to return to levels *slightly below* those. Political opponents of the KP pointed to the increased price of energy that compliance with the accord would entail along with (alleged) substantial job losses. Not surprisingly, the Senate voted against ratification by a large majority.

## Developments and Prospects since Kyoto

Notwithstanding determined opposition in the U.S. Senate and among certain economic interests to the KP, there are reasons for optimism for an effective climate agreement going forward. Changes in the political, economic, and legal environments may have modified the benefit-cost calculus in favor of international cooperation on climate change. Among these is a growing awareness in China of its own national vulnerability to the disruptions posed by global warming trends, particularly those related to rising sea levels that threaten the country's heavily populated coastal areas. The recent growth recession in China, and in other so-called emerging industrial economies such as India, has reduced the demand for fossil fuels and therefore their prices. Though depressed prices have complex impacts on the costs and benefits of GHG mitigation, they do provide an opportunity to raise taxes on their use that would be more difficult politically and economically in an environment of rising energy prices.

Changing perceptions in China on the need for international cooperation on climate change was an important contributing factor resulting in a recent bilateral agreement with the United States. Under the agreement, the United States expressed its intention to reduce its emissions by 26 to 28 percent of its 2005 level by the year 2025. China in turn announced its intention to achieve peak $CO2$ by 2030 and to increase the share of non-fossil fuels in primary energy consumption, in part via the institution of a carbon tax (Fransen et al., 2014). The 2014 U.S.-China announcement is important in its own right as evidence of an important shift in outlook on the urgency to combat climate change, but it was also a prelude to another international climate accord negotiated in November 2015. The Paris agreement is notable for the ambitiousness of its goal to reduce global average temperature to 1.5 Celsius above preindustrial levels—a half-degree C lower than the goal sought in previous international agreements. Achieving this goal will require that net anthropogenic emissions of carbon be reduced to zero by 2050, requiring in turn that new emissions be offset by carbon sequestration via carbon sinks, for instance, carbon-absorbing forests. The most contentious of the issues addressed by the Paris agreement, as always, concern the apportionment of responsibility for climate change and for the burden (cost) of its mitigation. While the Paris agreement stipulates that a financial transfer from developed to developing countries in the neighborhood of $100 billion will be needed to achieve its targets, it does not detail specific country contributions. In fact, it does not even specify which countries will count as contributors and which as recipients of these resources (Meyer, 2015a).

The recent apparent willingness of emerging countries to confront the problem of climate change via international cooperation is an important breakthrough both intrinsically and because it helps to overcome an important obstacle to the full engagement of the United States in that same effort. An important question, of course, is, will internal political and economic interests opposed to the costs of mitigating climate change derail recent progress? Recently, the U.S. Supreme Court ruled against the implementation of an important element of President Obama's Climate Action Plan that would have required new regulations on the emissions of coal power plants (Davenport, 2016). Moreover, the U.S. auto industry has recently switched production in favor of light trucks, SUVs, and minivans that are less subject to the stringent fuel efficiency standards that regulate passenger vehicles (Becker & Gerstenzang, 2016). These are precisely the kinds of U.S. domestic uncertainties that create doubt and ambivalence in the minds of climate negotiators in key partnering countries such as China and India.[9]

## ATMOSPHERIC BALANCE AND CLIMATE: PROVISION OF A PUBLIC GOOD, OR PRESERVATION OF COMMON PROPERTY?

As suggested earlier, the EE approach to the problem of environmental externalities typically regards environmental protection as a species of collective action problem subject to prisoner's dilemma incentives. A solution to this collective action problem favored by EE is to assign property rights to the relevant resource and then permit traders in a competitive market to allocate them to their highest-valued uses, namely "cap-and-trade" (CaT). Precedent exists for the successful application of CaT in the mitigation of sulphur dioxide (SO2) emissions. Under Title IV of the 1990 Clean Air Act Amendments, the United States created the first large-scale CaT system by setting an emission ceiling on SO2 from coal-fired power plants and allowing firms to buy and sell emissions permits. The result was a 43 percent reduction in emissions to levels below the program's initial target (Stavins et al., 2012). The attractiveness of CaT to economists is well known as it relies on the market mechanism to deliver cost effective pollution control without dictating specific control measures that may be technically and economically inferior.

The potential for CaT as a useful mechanism for global climate control has been noted by several commentators (Cole, 2002; Murray & Hosterman, 2009; Ranson & Stavins, 2013). The key to any CaT system consists in two of its key operational features. The first is setting the use (e.g., emissions) ceiling at an appropriate level to achieve the system's overriding goal of critical natural capital protection. The second consists of the initial allocation of use permits consistent with the predetermined use ceiling.[10] Applied to a global climate change agreement, the first of these requirements is essentially a technical-scientific one that has, for the majority of climate scientists, already been determined. The more difficult political-economic issue concerns the initial allocation of allowable emissions permits on a global scale. The answer to this challenge must take into consideration country-level GHG emissions, in both flow and stock terms; the differences in countries' abilities to provide for the basic needs of their populations, and thus the "growth imperative"; and provision of adequate incentives to induce participation in the agreement, particularly among the largest emitters. Support for a climate agreement may in the final analysis hinge on how this allocation problem is framed.

One possible such framing is to regard the purpose of an international climate change agreement as a vehicle by which to provide for a global public good. It may be argued that the allocation of emissions permits to use the atmospheric sink ought to be done strategically so as to enable the optimal use of the meta-commons. It could be further argued that allocating those permits according to current and historical CO2 emissions would provide incentive to the most important potential parties to the agreement to make a binding commitment to the agreement. Initial allocation could also follow a formula based on emission efficiency standards/improvements wherein countries and their affected industries would be awarded permits according to their abilities to devise methods of production that reduce the emissions per unit of output. This sort of approach would clearly be premised on EE principles.

An alternative framing of the issue based on EcE principals is to regard the earth's atmosphere, and its derivative subsystems that operate on the planet's climate, as the common property endowment of mankind. Conceived in this fashion the meta-commons dilemma is settled in favor of recognizing the global common property rights of humanity, including those that adhere to future generations (Risse, 2008; 2012). In this alternative vision, atmospheric-balance-as-climate-regulator trumps atmosphere-as-sink. The initial allocation of emissions permits then could follow a formula based on the distribution of global population.[11] Due adjustments to this formula could also be made based on prior stocks of emitted carbon, with heavier emitters receiving fewer permits than historically light emitters. By this approach, China and India would receive more permits than the United States and Europe. The international transfer of value inherent in this scheme is bound to encounter stiff political and economic resistance in developed nations, and especially so in the United States. The fact that the approach recognizes the particular needs and claims of poorer large emitters such as China and India, and induces them to engage in international cooperation, operates to remove an important political obstacle to U.S. cooperation (Meyer, 2015b). We might additionally hope that technical advancements in renewable energies will loosen the hold of fossil fuels on the U.S. economy so that the sale of emission permits itself comes to be regarded as a profitable line of market activity. Equally hopefully, it may become clear that the time has come to act before the human costs of climate change become catastrophic.

## NOTES

The author thanks the editors and two anonymous referees for helpful comments. They bear no responsibility for remaining errors.

1. Exemplars of the EE approach are Solow (1993) and Nordhaus (1994). That of the EcE include Daley (1996) and Costanza (1989).

2. A useful review of the WS/SS debate is provided by Neumayer (2010).

3. This scenario is widely associated with Hardin (1968) and referred to as "the tragedy of the commons." "Prisoners' dilemma" is derived from game theory and refers to

strategic decision making in which parties to an agreement find it collectively optimal to cooperate but have individual incentives to defect from the agreement. When these individual incentives dominate, the result is a collectively suboptimal outcome for all.

4. It is worth noting that property rights assigned to the state hardly guarantees that the general social welfare will be properly served inasmuch as the state and its agents may be as vulnerable to the shortsightedness and selfishness often characteristic of individuals. Cole (2002) refers to this problem as "the tragedy of the political commons."

5. Goetze (1987) arrives at essentially the same conclusion arguing that nonexcludability of a common resource such as the atmosphere dictates that a single decision about how exclusion, or access, is to be exercised. Such an authority would have to incorporate all the relevant interdependencies with multiple owners ceding their decision-making authority to a single body (193). As Cole (2002) makes clear, when exclusion is not possible there is no meaningful difference between common property and open access. Hence, Hardin's "tragedy of the commons" might as well be termed "tragedy of open access."

6. Some 'Deep Ecologists' will object to the privileged place that *human* life occupies in my argument as being unjustifiably anthropocentric. Adequate justification for my stance, I believe, is provided by Norton's (2005) "convergence" argument.

7. Herring (1990) employs the term *meta-commons* to refer to the second-order challenges in defining property rights and responsibilities in the face of overlapping and overarching local and global boundary claims.

8. The MP was amended in June 1990 in London and again in 1992 in Copenhagen to expand the list of banned substances, and to encourage the participation of developing countries in the Protocol. The latter was accomplished by the offer of financial and technical assistance from the developed countries. Today, the MP counts more than two hundred countries as signatories. A Register of the Status of Ratification of the Montreal Protocol and its Amendments can be found at http://www.environment. gov.au/protection/ozone/montreal-protocol/register-montreal-protocol-countries.

9. Recent Republican Party insistence that it will not consider *any* nominee from President Obama combined with statements by Republican presidential nominee contenders questioning, or *denying,* the facts on climate change adds further doubts on the sustainability of the Paris Agreement or any other international climate accord. Even more troubling is the decision by recently-elected President Donald Trump to withdraw U.S. participation in the Paris Agreement.

10. These two requirements do not exhaust the list of necessary conditions for an effective CaT system. There is a need, for example, for an effective compliance/monitoring system to ensure that parties to the agreement do not individually and collectively

violate the limits set on the use of the critical natural capital. Also, as Cole (2012, p. 84) notes, CaT presupposes the existence of the institutional prerequisites for market efficiency, which cannot be taken for granted particularly in less developed countries.

   11. Risse (2008) rejects the "equal per capita shares" argument as well as the "accountability for historical emissions" argument as bases for the initial allocation of property rights in the atmosphere in favor of an ability to pay principle that would assign greater burden to richer nations.

## REFERENCES

Barrett, S. (1999). Montreal versus Kyoto: International cooperation and the global environment. In I. Kaul, I. Grunberg, and M. Stern (Eds.), *Global public goods: International cooperation in the 21st century*, New York, NY: Oxford University Press for UNDP.

Baskin, Y. (1998). *The work of nature: How the diversity of life sustains us.* Washington, DC: Island Press.

Becker, D. F., & Gerstenzang, J. (2016). Stalling on fuel efficiency, *New York Times*, March 10, A23.

Cole, D. H. (2002). *Pollution & property*, Cambridge, UK: Cambridge University Press.

Common, M., & Stagl, S. (2005). *Ecological economics: An introduction*, Cambridge, UK: Cambridge University Press.

Daly, H. E. (1996). *Beyond capital: The economics of sustainable development*, Boston, MA: Beacon Press.

Davenport, C. (2016). Supreme Court's blow to emissions efforts may imperil Paris climate accord, *New York Times*, February 10, A10.

Fransen, T., Ge, M., & Damassa. T. (2014). The China-U.S. climate agreement: By the numbers. *World Resources Institute*, Retrieved from: www.wri.org/blog/2014/11/numbers-china-us-climate-agreement.

Hans, E. F. (2013). The Montreal Protocol in U.S. domestic law: A "bottom up" approach to the development of global administrative law. *International Law and Politics*, *45*, 827–860.

Herring, R. J. (1990). Rethinking the commons. *Agriculture and Human Values*, *7(2)*, 88–104.

Huesemann, M. H. (2003). The limits of technological solutions to sustainable development. *Clean Technologies and Environmental Policy*, *5(1)*, 21–34.

Meyer, R. (December 16, 2015). A reader's guide to the Paris Agreement, *The Atlantic*. Retrieved from: www.theatlantic.com/science/archive/2015/12/a-readers-guide-to-the-paris-agreement/420345/.

Meyer, R. (September 25, 2015). China, the world's biggest polluter, commits to cap-and-trade carbon emissions. *The Atlantic*. Retrieved from: www.theatlantic.com/science/archive/2015/09/the-worlds-largest-cap-and-trade-program/407371/.

Murray, B. C., & Hosterman, H. (2009). Climate change, cap-and-trade and the outlook for U.S. policy. *North Carolina Journal of International Law & Commercial Regulation, 34*, 699–720.

Norton, B. G. (2005). *Sustainability*. Chicago, IL: University of Chicago Press.

Ranson, M., & Stavins, R. N. (2013). Post-Durban climate policy architecture based on linkage of cap-and-trade systems. *Chicago Journal of International Law, 13* (Winter), 403–438.

Risse, M. (2012). *On global justice*, Princeton, NJ: Princeton University Press.

Rose, C. M. (1999). Expanding the choices for the global commons: comparing newfangled tradeable allowance schemes to old-fashioned common property regimes. *Faculty Scholarship Series*, Yale Law School Legal Scholarship Repository, Paper 1803. Retrieved from http://digitalcommons.law.yale.edu/fss_papers/1803.

———. (1986). On the intergenerational allocation of natural resources. *Scandinavian Journal of Economics, 88(1)*, 141–149.

———. (1993). Sustainability: An economist's perspective. In R. Dorfman & N. Dorfman (Eds.), *Economics of the Environment: Selected Readings*. New York, NY: Norton.

Stavins, R. N., Chan, G., Stowe, R., & Sweeney, R. (August 12, 2012). The U.S. sulphur dioxide cap and trade programme and lessons for climate policy. *Vox*. Retrieved from: http://www.voxeu.org/article/lessons-climate-policy-us-sulphur-dioxide-cap-and-trade-programme.

Sunstein, C. R. (2007). Of Montreal and Kyoto: A tale of two protocols. *Harvard Environmental Law Review, 31(1)*, 1–65.

Wirth, D. A. (2015). The international and domestic law of climate change: A binding international agreement without the Senate or Congress. *Harvard International Law Review, 39*, 515–566.

# 6 Changing Historic Concepts of Water Rights and Water Ownership

KAREN Z. CONSALO

Despite its fluid and abundant nature, water, like everything else on earth, can be owned as property. However, the nature of ownership of water is usually highly complex. When evaluating property rights, scholars often refer to a "bundle of rights" (Baron, 2014). Such a "bundle" is a reference to the various ownership rights that may be available: the right to access the property, the right to exclude others from it, the right to build over and drill under the property, and so on (ibid.). Each ownership right is one "stick" in the "bundle" of property rights. The many different forms of property ownership include various combinations of "sticks" to make up a particular "bundle" of property ownership. The concept of a "bundle of sticks" can be applied to water, too. The sticks in the bundle of water ownership often vary greatly from those found in ownership of dry land (ibid.).

Due to its fluidity, water is always in flux. In the most elementary water cycle, that of condensation to precipitation to evaporation and back to condensation, water passes from an uncontained gaseous form high in the atmosphere to a containable earthbound liquid and then back into the atmosphere again as a rising gas (Baron, 2014). This cycle can be altered by weather patterns as well as by human interference (ibid.).

Generally speaking, water is only property when it is present on the earth. Yet even earthbound water presents a multitude of complexities to possession and ownership. Consider the difficulties in accessing the vast extent of water present on the earth. In its liquid form, most water is utterly unreachable, at the depths of a lake or ocean. When in solid form, water may be suspended deep within an iceberg or glacier. In gas form, as steam or fog, water is nearly as ephemeral as the wind. It is challenging, if not impossible, to capture and quantify water for ownership purposes.

Even when an ascertainable amount of earthbound water is quantified for the purposes of ownership, such ownership is usually transitory. If water is used to irrigate crops, the moment it sinks into the ground it is lost to the farmer who briefly owned it. If used for personal hygiene, the moment it washes down the drain it is lost to that fleeting owner. If flowing through a chain of lakes or rivers, any claim of ownership by an adjacent landowner or government authority lasts only so long as the water remains within that particular lake or river before migrating to another.

In addition to complexities created by its fluid and transitory nature, complications to water ownership are often related to the ownership of land adjacent to or under the water body. Land adjacent to a water body is known as riparian land. Land under the water is known as "submerged land." In one's bundle of sticks of water ownership, is the submerged land underneath the water included? If so, does one owner possess all the submerged lands, or is all submerged land shared by several owners, or do several owners have claims to different geographical areas of the submerged land? What if drought or flood alter the nature of the land from submerged to riparian or vice versa?

Consider this simple and common illustration of the fluid and ephemeral nature of water ownership: water falls as rain from multiple clouds above a state. This rain lands on both private and public property. Some of the water immediately seeps into the soil as natural irrigation. Some of the water is captured by private landowners in rain barrels or similar storage apparatus. Much of the water will be directed through human-made gutters and sewer systems to flow into government-owned reservoirs. Rainwater that is not captured by private or public entities percolates into the ground and eventually flows to various lakes, rivers, ponds, or oceans. Some will flow into underground aquifers accessible only by public and private wells or the occasional cave diver.

In this example, the single rainstorm creates a multitude of scenarios for ownership of water. The rain that falls onto private property may be owned by that landowner for only that period during which the water is present on the property. The water that is intentionally captured by individuals or institutional uses can be stored and owned for weeks, months, or even years. The water that flows into the lakes and rivers may become property of the jurisdictional government and subject to government ownership and regulation—yet with certain property rights reserved to the public for recreation, fishing, or navigation. The rainwater that eventually flows into a reservoir will also be owned by a government entity but distributed, for a nominal cost, to the public utility users of that government. Once the water is distributed by the utility into private homes and businesses, it transfers into private ownership to be used immediately or stored for personal needs.

Yet all forms of water ownership in this scenario are temporary. Once the rainwater has been used for drinking, bathing, irrigation, or other uses, it passes biologically back into the environment through natural or human-engineered processes. Even if the rainwater remains unused in lakes, streams, or reservoirs, forces of heat and evaporation will naturally cause the water to pass back into the atmosphere as an uncontained gas. Even when the water is contained and owned, it is nearly impossible for the owner to isolate a single molecule of the water that could be clearly identified and designated as within their scope of ownership.

With such inherent complexities of water ownership in mind, this chapter will explore a few of the common frameworks that have evolved for water ownership, both fresh and salt water, within the American legal system. These structures for water ownership include: (1) common usage, (2) government ownership as a public trust, (3) ownership through riparian rights, and (4) ownership through prior appropriation. This chapter also describes arising frameworks for water jurisprudence which may have dramatic impact on the allocation and availability of potable water resources both domestic and internationally.

## CURRENT GLOBAL CONCERNS REGARDING FRESH WATER SUPPLY

The world's oceans, lakes, rivers, and other water bodies have shaped human civilization (Draper, 2008). While the saline ocean waters have a great value for navigation and fishing, fresh, or "potable," water is a more precious resource for human survival as it is necessary for drinking, cooking, and irrigation. Yet, fresh water only accounts for 2.5 percent of the world's water supply (Freshwater Crisis, n.d., para. 4). Of this 2.5 percent, only 1 percent is readily accessible rather than contained far underground or frozen in glaciers (ibid.). As a necessary but comparatively scarce resource, fresh water has an immense value. Yet throughout human history, our laws have allowed the pollution and waste of fresh water supplies. Currently, more than 2.3 billion people live in areas of chronic water shortage (Marston & Cai, 2016). Further, current legal structures have rendered fresh water abundant and cheap to some while nearly inaccessible or prohibitively expensive to others (ibid.).

In America, one might believe that clean water is a basic right of all citizens. Unfortunately, such belief is misplaced. Regardless of geographic, racial, or socoeconomic status, clean water is a scarcity in America. For proof, look no farther than the local grocery store, which stocks bottle after bottle of "clean" drinking water for sale to Americans who do not feel safe drinking the public water supply. For less anecdotal evidence, open any periodical or newspaper to find articles regarding the lack of clean, safe drinking waters across the country. The last few years have brought headlines describing a state of emergency due to unsafe levels of lead in the public drinking water supply for Flint, Michigan (Hulett, 2015); a massive chemical spill of methylcyclohexanemethanol into the Elk River and the municipal water supply of Charleston, West Virginia (Conte & Francis, 2014); and a release of more than three million gallons of toxic sludge containing both lead and arsenic from an abandoned mine into the Animas River—a feeder to the reservoir that provides drinking water to residents of Durango, Colorado (Turkewitzaug, 2015). The last decade has also brought headlines relating to a four million gallon oil spill in the Gulf Coast, used hypodermic needles washing up on East Coast beaches, and severe droughts, including an ongoing four-year drought in California (Griffin, Black, & Divine, 2015). When each week brings to light a new case of water pollution or water shortage, it is no longer possible for a reasonable mind to view these as isolated events involving a few unlucky communities. Rather, these situations represent an epidemic across our country, demonstrating that the right to clean water no longer exists in America.

But America is not alone in our struggle to maintain clean, safe, and plentiful water supplies for our citizens. In countries across Asia, entire families have no choice but to draw their water from the same water bodies that have been used as toilets for people and livestock. In many areas of Africa women waste hours of their day and even run the risk of assault to obtain drinking water for their families from the nearest public source. International disputes over water access lead to more and more frequent conflicts (Kristof, 1997). Ownership and control of clean water is quickly becoming one of the most sought after and privatized property rights around the globe. Many experts and commentators have forecast that in the near future, wars will be fought not for oil but for water (Judge, 2013).

## AMERICAN JURISPRUDENCE FOR WATER OWNERSHIP

The United States has always attempted to balance the public's right to access and use American water bodies with private rights to access, use, and even exclude others from "owned" water bodies. This balance between public access rights and private ownership rights has been struck in a variety of ways across the fifty states; however, a few core tenets of water jurisprudence have arisen. These core tenets have led to certain frameworks for water ownership, including common access, public trusts, prior appropriation, and riparian rights.

The longest-standing legal doctrine is the common right of citizens to access and use nearby water bodies and water supplies. Such common rights date back to the dawn of human civilization and boil down to the basic philosophy that water resources, like air and sunlight, belong to everyone and to no one. This perspective that water is subject to common ownership is evidenced through use of communal wells for people and livestock and through culturally accepted public access to many lakes and rivers for drinking, recreation, fishing, and hunting.

However, through time, private individuals began to claim more "sticks" in the bundle of water rights and thereby assert more extensive private claims to own and control water supplies. New ways of owning water evolved across the country in jurisprudence that was based, primarily, upon the relative availability of water (Craig, 2012). In the dry Midwestern and Western states, those first to access and use a water body gained certain ownership rights to the waters within. This became known as the Prior Appropriation Doctrine. In the more hydrated Eastern states, those who purchased land adjacent to a water body obtained certain ownership rights to both the water body and the waters within, through what became known as Riparian Rights.

So, too, have the federal and state governments sought to exert ownership rights over water bodies and water supply through sovereign rights and policies of protecting public resources. This authority is often expressed in state constitutions, federal and state regulations, and public trust doctrines. Each of these frameworks for water ownership is discussed in greater detail below.

## PUBLIC OWNERSHIP, AKA TRAGEDY OF THE COMMONS

Throughout much of human history, water supply has been freely open to the public—without the need to purchase the water body or the land adjacent to it (Craig, 2012; Zellmer, 2008). Natural resources that were subject to open and shared ownership were considered to be common property, or "the Commons." When applied to local water bodies, this common ownership allowed all community members to possess a few sticks in the bundle of property rights, such as the rights to access and to use the water. Yet no member of the community would possess all the sticks in the bundle of property rights, and therefore no member of the community could exclude others from the water supply or appropriate all of the water for their sole usage. The benefits of such common ownership is clear: every member of the community could access the water necessary for the survival of themselves, their families, and their livestock, thus enhancing the community as a whole.

The "sticks" of ownership included under common ownership also allowed less sanitary purposes. Often, citizens had the right to use local lakes and rivers for bathing, as toilets for humans and livestock, and as disposal for other waste products including the remnants of butchery and tanning. While advancing health laws and sanitation technology eventually limited the use of common waters as large toilets, advancing technology also led to new and more toxic waste products being disposed of in the commonly owned waters.

One famous international example of common usage destroying a valuable community water body was the Thames River in London. Historic common usage of this water body granted a property right to all citizens to dump human sewage directly into the river, as well as the right of laundries to dump their biological and chemical waste products directly into the river. By the mid 1800s, the Thames River, vital to the city of London, was so terribly polluted that it was nicknamed the "Great Stink" (Lemon, n.d.). In addition to emitting a smell so noxious that it led to the suspension of Parliament in 1858, the hazardous cocktail created by this common dumping led to a terrible cholera outbreak among citizens who used the polluted common waters as their drinking supply (ibid.).

In America, we have a more recent example of common usage nearly destroying the largest lake in Florida, Lake Apopka. This lake was famous in the 1800 and 1900s for its abundant and enormous bass. However, the large lake was surrounded by privately owned farms which each asserted a common property right to use the lake as a drainage and sewage tank for the agricultural runoff, including arsenic, pesticides, and fertilizers. The continual runoff of waters contaminated with fertilizers and pesticides from the dozens of farms over many years led to a chronic algal bloom, which suffocated the lake waters and killed the bass stocks ("History of Lake Apopka," 2013). By the end of the twentieth century, the famous bass stocks were destroyed and the lake was a soup of peagreen muck (Hatzipangos, 2006).

Corporate entities also used common ownership of water resources to advance their business interests. With little or no investment in a water body, nor any obligation to maintain it, corporate entities used marshes, streams, and rivers as dumping grounds for everything from solid and chemical to biological waste (Hardin, 1968). One famous example of such corporate usage of the common waters was the dumping of various carcinogens, including trichloroethylene, which caused a terrible cluster of childhood leukemia victims in Woburn, Massachusetts (Harr, 1996).

The Tragedy of the Commons is a story that has repeatedly played out across the globe through the centuries and continues today. Common ownership and usage of water bodies for drinking, fishing, bathing, and defecation is still common in developing countries. So, too, are the adverse effects of such common ownership, including water pollution and waterborne illness ("Global WASH-Related Diseases and Contaminants," n.d.). When all people have the right to access and use a water resource yet none have the responsibly to maintain it, the water supply inevitably becomes overused, polluted, and eventually even destroyed.

## PUBLIC TRUST/PUBLIC USAGE DOCTRINES

In an attempt to continue the public benefit of common ownership but limit the adverse effects caused by unrestricted usage, many state governments have adopted some limited variation of a public trust or public use doctrine (Salsich, 2003; Zellmer, 2008). Yet the manner and extent to which public right to water usage may be exercised varies greatly (Zellmer, 2008). Such variation is guided by the prevailing water jurisprudence adopted in individual states, as well as the different constitutional protections afforded to property rights and to natural resources in each state (Zellmer, 2008).

Many states, through regulation or contractual rights, have reserved a level of water ownership to the state or federal government to regulate and distribute as it deems appropriate (Reimber, 2001). This doctrine is based in the historic European concept that all land and water originally belonged to the sovereign (Frank, 2012). Such jurisprudence was brought to America where, rather than royalty, the sovereign was federal and state governments. The federal government has used this concept of sovereign authority to regulate all navigable waters of the United States under the Clean Water Act. In addition, many states assume a dual role as both owner and regulator of jurisdictional water bodies.

The American concept of sovereign ownership is universally tied to use of the water for the public good, hence the nomenclature: Public Trust Doctrine (Frank, 2012). This doctrine is typically established by the state's constitution and enabling legislation that establishes the state's ownership and control over certain jurisdictional water bodies for the benefit of its citizens (ibid.). Thus, while the state owns the waters, the bundle of property sticks is restricted by an obligation to use and maintain the waters for the public benefit (ibid.).

Ownership under a public trust framework can take a variety of forms. In some states, the government owns both the submerged lands and the water above while in other states the government owns just the water but not the submerged lands underneath (which can be owned by private interests). Other variations of the public trust structure allow various levels of shared water ownership between the government and private parties. The exact structure and extent of state ownership is typically created in broad strokes within the state's constitution and then further specified in codes and other regulations.

This concept rarely translates to pure conservation of public trust water bodies. Rather, it is quite common for public trust waters to be used for public drinking water, fishing, and recreation (Restatement, 2017). It is also common to find that public trust waters may be, in part, converted to private use. It is not uncommon for states to allow private and commercial boat docks and marinas built into the public waters. Nor is it uncommon for states to allow largescale water withdrawal by private industrial and commercial users, including utilities, bottling franchises, and even theme parks (Consalo, 2016).

This sale of public trust waters for commercial resale illustrates the fluid and temporary nature of water ownership. The waters are initially owned by the state but subject to certain public rights to use the water. They are sold to a private commercial entity becoming the property of that entity. Yet often, the water is simply bottled and distributed to purchasers across the county. Once purchased, the consumer becomes the temporary owner until the water is drunk and biologically "deposited" into the possession of the local utility company where it can be sanitized to various degrees to be resold as potable water for drinking and bathing or as reclaimed water for irrigation. Thus, the cycle of temporary ownership and continual transfer of water continues.

## PRIOR APPROPRIATION

In the American West, water has always been a scarce natural resource (Grantham & Viers, 2014; Padlock & Doyle, 2015; Tarlock, 2001). While there are a few large water bodies, such as the Colorado and Snake Rivers, most of the West is arid land with little rainfall (Tarlock, 2001). The scarce nature of fresh water in this part of the country led early settlers to make ownership claims for exclusive, or at least priority, use of water resources (Tarlock, 2001). The legal doctrine governing water ownership in the American West is known as the Doctrine of Prior Appropriation. In common vernacular, it is known as "first in time, first in line" (Grantham & Viers, 2014; Podolak & Doyle 2015; Tarlock, 2001).

The term *appropriation* refers to the physical taking of water from its source and conversion of this water to a beneficial use. Under the Prior Appropriation Doctrine, the first person or entity to appropriate water from a particular water body for a beneficial use obtained a priority right to use the waters of that water body, often in perpetuity (Davis, 2001; Tarlock, 2001). Such ownership, once recognized by court order, entitles the first appropriator certain rights to the water which must be satisfied before any latter appropriators may use the water body, hence the term "first in time, first in line."

Such appropriations are limited only by how much water the appropriator can obtain and convert to a beneficial use. After the first appropriator takes possession of as much water as they can obtain and convert to a beneficial use, the next appropriator in time takes the next place in line to assume as much of the remaining water as they can obtain and convert to a beneficial use. The process continues until all the waters are appropriated to private or public ownership. The doctrine of Prior Appropriation has been used since the 1850s and is codified into the laws of most Western states. Under most laws, there is a significant stick missing from the ownership bundle of property rights: the appropriator does not own any part of the water body itself (Davis, 2001; Tarlock, 2001). Ownership of the water body vests with the federal or state government. The appropriator only possesses the right to withdraw and privatize a certain amount of water from that water body (Davis, 2001). Once the water is withdrawn, it becomes the property of the appropriator to use as they see fit (Davis, 2001; Tarlock, 2001).

During the last hundred years, overallocation of waters in the American West (driven by exponential growth of urbanized areas and allowed by the Doctrine of Prior Appropriation) has led to severe drought, water shortages, and ecological destruction of the limited fresh water resources. Almost every major water body in the West has been overappropriated, meaning the claims to ownership of the waters exceed the amount of water that actually exists within the water body (Davis, 2001; Tarlock, 2001). These adverse effects become more pronounced during seasonal dry periods and natural drought periods.

Ironically, overappropriation is exacerbated by the common knowledge that in the American West drought periods are always just around the corner and thus, appropriation holders often appropriate and store the valuable waters in tanks and reservoirs for long periods of time, further starving the water body of necessary waters (Tarlock, 2001). It is a destructive cycle in which appropriation and hoarding of water leads to less water flowing naturally in the water bodies, which leads to more drought and more hoarding of water resources. Sadly, even when the water body still retains some water after the appropriations are taken, the amount of water left may not be enough for the water body to function hydrologically or support aquatic life (Water in the American West, 2012).

The Prior Appropriation Doctrine has also led to modern legal battles regarding water ownership. These legal battles are often waged on a grand scale, involving states fighting with other states and cities fighting with other cities, with widespread financial and geopolitical ramifications (Davis, 2001). It has been aptly observed of the current state of Western water supply: "Nineteenth-century water law is meeting 20th century infrastructure and 21st century climate change and it leads to a nonsensical outcome" (Hiltzik, 2014, para. 10).

## RIPARIAN RIGHTS

A different concept of water ownership, known as the Riparian Rights Doctrine, arose in the Eastern states, where water is far more abundant (Craig, 2012; Null, 2016; Restatement, 2017; Zellmer, 2008). Under this doctrine, a person or company that own land adjacent to a water body, known as a "riparian owner," possesses a large number of sticks in the bundle of property rights to waters on, adjacent to, or under their property (Craig, 2012; Lauer, 1963; Waite, 1969). While riparian rights vary by state, such sticks generally include the right to access the water body and to exclude others from it, the right to use the waters, the right to appropriate the water and aquatic wildlife, and the right to build boat docks and marinas upon the submerged lands (Consalo, 2015; Craig, 2012). Cases in some states suggest there may even be an expansion of the riparian doctrine to include the right to a certain water quality (Craig, 2012). At its core, the Riparian Rights Doctrine allows the riparian landowner to use the adjacent water body in any reasonable fashion that does not directly harm other riparian land owners (Davis, 2001; Hitlick, 2014; Wines, 2014).

However, problems arise when riparian owners use their extensive property rights to the water body as a license to pollute or withdraw extensive amounts of water. Until the 1970s, a riparian owner was essentially allowed to use the adjoining water body in any manner that did not give rise to complaints from other riparian owners. If there were no other riparian owners near the water body, this doctrine allowed the sole riparian owner an extensive bundle of property rights to the water, including activities that would endanger the continued viability of the water body either through pollution or excessive water withdrawals. It was quite common, therefore, for some of the most noxious commercial users, such as chemical factories and tanneries, to purchase riparian lands and then use the adjacent water bodies as a landfill and ad hoc sewage system (Salzman & Thompson, 2014). If a use was so toxic that downstream riparian owners might object, the solution was simply to purchase all riparian land along the water body so that there were no other riparian owners to raise objection. In such cases, the riparian rights were essentially unlimited. This led to significant environmental problems due to overwithdrawals and pollution. It also resulted in unexpected financial ramifications to future riparian owners who assumed liability for cleaning up the contaminated waters, once discovered.

Another ecologically damaging right of traditional riparian systems is the riparian owner's right to drain, and thus destroy, the water body entirely. Until recent decades, ecological and economic value of wetlands was not fully understood. Therefore, many riparian owners viewed wetlands as obstacles to be drained and filled with dry land. Many towns and railroad lines across the East were realized by purchase and subsequent drainage of extensive wetlands (Conradt, n.d.). In addition to long-term environmental impacts, such drain and fill actions led to adverse financial ramifications for future purchasers, since the former wetlands were often subject to regular flooding (Grunwald, 2006).

RECENT LEGAL FRAMEWORKS FOR WATER CONTROL

While the legal frameworks of common use, public trust, prior appropriation, and riparian rights have established the rights to own, access, use, and sell water supplies, these frameworks have not prevented the pollution of our world's water supplies, nor have they ensured a clean and abundant fresh water supply. Even those fortunate enough to have some level of ownership over fresh water supply, either through the doctrine of common rights, riparian ownership, prior appropriation, or as the beneficiary of the public trust, often struggle to secure a sufficient, and clean, supply of the water. Each doctrine of water ownership allows a few parties to pollute or overappropriate the available water supply such that insufficient supply is left for the viability of the water body and other potential uses. Yet, there are additional legal frameworks for water ownership, which can be used in a variety of combinations to achieve the goal of protecting property rights to water while preserving the quality of waters on this earth.

Regulations

Both common public usage and abusive private usage led to significant degradation of American water supplies by the 1960s and '70s. These decades brought the human health tragedy of Love Canal, where careless use of a human-made canal as an industrial waste sewer resulted in a freakishly high number of victims of leukemia and birth defects (Beck, n.d.). The quality of Cleveland's water supply was so terrible that the Cuyahoga River actually caught fire (Scott, 2009).

As a result of these health and environmental tragedies, in the early 1970s Congress enacted a variety of federal regulations to limit the extent to which water ownership rights included the right to overuse and pollute water supplies (Comprehensive Environmental Response, Compensation and Recovery Act, 1980; Resource Conservation and Recovery Act, 1978; Safe Drinking Water Act, 1974). Laws such as the Clean Water Act, the Safe Drinking Water Act, the Resource Conservation, and Recovery Act (RCRA), and the Comprehensive Environmental Response, Compensation and Liability Act (CERCLA, commonly known as "Superfund") created an extensive net of federal regulations that governed most aspects of public and private water ownership and usage (1980, 1978, 1974). These laws were so extensive and detailed that the federal Environmental Protection Agency did not have sufficient personnel to enforce the regulations. Therefore, much of the responsibly for supervision and enforcement was delegated to the fifty states. The states, in turn, were able to enact even stricter regulations on water ownership and use.

A core tenet of most of these regulations was the imposition of permitting requirements for most activities that could involve adverse effects to water bodies, regardless of whether such water body was privately owned. Through this permitting authority, federal, state, and local governments gained the power to protect all water bodies. Today, the types of water usage that require government permits under the various regulations range from polluting the waters to removal of water, soil, or sand from the water body, and to construction of boat docks and marinas.

As might be imagined, in the early years of enforcement of this extensive government regulation over water rights, there was a vast amount of litigation regarding the constitutionality of such restrictions. However, for the most part, the provisions of federal and state water regulations have been upheld and remain in force today. While these regulations do restrict the extent of water rights to varying degrees, they have cumulatively resulted in dramatic improvements to American water bodies over the last four decades (Salzman & Thompson, 2014).

## Earth Jurisprudence

In recent years, a new water framework has arisen, known as Earth Jurisprudence (Cullinan, 2011). Earth Jurisprudence acknowledges that various natural resources belong to all living beings—not just human beings (ibid.). In so acknowledging, Earth Jurisprudence requires that certain property rights of nonhuman entities be recognized and protected (ibid.). Such rights would include the right to access and use water supply, as well as the right to prevent pollution or overwithdrawal from such water supply. This framework is a dramatic paradigm shift from the anthropocentric jurisprudence of most of human civilization with regard to water bodies and water supply.

Under an Earth Jurisprudence framework, laws relating to water would need to be drafted to incorporate a recognition of these property rights of nonhuman entities such as fish and animals. Earth Jurisprudence would therefore limit the existing rights of certain human and corporate entities to withdraw and pollute waters. (As a side benefit of this redistribution of rights, human entities would also benefit from more abundant, clean, freshwater supplies.)

While certain ownership rights for nonhuman entities might be effectuated through minimum standards of water cleanliness and water supply reservations, it is likely that human trustees would need to be appointed to enforce more specific rights of nonhuman entities, such as the right to sue. The use of trustees to protect property rights has been used for centuries in regard to children, incapacitated persons, and even pets. Recognizing the dramatic redistribution of property rights necessary to implement an Earth Jurisprudence framework, it is not surprising that such revolutionary notions have not been adopted by any regulatory code in the United States. However, the movement has great potential to achieve the societal goal of abundant, clean water for both humans and wildlife.

## Transferrable Water Rights

With legal frameworks governing a source of water owned by a private entity, market incentives can be implemented to limit waste and pollution by allowing such rights to be bought and sold on a "water market" (Draper, 2008; Null, 2016). Such a framework requires clearly defined and exclusive rights to access and use water, which in turn, may then be sold in allocated units to an end user (Draper, 2008; Null, 2016). By deeming water rights transferrable, the owners of the water have greater incentive to conserve water so that it may be resold. Similarly, the initial owner has an incentive to keep such water clean for as long as it is within their possession, in order to keep the resale value highest. Several countries, including the United States, Canada, Australia, and Mexico, have implemented various forms of transferrable water rights (Marston & Cai, 2016).

## Twenty-First Century Decision Making

Population explosion and technological advancements have rendered our reliance on historic legal frameworks of water ownership untenable for the long-term sustainability and availability of clean water sources. (Marston & Cai, 2016). Our world requires new and perhaps revolutionary thinking to establish legal frameworks that allow for public and private ownership while still protecting this valuable natural resource. A starting point for such a legal framework is the realization that fresh water is a limited resource. Any legal doctrine that allows for pollution, overusage, and hoarding is incompatible with the goal of an abundant clean water supply. Further, evaluation of current and future water supply stores must take into account the needs of all water-dependent creatures, not solely human demands.

In addition to selection of a legal framework that recognizes an intrinsic value of water, it is also necessary to place an accurate economic value on water as both a public resource and as a private property right. Such economic value attached to the right to access and use water fairly must represent all aspects of such water usage, including the constant consumer demand for water (whether that consumer be human or nonhuman), the finite supply of fresh water to meet consumer demand, and the depreciated value of a degraded water supply, either saline or fresh. The right to obtain water rights should require payment at a rate sufficient to compensate for and correct adverse effect of such usage on water quality.

It is unlikely that a single legal framework for water ownership can be used by all states to improve water quality and water supplies. As described above, different areas of the county have different water supplies, both in abundance of renewable water and in the nature of the water bodies available (Craig, 2012). Further, every state already has certain existing frameworks for water ownership. Yet, our current water shortages and water pollution problems make it clear that traditional legal frameworks for water ownership must be updated and blended with more innovative concepts of ownership, such as earth jurisprudence or transferrable rights, in order to ensure that water resources are maintained in a manner which protects one of the most valuable natural resources on our planet for all potential users.

## REFERENCES

Baron, J. B. (2014). Rescuing the bundle of rights metaphor in property law. *University of Cincinnati Law Review*, 82.

Beck, E. C. (n.d.). Love Canal tragedy. Retrieved from www.epa.gov/aboutepa/love-canal-tragedy.

Berry, T. (1999). *The great work: Our way into the future.* New York, NY: Bell Tower.

Centers for Disease Control and Prevention. (n.d.) Global WASH-related diseases and contaminants. (n.d.). Retrieved from: www.cdc.gov/healthywater/wash_diseases.html.

———. (2014). 2014 West Virginia chemical release. (n.d.). Retrieved from: http://emergency.cdc.gov/chemical/MCHM/westvirginia2014/ Centers for Disease Control and Prevention.

Clean Water Act, §§ 3312511387 (1972).

Comprehensive Environmental Recovery, Liability and Compensation Act, 42 §§ 9601–9675 (1980).

Conradt, S. (n.d.). Why Walt Disney built a theme park on swampland. *MentalFloss*. Retrieved from http://mentalfloss.com/article/28174/why-walt-disney-built-theme-park-swampland.

Consalo, K. (2016). Selling Florida's water up the river. *Florida State University Journal of Land Use and Environmental Law*, 31.

Conte, M. & Francis, E. (2014). Charleston told not to drink water after chemical leak. ABC News. Retrieved from http://abcnews.go.com/US/charleston-told-drink-water-chemical-leak/story?id=21493603.

Craig, R. (2012). Defining riparian rights as 'property' through takings litigation: is there a property right to environmental quality?. *Environmental Law*, 42, 115-155.

Cullinan, C. (2011). *Wild law: A manifesto for Earth justice.* White River Junction, VT: Chelsea Green.

Davis, S. K. (2001). The politics of water scarcity in the western states. *The Social Science Journal, 38(4)*, 527–542.

Domonoske, C. (n.d.). Obama declares state of emergency over Flint's contaminated water. *National Public Radio*. Retrieved from www.npr.org/sections/thetwo-way/2016/01/16/463319454/obama-declares-state-of-emergency-over-flints-contaminated-water?sc=17&f=1001&utm_source=iosnewsapp&utm_medium=Email&utm_campaign=app.

Draper, S. (2008). Limits to water privatization. *Journal of Water Resources Panning and Management*, 134, 493-503.

Frank, R. (2012). The public trust doctrine: Assessing its recent past and charting its future. *Davis Law Review*, 45.

Freshwater Crisis. (n.d.). *National Geographic*. Retrieved from http://environment.nationalgeographic.com/environment/freshwater/freshwater-crisis/.

Griffin, D., Black, N., & Devine, C. (2015). 5 years after the Gulf oil spill: What we do (and don't) know. *CNN News*. Retrieved from: www.cnn.com/2015/04/14/us/gulf-oil-spill-unknowns/.

Grunwald, M. (2006). *The swamp: The Everglades, Florida, and the politics of paradise*. New York, NY: Simon & Schuster.

Hardin, G. (1968). The tragedy of the commons. *Science*, 162 (3859), 1243–1248.

Harr, J. (1996). *A civil action*. New York, NY: Random House.

Hatzipanagos, R. (April 24, 2006). Lake Apopka's water war. *Orlando Business Journal*. Retrieved from: www.bizjournals.com/orlando/stories/2006/04/24/story2.html?i=38087.

"Helping Girls and Women Stay Safe in Mba Mondo." (n.d.). Retrieved from www.wateraid.org/uk/what-we-do/stories-from-our-work/helping-girls-and-women-stay-safe-in-mba-mondo.

Hiltzik, M. (2014). Water war bubbling up between California and Arizona. *Los Angeles Times*. Retrieved from: www.latimes.com/business/hiltzik/la-fi-hiltzik-20140620-column.html.

"History of Lake Apopka" (2013). Retrieved from: http://floridaswater.com/lakeapopka/history.html St. Johns Water Management District, State of Florida.

Hulett, S. (October 5, 2015). High lead levels in Michigan kids after city switches water source. *National Public Radio*. Retrieved from: www.npr.org/2015/09/29/444497051/high-lead-levels-in-michigan-kids-after-city-switches-water-source.

Judge, C. (2013). The coming water wars. *U.S. News & World Report*. Retrieved from www.usnews.com/opinion/blogs/clark-judge/2013/02/19/the-next-big-wars-will-be-fought-over-water.

Kristof, N. (1997). For third world, water is still a deadly drink. *New York Times.* Retrieved from www.nytimes.com/1997/01/09/world/for-third-world-wate r-is-still-a-deadly-drink.html?pagewanted=all.

Lauer, T. E. (1963). The common law background of the riparian doctrine. *Missouri Law Rev*iew, 28.

Lemon, J. (n.d.). The great stink. Retrieved from: www.choleraandthethames.co.uk/ cholera-in-london/the-great-stink/ City of Westminster Archives; 1800–1900.

Marston, L. & Cai, X (2016). An overview of water reallocation and the barriers to its implementation. *WIREs Water*, 3, 658-677.

Null, S.E. & L. Prudencio (2016). Climate change effects on water allocations with season dependent water rights. *Science of the Total Environment*, 571, 943-954.

Reimber, M. (2001). The public trust doctrine: Historic protection for Florida's navigable rivers and lakes. *The Florida Bar Journal*, LXXV.

Resource Conservation and Recovery Act, 42 §§ 6901–6992 (1976).

Restatement (Second) of Torts § 856 cmt. (Am. Law Inst. 2017).

Safe Drinking Water Act 42 § 300 (1974).

Salzman, J., & Thompson, B., Jr. (2014). *Environmental Law and Policy* (4th ed.). St. Paul, MN: Foundation Press.

Scott, M. (2009). Cuyahoga River fire 40 years ago ignited an ongoing cleanup campaign. *The Plain Dealer*. Retrieved from: www.cleveland.com/science/ index.ssf/2009/06/cuyahoga_river_fire_40_years_a.html.

Stevens, M. (2015). Water, 2015, California: The no good, very bad year—Now, "Pray for Rain." *Los Angeles Times*. Retrieved from: www.latimes.com/local/ lanow/la-me-ln-water-year-20150929-story.html.

Tarlock, A. D. (2001). The future of prior appropriation in the New West. *Natural Resources Journal*, 41, 769–793.

Turkewitzaug, J. (2015). Environmental agency uncorks its own toxic water spill at Colorado Mine. *New York Times*. Retrieved from: www.nytimes. com/2015/08/11/us/durango-colorado-mine-spill-environmental-protectio n-agency.html?_r=0.

Waite, G. (1969). Beneficial use of water in a riparian jurisdiction. *Wisconsin Law Review*, 864.

Wines, M. (2014). West's drought and growth intensify conflict over water rights. *New York Times*. Retrieved from www.nytimes.com/2014/03/17/us/wests-dr ought-and-growth-intensify-conflict-over-water-rights.html?_r=0.

"Water and Violent Conflict" (2005). Retrieved from: www.globalpolicy.org/ images/pdfs/052605waterconflict.pdf.

Zellmer, S. & Harder, J. (2008). Unbundling property in water. *Alabama Law Review* 59, 679-745.

# 7 An Exploration of Coastal Property Rights in the United States under Conditions of Sea Level Rise

CHAD J. MCGUIRE

The kind of property that is the focus of this chapter is *real* property, that is, tangible real estate or land. In the United States, the rights and obligations associated with land are steeped in legal doctrine. Common law principles are inherited from our European neighbors (mainly England), and many of those property rights derive from earlier Western civilization including Roman law (Hausmaninger & Gamauf, 2012). This is particularly true of coastal areas. Subject to gravitational forces, wind, and currents, the line between land and ocean is dynamic and ever changing. Our earliest legal traditions distinguished between private and public ownership. Subject to certain exceptions, only the public could own land under the ocean, referred to under common law tradition as the *jus publicum*. Otherwise, land not constantly submerged (tidelands), or the dry land touching tidelands could be privately held, legally referred to as the *jus privatim* (Nixon, 1994, p. 42).[1]

Bounded by principles of tangible property, legal definitions of coastal land were created under the expectation that natural conditions could change the legal characteristic of the property right. For example, slow and natural additions of sediment over time could move the land-sea boundary farther out to the ocean. This *accretion* of land can alter property rights. What was publicly owned submerged land is now privately owned upland. Similarly, a gradual and natural erosion of land to the sea, often referred to as *reliction,* legally transforms what was dry private land to submerged public land (Flushman, 2002, pp. 95–98).

Rather than relying on specific geospatial boundaries, the property rights of coastal areas are more malleable, mirroring the dynamic conditions of changing coastlines. But today is different. Many coastlines in the United States are experiencing intensified change. While coastlines have always been dynamic, climate change increases the variability and, ultimately, the extent of change. Specifically, a warming Earth brings with it the conditions for coastal disruption. Rising seas impact low-lying coastlines that have a gradual slope. Increasing storm frequency and intensity accelerate the reshaping of our coastlines (Church et al., 2013).

In sum, climactic changes have implications for how we define and interpret property rights relating to coastal land. This chapter will focus on examining two conceptual categories of property rights, referred to for purposes of this analysis as a *Lockean view* and a *Modern view*. These two categorical views of property rights will be used as counterpoints to look at how current case law is interpreting land rights within a changing coastal zone. The goal is to highlight how the contextualization of property rights will likely impact how those rights are defined at the coastline in an era of climate-induced sea level rise.

## FOUNDATIONS OF PROPERTY RIGHTS

The concept of property rights is, fundamentally, a human creation derived from agreed-upon social norms legitimized by the power of law. Land, of course, exists outside of these social norms. Thus, property rights in relation to real property, or physical land, combines the essential objective aspects of land (physical dimensions) with expressions of societal norms. The land itself is generally not subject to change over time (absent qualifications noted earlier such as the phenomenon of sea level rise). But social constructs are subject to change based on the values, beliefs, and norms of the populace over time (Stern et al., 1999). As such, property rights may be divided into two categorical characteristics: the physical land itself, and the non-physical manner in which the land is defined by society.

Elinor Ostrom's work is helpful in understanding the nonphysical aspects of property rights (Ostrom, 1990). Some of her work focused on two characteristics that can be applied to property rights: divisibility and excludability. Using these two characteristics and creating a spectrum from high to low, Ostrom was able to identify four fundamental, human-derived, categories of property rights: public goods, toll goods, private goods, and common pool resources. A representation of these four categories of property rights is shown in Figure 7.1.

Figure 7.1 shows how societal norms play a critical role in defining property rights. For example, private property rights share the essential characteristics of private goods; both exhibit characteristics of high excludability and high divisibility. High divisibility, in this context, means the land is discrete and unique. One parcel of real property is easily distinguished from another based on its unique location: no two parcels can share the same space. The other characteristic—high excludability—suggests the owner of the parcel has one of the most important rights of private property ownership under real property law: the right to exclude others. These two characteristics together establish the unique aspects of real property rights which, in turn, reflect social values. The divisibility characteristic of real property is an inherent trait. The excludability characteristic is a preference reflecting our societal values. Coincidentally, high excludability is a fundamental reason we imbue significant monetary value into real property.

According to Figure 7.1, a common pool resource is an alternative property right characteristic for things like real property where the inherent characteristic is high divisibility. The traditional example of a property with high divisibility but low excludability is a commons: a discrete physical space where there is no right to exclude others. Garret Hardin used the example of a commons to identify some of the base triggers of environmental harm in his article *The Tragedy of the Commons* (Hardin, 1968). The values associated with the land exist, but the incentives to manage the land in a way that ensures its long-term sustainability can be limited by exploitation. The right to exclude allows an individual to capture the potential values of the land without having to worry about others usurping their plans. A long history exists in the United States that identifies private property rights as an important value, often linked to both the political and cultural ideology of the country (Rose-Ackerman, 1985).

Without defined property rights, land is essentially a common pool resource (see Figure 7.1). Again, putting aside the social constructs placed on how property rights to land are valued, we can observe that in a pure state of nature no human really owns land, because the notion of ownership itself is derived from social constructs enforced, ultimately, by the power of law (McGuire, 2014, p.102). If

|  | Low          Excludability          High | |
|---|---|---|
| **Low** | PUBLIC GOOD | TOLL GOOD |
|  | National Defense | Private Club |
|  | Gravity | Park (Zoo) |
|  | Low Excludability | High Excludability |
|  | Low Divisibility | Low Divisibility |
|  | Government Control | Mixed Control (Govt./Private) |
| **Divisibility** | COMMON POOL RESOURCE | PRIVATE GOOD |
|  | Air | Homes |
|  | Ocean | Consumer Goods |
|  | Low Excludability | High Excludability |
|  | High Divisibility | High Divisibility |
| **High** | Mixed Control | Free Market |

Figure 7.1. Representation of four main categories of property rights based on the characteristics of divisibility and excludability

we removed all social and legal constructs from real property, we would be left with a fixed piece of land that is highly divisible but has low excludability.[2] Under such conditions there are really no constraining factors on human actions; each individual preference will drive the actions of each actor. Thus, if we assume all actors want access to the common piece of land, then we can also assume that individual self-interest will drive the commons to overutilization for the same reason Hardin explained in his essay; each person's self-interest will lead to rational decisions at the individual level that, at the collective level, yield an irrational result—the overexploitation of the commons. The only limits on this irrational result are the decisions by individuals to band together and, as a group, create and enforce certain protections for the commons. These nascent rules, moving from informal to formal, are founded in common agreement between societal members. They are subject to change as circumstances demand.

Rules, both formal and informal, collectively form the foundations of property rights. They exist fundamentally through agreement; they have no real existence in an ontological sense. The values, beliefs, and norms of the group members establish the essence of the property right. In this way the property right is more epistemological, based on human experience. This is particularly true for those kinds of property rights that are characterized as "highly divisible" as noted in Figure 7.1. Formal institutions have existed for millennia to control real property. But there are also numerous examples of informal institutions developed by subgroups based on how they interact and value the resource (for example, see Acheson, 1988). Common in these examples is a basic judgment being made about the role of land use in relation to individual and group norms, values, and beliefs. And it is these norms, values, and beliefs that help to form the ongoing debate we have over real property rights, and in particular, how those "rights" are impacted under changing circumstances such as climate-induced sea level rise.[3]

## TWO NORMATIVE VIEWS OF PROPERTY RIGHTS: THE LOCKEAN VIEW AND MODERN VIEW

In an attempt to look at the issue of property right dynamics in an era of sea level rise, two categorical views of real property rights are being defined for analysis: a Lockean view and a Modern view of property rights. For purposes of this chapter, a Lockean view perceives property rights as existing outside of societal norms. Alternatively, a Modern view places property rights wholly within societal norms. A visual representation of Lockean and Modern views of property rights in relation to societal norms in presented in Figure 7.2.

For this analysis, a Lockean view sees property rights as fixed and not subject to interpretive changes even as social norms may change over time. A Modern view represents the opposing view, seeing property rights as subservient and contingent to societal norms. The Lockean view derives from the work of John Locke, in particular a theory of property rights that is connected to natural law (Simmons, 1992). With this theory, property rights derive from direct human action (generally labor) on land. As such, the property right establishes itself by the influence of human action and is immutable from that action. Just as a person owns oneself from a biblical standpoint, that person also owns their own labors: the natural results of their actions. Thus, common land becomes privately owned by the application of labor. But like the free will of the person, that ownership cannot be diminished so long as the land is not abandoned.

A Modern view focuses more on property rights from an economic and even social optimization perspective (Alexander & Penalver, 2012). In legal parlance, the right to real property is often referred to as a bundle of rights (Johnson, 2007). A right to real property is not a singular or absolute right, but rather a set of rights that are divisible. Examples include many of the public and private land use planning tools used today. This includes an array of public instruments such as zoning that limit land mainly based on master public planning and founded in protecting the health, safety, and welfare of the citizenry. Also included are private instruments such as easements and covenants that provide allowances and create restrictions on the use of land.

For the purposes of this chapter, the key distinction between the Lockean and Modern views of property rights focuses on how they apply differently toward

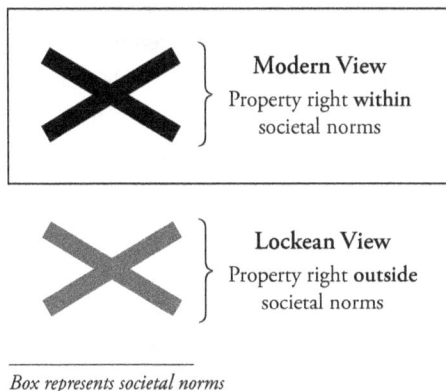

Modern View
Property right **within**
societal norms

Lockean View
Property right **outside**
societal norms

*Box represents societal norms*

Figure 7.2. A representation of Lockean and Modern views of property rights in relation to societal norms

attempts to alter existing property rights. Or, as a more particular question to the subject matter of this chapter, what kinds of property right expectations should a coastal landowner have in an era of sea level rise? Should they expect their established rights at the time of ownership to be immutable, or are those rights subject to change based on the internalization of new information about coastal dangers that become reflected in societal norms? Within a Lockean view, the right to alter existing property rights would be close to nonexistent. Using a Modern view, existing property rights are malleable, conforming to societal expectations. Thus, if social norms change over time, then those changes can be imbued into the regulation of property rights. The bundle of rights is altered. But with a Lockean view, property rights exist outside of societal norms. Thus, a change in societal norms will not result in a change to private citizens' property rights.

The distinction between a Lockean and Modern view is important because it helps to highlight how formal legal structures in the United States have attempted to address private real property rights in a variety of settings. Case law precedent, mainly from the United States Supreme Court, provides a compelling window into the evolution of property rights over time. By reviewing key cases under the property right framework juxtaposing Modern and Lockean views as described above, insights can be gained into the association between societal norms and property rights. And these insights are critical when considering how expectations toward property right may need to change to deal with evolving coastal zone risks due to climate change.

## JUDICIAL INTERPRETATIONS OF PROPERTY RIGHTS IN PRIVATE LAND

Before looking at specific cases, one additional conceptual framework is presented. This framework looks at the relationship between portions of the Fifth and Tenth Amendments to the United States Constitution. One can think of this as a spectrum with the Fifth Amendment at one end and the Tenth Amendment at the other end. A visual representation of this spectrum is shown in Figure 7.3.

For purposes of Figure 7.3 and this chapter, the Tenth Amendment represents the lawful power of government to regulate (restrict) land use. The U.S. Supreme Court opinion in *Euclid v. Ambler,* 272 U.S. 365 (1926) stated that government has the right to regulate land, especially when those regulations are shown to directly protect from dangers common to the public. At the other end of the spectrum is the Fifth Amendment, which, for purposes germane to this chapter, focuses on the limitations of government to regulate land. Supported by the takings provision of the Fifth Amendment, the United States Supreme Court opinion in *Pennsylvania Coal v. Mahon,* 260 U.S. 393 (1922) held that while government has the power to regulate private property under certain circumstances, if the government regulation goes "too far," then the regulation will be recognized as a taking of private property within the meaning of the Fifth Amendment. Government regulations that are found to be takings of private property rights are generally referred to as *regulatory* takings.

If an action is deemed to be closer to the Fifth Amendment side of the spectrum in Figure 7.3, then a regulatory taking of private property is more likely to be found. In addition, actions that are deemed regulatory takings are more likely, but not always, to be supported by a Lockean view of property rights. Alternatively, an action deemed closer to the Tenth Amendment side of the spectrum in Figure 7.3 will more likely be seen as a valid exercise of government powers to protect the health, safety, and welfare of its citizenry. Such actions will also tend to be supported by a Modern view of property rights, especially actions that interfere with existing property rights, for example, changing zoning laws that impact existing property rights.

Case law helps us interpret when certain actions are safely within government power (actions at the end of the Tenth Amendment side of the spectrum in Figure 7.3), and alternatively when actions are likely to be adjudged regulatory takings. But even with case law, there is a good deal of ambiguity concerning whether an action will be seen as either a legitimate exercise of police power or an illegitimate regulatory taking. This space of the "unknown" is represented by the shaded square in the center of Figure 7.3. The regulation of coastal areas to deal with sea level rise is new, as the condition of sea level rise has been observed and

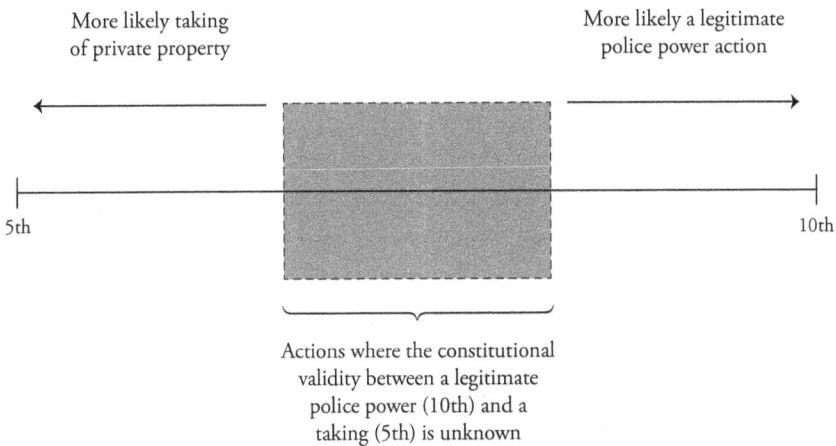

Figure 7.3. Spectrum showing government power and limits to that power under the Fifth and Tenth Amendments to the United States Constitution

understood in our very recent history. Thus, planning for sea level rise that includes potentially altering existing understandings of property rights will undoubtedly fall somewhere in the middle of this spectrum. And whether planning results in a regulatory taking or legitimate government action will depend in large part on the view of property rights supporting the action. But before entertaining that question in more detail, a review of key case law decisions will aid in understanding how planning for sea level rise will be impacted by an application of a Lockean versus Modern view of property rights.

Case law supporting the fundamental power to regulate land (zoning) was already mentioned earlier, in the *Euclid* case. A limitation to regulating land was also identified earlier in the *Pennsylvania Coal* case. Focusing on regulatory takings and using case law precedent, three categories of regulatory takings are identified for further examination in the context of coastal property rights: permanent physical occupations, regulations that deprive landowners of all economic use of their property, and regulations that deprive landowners of some use of value of their land (McGuire, 2014, p. 292). Each category is highlighted below using the foundational case(s) identifying each category of regulatory takings.

The foundational case for government-sanctioned physical occupation of private land is *Loretto v. Teleprompter Manhattan CATV Corporation*, 458 U.S. 419 (1982). *Loretto* involved a city ordinance allowing boxes owned by cable companies to be attached to private residences regardless of the landowner's acquiescence. The U.S. Supreme Court saw the ordinance as a public sanction of a physical occupation of private property. The Court determined such a sanction to be a de facto taking of private land requiring just compensation for the portion of the building "occupied" by the boxes under the Fifth Amendment. The holding shows how a government action (in this case "action" through the legislative process) can lead to a physical occupation of private land, and, further, how that occupation results in a taking even when the intent of the legislation was not to use the government's eminent domain power.

The second category of regulatory takings cases—regulations that deprive a landowner of all viable economic use of their property—is highlighted by the U.S. Supreme Court case *Lucas v. South Carolina Coastal Council*, 505 U.S. 1003 (1992). In *Lucas*, the owner of an undeveloped but buildable lot on a barrier beach island in South Carolina sued after a government agency—the South Carolina Coastal Council—passed a regulation banning property on barrier beaches from development. The landowner, Lucas, claimed the regulation had the effect of "taking" his property because it significantly diminished the value of the land because it was no longer capable of being developed. The U.S. Supreme Court held that any government action that results in a landowner from being deprived of all viable economic use of the property is a categorical taking requiring just compensation under the Fifth Amendment. The case was remanded to the South Carolina state court system for a factual determination as to whether the regulation removed all viable economic use of Lucas's property.

A third category of regulatory takings jurisprudence—regulations that deprive a landowner of some use or value in their land—was defined by the U.S. Supreme Court in *Pennsylvania Central Transportation Company v. New York City*, 438 U.S. 104 (1978). In what became known at the *Penn Central* test, the Court identified the following three factors to use when determining if a government action results in a regulatory taking: (1) the economic impact of the regulation on the landowner; (2) the extent to which the regulation interferes with legitimate investment-backed expectations; and (3) the character of the government interaction. Rather than develop per se categories of takings as it later did in *Loretto* and *Lucas*, the Court here noted that government regulation often impacts the value and rights of private property, and thus impact alone cannot be the basis for declaring a regulatory taking. Rather, a context-specific analysis incorporating the three factors above is necessary to contextualize the genesis of the government regulation and its impact on private landowners. If the government regulation is loosely connected to a Tenth Amendment police power of the state, but yet has significant impact on the value and rights of private property, then it is more likely a regulatory taking will be found. Alternatively, if the government action is closely connected to its police power and yet has limited impact on the values and rights of private property, then it is more likely no regulatory taking will be found.

These three cases—*Loretto*, *Lucas*, and *Penn Central*—provide a contextual starting point for analyzing coastal property rights under conditions of sea level rise, including recent case law that highlights the importance of whether the Court is interpreting property rights from a Lockean view versus Modern view lens. Before viewing specific cases in relation to coastal property rights, let us place these three foundational cases within the context of our spectrum of limits to government power under the Fifth and Tenth Amendments. Figure 7.4 uses the spectrum identified in Figure 7.3 but places the three cases in relation to where they may exist on the spectrum.

As Figure 7.4 shows, the *Loretto* case sits squarely near a Fifth Amendment taking of private property. The case supports a Lockean view of property rights, where any physical occupation of the building is a per se violation of Fifth Amendment protections. Both *Lucas* and *Penn Central* have been placed in the center of the spectrum, with *Lucas* closer to the Fifth Amendment side and *Penn Central* closer to the Tenth Amendment side of the spectrum. Both of these cases derive tests requiring some balancing of interests to determine if the government action is so obtrusive and unrelated to an important government interest that a regulatory taking must be found. But as tests the cases are fact sensitive and therefore fail as clear litmus test to determine just when government action goes too far in regulating a private property right. However, we can analyze some recent coastal cases to provide further context on when property rights lawfully yield to government regulation.

## ANALYZING COASTAL PROPERTY RIGHTS WITHIN CONDITIONS OF SEA LEVEL RISE

As noted earlier in this chapter, coastal zones are dynamic areas where the property lines between land and sea are in constant flux. But the rate and extent of flux is being impacted by climate change and, as a direct consequence in many coastal areas, sea level rise. As a result, recent cases have been decided that highlight the difficulties inherent in government action to protect against the negative effects of sea level rise, in particular the impact government action sometimes has on private property rights. This section attempts to review a few of these cases in the context of the Lockean-Modern property right paradigm. The analysis begins by returning to *Lucas* and an important qualification noted by the U.S. Supreme Court in its opinion.

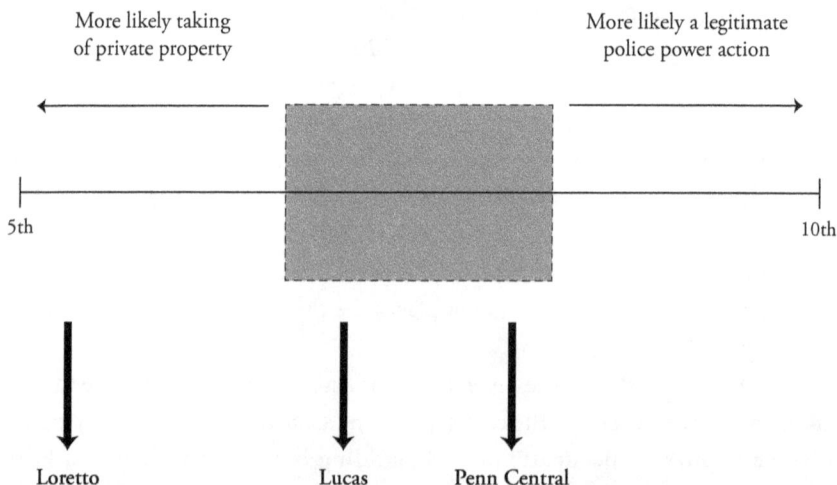

Figure 7.4. Spectrum showing government power and limits to that power under the Fifth and Tenth Amendments to the United States Constitution with regulatory takings cases placed within spectrum

*Lucas* stands for the proposition that a government action resulting in the diminution of all viable economic use of land will result in a categorical regulatory taking. But in its decision, the U.S. Supreme Court qualified its determination that a categorical regulatory taking always occurs when government act removes all viable economic use of the property. The Court noted, "[W]here the State seeks to sustain regulation that deprives land of all economically beneficial use, we think it may resist compensation only if the logically antecedent inquiry into the nature of the owner's estate shows that the proscribed use interests were not part of his title to begin with" (*Lucas v. South Carolina Coastal Council*, 505 U.S. 1003, 1027 (1992)). What the Court is referring to here is the state's power to protect against a public nuisance. As stated by the Court, "A law or decree with such an effect must, in other words, do no more than duplicate the result that could have been achieved in the courts—by adjacent landowners (or other uniquely affected persons) under the State's law of private nuisance, or by the State under its complimentary power to abate nuisances that affect the public generally" (*Lucas v. South Carolina Coastal Council*, 505 U.S. 1003, 1027–28 [1992]).

The Court in *Lucas* is identifying the public nuisance exception to a regulatory taking claim. Under background principles of state property law, private landowners are prohibited from taking actions that would result in a public nuisance. For example, starting fires in a densely populated residential neighborhood may, as a matter of background principles of state property law, be prohibited because such actions have a strong likelihood of harming the public. Thus, government regulations that limit the use of private land to protect against actions deemed public nuisances are categorically outside of a regulatory takings challenge because the private landowner never obtained a legal right to commit a public nuisance on their land. Or said another way, uses of private land that can be shown to be public nuisances are not "rights" that attach to the land.

The Modern view of property rights supports the public nuisance exception to a regulatory taking. Recall the Modern view looks at property rights through an economic and social optimization lens. It identifies a "bundle of rights" in relation to land use. Owners receive a number of rights, such as the right to possess the land and exclude others. But the right to the land is not unlimited. Certain uses are not allowed because they interfere with societal norms. In this case the societal norms are reflected in the doctrine of public nuisance. No landowner has a right to commit a public nuisance, and therefore a public nuisance is not included in the bundle of rights afforded private land ownership. The Modern view of property rights supports the exception outlined by the U.S. Supreme Court in *Lucas* and also provides insight into how the theory operates in a way that makes property rights contextual. Starting a fire on one's private property may be a right included in the "bundle of rights" afforded private landownership. But making a large fire, or making a fire when the weather is windy may contextually be off-limits because those actions are equivalent to a public nuisance. Thus, the action of making a fire is separated from the property right, and it is the context in which the fire is made that matters, particularly when the context speaks to the societal norms and expectations of the community. Or, in legal parlance, the context makes the action a public nuisance rather than a private act within the property rights held by the landowner.

The idea that property rights in land can be contextual is supported through the Modern view of property rights. Rather than making activities absolute ("I can use my land in these ways"), the right to use land is made subservient to the public good. So private property rights are not seen as absolute rights outside of social norms (as the Lockean view would suggest—see Figure 7.2), but rather as a set of rights that are subject to changes in social norms. Examples of the fluid nature of property rights as defined through activity (a property right as the right to engage in specific activities) exist in case law interpretations of public nuisance doctrine.

*Boomer v. Atlantic Cement Company*, 26 N.Y.2d 219, 309 N.Y.S.2d 312 (N.Y. 1970) established the *balancing of interests* test that today is used when determining damages related to public nuisance. In *Boomer* the Atlantic Cement Company created, as a consequence of its operations, air particulates that affected a nearby residential neighborhood. The Court found the activity was a public nuisance as the legal requirement for a nuisance is the unreasonable interference in the use and enjoyment of one's property, and per the Court's determination, the cement soot created an unreasonable interference in the use and enjoyment of the residential properties. Historically, the finding of a public nuisance would result in an injunction of the offending activity and damages to the offended parties. But in this case the court noted the economic activity of the company was substantial (millions in annual revenue and employing hundreds of people), while the harm to the residential neighborhood was real but less than the benefits of the continued operation of the business. Thus, in balancing the interests of the parties, the court fashioned a remedy that allowed the cement company to maintain operations while paying for the damages caused to the residential neighborhood.

There are a few insights from the *Boomer* case relative to the fluidity of property rights (in terms of activities allowed) and also how the preexisting activities are reconciled with changed circumstances. We can assume the cement company was engaging in a lawful industrial enterprise in its location; in other words, it had the right to create cement on its property. But the right to create cement was altered when its production was found to unreasonably interfere with the use and enjoyment of other properties. One can say that the property right is to engage in "lawful" activities on their property. But if and when an activity is deemed unlawful, then the activity ceases to be one of the property rights granted to the landowner. In this case, the activity itself is lawful (making cement). What makes it "unlawful" is that, as a byproduct of creating cement, the company engaged in actions that were, as a matter of public nuisance law, deemed unlawful.[4] If the residential neighborhood did not exist, then the nuisance action would likely not exist and the process of producing cement would be lawful.

The *Boomer* case shows that property rights, at least regarding nuisance claims, are defined more by the *context* of the activity than by the activity itself. This follows a more Modern view of property rights, where rights are interpreted within the context of societal norms. This is further exemplified in the *Boomer* case as the Court, for the first time, balances the interests of the parties when fashioning a remedy to the proven nuisance. In this case, the social value of the economic activity outweighs the harm at least to the extent that the offending activity is allowed to continue. One can argue the heightened importance of economic activity by society over time created the change in social norms that allowed for the continuance of the activity even though it was judged a nuisance. Thus, even within the law of nuisance, social norms can play a role in how certain property rights (for example, the right to the reasonable use and enjoyment of one's property) are interpreted and judged.

A more recent U.S. Supreme Court case speaks to the fluidity of property rights in a coastal zone setting. In *Stop the Beach Renourishment, Inc. v. Florida Department of Environmental Protection*, 560 U.S. 702 (2010), the United States Supreme Court held that coastal landowner property rights were, effectively, subservient to the needs of the public when protecting against the effects of coastal erosion. In this case, landowners owned coastal property immediately adjacent to the ocean. The State of Florida, acting under a statute authorizing public projects to protect against the loss of coastal land, engaged in a nourishment project that added sand between the landowners' properties and the ocean. Florida claimed ownership of the newly created landmass, cutting off the private landowner's property from touching the ocean. The private landowners claimed the action, supported by Florida law, resulted in a taking of their property rights. The U.S. Supreme Court held there is no such taking. While the details of the ruling are complex (including an analysis of a *judicial* taking), the essential legal basis for the ruling was supported by background principles of property law. In essence, the Court saw the submerged land as public property and, as such, held the Florida was entitled to fill the land and maintain title under the State's historical principles of property law.

Beyond the holding itself, the Court's analysis in *Stop the Beach Renourishment* provides some important details vis-à-vis competing property rights. For example, the analysis paid little attention to the well-established property rights of coastal landowners under common law, often referred to as littoral or riparian rights (Policicchio, 2011). One of the critical rights of coastal landowners is to have their private property extend to the water's edge ("touch" the water). This property right is economically significant. Indeed, as a general rule, the price willing to be paid for coastal property is enhanced when that property directly abuts the ocean (Bin, Kruse, & Landry, 2008). The U.S. Supreme Court in this case effectively chooses to ignore the private property right and simply focus its analysis on the public property rights of the State of Florida. Why? Likely because the Court is framing its analysis through a Modern view of property rights. The State is taking action to prevent the erosion of its shorelines. This is a clear Tenth Amendment function to protect the citizenry. Thus, the State is proactively protecting against a public nuisance in the form of coastal erosion. If a more traditional Lockean view of property rights dominated the Court's analysis, then it likely would have held, like the lower state court had, that the actions of Florida were a taking of a clear property right: the ability of coastal landowners to touch the shoreline.

## CONCLUSION

*Lucas, Boomer,* and *Stop the Beach Renourishment* provide important insights into the dynamic and evolving nature of property rights in coastal areas. What the cases show is that property rights are not as certain as one might first imagine. Rather, they tend to be contextually defined based on the circumstances presented. As *Lucas* showed, even a clear regulatory taking can be excused when the purpose of the government action is based on fundamental Tenth Amendment powers, particularly, protecting against a nuisance. *Boomer* adds to our understanding by defining the contextual nature of a public nuisance. An act may be lawful in certain contexts, but determined to be unlawful in other contexts. Thus, we cannot easily define property rights through actions in absolute terms. Rather, the actions themselves may be subject to regulation based on the circumstances presented. A cement factory far removed from development may operate lawfully. But that same factory located near development may not operate in the same fashion. The right to act in some manner on one's property is contingent and not absolute. Or in the Modern view of property rights parlance, the property right is subject to societal norms, including changes to those norms over time.

*Stop the Beach Renourishment* places the contingency of private property rights in additional context. The established right to touch the water becomes subservient to the state's right to protect its citizenry from hazards so long as the reasoning emanates from the state acting on its own property rights, rather than viewing the issue as the state impeding on an established private property right. This seems to be precisely the reasoning employed by the U.S. Supreme Court in this case. And this reasoning is supported from a Modern view of property rights, namely, that state action supported by current public values, beliefs, and norms will tend to trump a Lockean view of property rights that uphold a private right regardless of how it impacts those values, beliefs, and norms.

This brief analysis leads us to a view of real property rights that will likely be subservient to public welfare in an era of climate-induced sea level rise. The case history presented suggests a future where actions will need to be taken to realign perceptions of coastal development and coastal living. If the state can move forward supported by clear Tenth Amendment principles, then it will be much easier to develop proactive policies without the fear of impeding legitimate private property rights. Of course, this depends on a number of factors that center on how these property rights are viewed. The path toward regulation and action will be clearer under a Modern view of property rights. The right of state action to impede private property rights will be less clear under a Lockean Theory of property rights. What is certain is that property rights in land, and in particular coastal property rights, will likely continue to be judged in a more contextual sense. Presumably, then, as climate change and sea level rise become more accepted into the social fabric, the ability of government to regulate coastal land without fear of a taking challenge will likely increase, at least as long as our judicial system views property rights from a Modern perspective.

## NOTES

1. The legal relationship between wet and dry lands has a long and detailed history. It has its roots in Roman civil law, adopted by Emperor Justinian between AD 529 and 534 but derived from the Roman jurist Gaius (second century AD) who in turn incorporated principles of natural law from earlier Greek philosophy. Book II of the Institutes of Justinian states the following with respect to coastlines:

> By the law of nature these things are common to all mankind—the air, running water, the sea, and consequently the shores of the sea. No one, therefore, is forbidden to approach the seashore, provided that he respects habitations, monuments, and the buildings, which are not, like the sea, subject only to the law of nations.

English common law adopted many aspects of Roman civil law with respect to property rights along coastlines after the passage of the Magna Carta. In turn, the

United States inherited most of these principles due to its European settlement history beginning as English colonies.

2. Excludability used in this sense means the ability to exclude others *without* using force, but rather excluding through *legal* means—by virtue of some rule of law. Obviously, one can physically exclude others from real property, but their ability to do so is proportional to the means they can employ to maintain the exclusion. If others who are more powerful want to access the property, then the ability to exclude diminishes. In other words, the ability to exclude is directly proportional to the relative amount of force capable of holding the property in relation to others.

3. James Acheson, through a detailed ethnography of lobstering practices in Maine, was able to show complex interactions and social relationships that developed in relation to fishing rights. In essence, local lobster fishermen created "gangs" to limit access to lobsters in given coastal areas. These gangs developed and enforced local informal rules that, in many cases, usurped the official government laws and regulations. For example, one with a state license to catch lobster may be prevented from doing so by local lobstermen. In many ways the locals saw the lobster resource with a slightly different set of values, beliefs, and norms. Thus, they enforced a set of property rights that were not officially sanctioned by government.

4. One must concede that Atlantic Cement, in making cement, was engaging in the reasonable use and enjoyment of its property. But once the particulates moved through the air to the residential neighborhood, those particulates prevented the residents from the reasonable use and enjoyment of their properties (the ability to be outside in the backyard, etc.). Atlantic Cement's right to enjoy its property uninhibited likely ends at the property line of the residents in the neighborhood, and vice versa.

REFERENCES

Acheson, J. M. (1988). *The lobster gangs of Maine*, Hanover, NH: University Press of New England.

Alexander, G., & Penalver, E. M. (2012). *An introduction to property theory.* New York, NY: Cambridge University Press.

Bin, O., Kruse, J. B., & Landry, C. E. (2008). Flood hazards, insurance rates, and amenities: Evidence from the coastal housing market. *The Journal of Risk and Insurance, 75(1)*, 63–82. http://dx.doi.org/10.1111/j.1539-6975.2007.00248.x.

Church, J. A., et al. (2013). Sea level change. In Stocker, T. F. et al. (Eds.), *Climate change 2013: The physical science basis. Contribution of Working Group I to the Fifth Assessment Report of the Intergovernmental Panel on Climate Change.* Cambridge, UK: Cambridge University Press.

Flushman, B. S. (2002). *Water boundaries: Demystifying land boundaries adjacent to tidal or navigable waters*. New York, NY: John Wiley and Sons.

Hardin, G. (1968). The tragedy of the commons. *Science, 162 (3859)*, 1243–1248. http://dx.doi.org/10.1126/science.162.3859.1243.

Hausmaninger, H., & Gamuf, R. (2012). *A casebook on roman property law*. New York, NY: Oxford University Press.

Johnson, D. R. (2007). Reflections on the bundle of rights. *Vermont Law Review, 32(2)*, 247–272.

McGuire, C. (2014). *Environmental law from the policy perspective: Understanding how legal frameworks influence environmental problem solving*, Boca Raton, FL: CRC Press.

Nixon, D. W. (1994). *Marine and coastal law: Cases and materials*, Westport, CT: Praeger Publishers.

Ostrom, E. (1990). *Governing the commons: The evolution of institutions for collective action*. Cambridge, UK: Cambridge University Press.

Policicchio, J. (2011). Stop the beach renourishment, inc. v. florida department of environmental protection. *Harvard Environmental Law Review, 35 (2)*, 541-554.

Rose-Ackerman, S. (1985). Inalienability and the theory of property rights. *Columbia Law Review*, 85 (5), 931–969. http://doi.org/10.2307/1122458

Simmons, A. J. (1992). *The lockean theory of rights*, Princeton, NJ: Princeton University Press.

Stern, P.C., Dietz, T., Abel, T., Guagnano, G.A., & Kalof, L. (1999). A value-belief-norm theory of support for social movements: The case of environmentalism. *Human Ecology Review*, 6 (2), 81–97.

# 8 Using Property Rights as a Metaphor to Understand Personal Place Brand Identity

STACI M. ZAVATTARO

Before delving into the ideas I present here, I need to make a confession: I am neither a lawyer nor a law professor. My training is in public administration, and I study place branding in local governments. My interest in property came from the way Ann Davis wrote her description of the property camp we mentioned at the outset of this volume. She crafted a story of property as ever changing, diverse, sometimes even elusive. My training is highly theoretical and conceptual (as opposed to quantitatively methodological), so I was intrigued by learning more about the image-laden aspects of property. For me, the property lens is not widely applied in my field, unless of course it is to issues of real property (commons concerns, eminent domain, etc.). What I do in this chapter is use property as a way of understanding and theorizing why a place, a neighborhood, a street, becomes so important to someone—why it becomes part of their personal identity.

At a local level, cities always are trying to find ways to meaningfully involve stakeholders in governing practices. Place branding, as it becomes a key governance strategy (Eshuis, Braun, & Klijn, 2013), is no different. The process and outcomes must be meaningful to vastly different audiences, which is no easy task. When done wrong, branding can alienate people and lead to distrust in government (Zavattaro, 2014). This chapter takes a deeper look at why people would get angry if their place were misrepresented or somehow changed.

The idea of private property is one that has been long contested and that still causes worry, strife, and potential divisions in societies globally. With constant innovation, coupled with the expansion of digital technologies that allow for rapid information sharing, there is a worry about protecting a less-tangible form of property: intellectual property. Property often is understood as a "bundle of sticks" that imposes certain rights and corresponding duties on people, though even this understanding can prove problematic because of conceptual uncertainty (Penner, 1996).

Local residents develop an attachment to place, be it a country, a state, a city, even a neighborhood. People become passionate when someone or something tries to change that deeply held sense of place identity. Using the lens of property can help place brand managers and scholars understand the implications of shifting a place's identity—and even why residents themselves cling tightly to a sense of place. While this idea might not seem novel, using property rights as a metaphor for viewing place branding shows the personalization that takes place when people socially construct their sense of selves around their chosen places.

The personification of place (Brown & Campelo, 2014) allows for such an inquiry, as places tend to take on personalities all their own. If those living in a place (neighborhood, city, state, country) anthropomorphize their locales, then those have the ability to become part of their personal selves (Zavattaro, 2013). "Indeed, the regard for property is inextricably linked to the regard for location" (Tyson, 2014, p. 652). Therefore, the purpose of this chapter is to build upon the personalization of place using property rights as a metaphor to generate a theoretical framework based upon Kavaratzis and Hatch's (2013) identity-based view of place branding. To do so, two constructs are used: spatial-relational and legal-rational views of property. A spatial-relational view of property moves property beyond a legal-rational viewpoint. Spatial-relational views of property take into account the socially constructed, reciprocal nature of property.

Property, when seen as a bundle of rights, imparts rights and duties upon individuals. If I own a car, it is my right to drive it and your duty not to steal it. Legal-rational aspects of property often are tied closely with property as a physical thing rather than the relational aspects of property. An example of a legal-rational view of property would be owning land and not expressly taking into account the commons surrounding the land. As such, all property is legal-rational though not all property is spatial-relational. The concern herein is with the spatial-relational aspects of property, in that personal property can be internalized as an integral part of a person's worth. A place, it is argued herein, then becomes an important part of a person's spatial-relational identity with a place and helps build a sense of self.

The chapter begins with an overview of metaphor use in scholarly literature and real-life encounters, as well as property rights as understood for purposes of this theoretical development. Second, place-branding literature is introduced with a specific focus on the Kavaratzis and Hatch (2013) framework. The third section of the chapter presents an updated framework using the property rights lens, while the conclusion offers avenues for future research.

## METAPHOR IN LIFE AND RESEARCH

Metaphors serve as more than mere rhetorical devices. Metaphors are indeed key ways in which we organize our worlds (Lakoff & Johnson, 2003). Within public administration, Morgan (2006) perhaps popularized the use of metaphors to understand the living world. Metaphors are *"a way to thinking* and *a way of seeing* that pervade how we understand our world generally" (Morgan, 2006, p. 4; emphasis in original). As Lakoff and Johnson (2003) add, metaphors allow us to understand one thing in terms of another. It is through this linkage that we create "new, emergent meaning that is not compositional; instead, there is new meaning constituted in and through the metaphor" (Cornelissen, Kafouros, & Lock, 2005, p. 1548). A key to making metaphors work for our understanding of certain phenomena is both the elements must be readily recognized (e.g., rock and hard place). Not having these easily recognizable parts risks the metaphorical comparison collapsing (Cornelissen & Kafouros, 2008). Metaphor relies upon existing knowledge (Nonaka, 1994) to create something new, a different lens through which to explore phenomena (Tsoukas, 1993). For metaphors to be effective, they necessarily do more than compare Thing A to Thing B to create Thing C (Cornelissen, 2005). By using metaphor in organization or administrative theory, "we infer an abstract ground for it, and this ground does not consist of shared features, previously associated with the target and source, but is something new all together" (Cornelissen, 2005, p. 755).

Returning to Morgan (2006), he offers several metaphors through which to view organizations of all kinds. Perhaps the most famous is an organization as a brain, noting how important organizational learning is to growth and success. In another metaphor, he conceptualizes organizations as machines, hearkening to the organization going about its business in a methodical matter. In practice, one might expect to see that style of individual and organizational behavior playing out, especially in a large bureaucracy with its methodical processes. Morgan does not have a monopoly on using metaphor in administrative and organizational theory. In other examples, public organizations and administrators have been likened to theater participants (Terry, 1998), gamesmen (Lynn, 1982), and garbage cans (Cohen, March, & Olsen, 1972). Metaphors such as these, again, are meant to convey an image about the kinds of organizations and individuals— and their expected behavior. A metaphor used in the public sector "must express the integrative function of relating the government to the governed" (Sementelli & Abel, 2007, p. 365).

It should be noted here that metaphor is not perfect for understanding social reality. There are indeed shortcomings (Cornelissen & Kafouros, 2008). Cornelissen and Kafouros (2008) argue that metaphors fail when the two entities do not have enough conceptual difference—yet the key is that the comparatives cannot be *too* distant either. There is no guidance, though, for striking that "perfect" balance for understanding. For example, they argue that understanding an organization as a machine is much easier than understanding one as a soap bubble because of the A and B comparatives. In other words, seeing an organization as a well-tooled, systematic machine makes more sense than an amorphous, fleeing soap bubble. Despite criticism, Nonaka (1994) lauds metaphor in organization theory because it can transform tacit, expert knowledge into a useful explicator of organizational occurrences. Metaphor "constitutes an important method for creating a network of concepts which can help generate knowledge about the future by using existing knowledge" (Nonaka, 1994, p. 21).

This brief outline of metaphor is used to set the stage for using property as a metaphor for understanding place brand identities. As noted earlier, the key argument is that we can understand place brand identity through the lens of property because people become so attached to a place—and that identity becomes ingrained in their sense of self and place in the world. In the next section, another brief introduction to property is offered. It should be noted that this chapter does not take a purely legal view, so the review does not pretend to be exhaustive. Instead, it sets the stage for the core argument outlined just above.

## PROPERTY RIGHTS: SOCIORELATIONAL VERSUS LEGAL-RATIONAL

For this chapter, property is viewed through a communal, relational lens rather than individualistic and legal. Shoked (2011) advances this line of thought by citing a case from Illinois where a property owner, who stood to benefit financially from a city rezoning ordinance, challenged said ordinance on the grounds of depriving her of the social, community value she derived from her private ownership. The Illinois Appellate Court reversed a lower court decision that dismissed the claim, thus extending private property rights into the community, shared realm.

As Shoked notes (2011), such a communal view is novel, as private property rights often are viewed as grounded in legal precedent—and legal precedent alone. When discussing property rights and ownership duties, Honoré's standard incidents often provide the grounding. Some of his standards include the right to possess, right to manage, right to use, right to capital, right to security, prohibition of harmful use, and right to income. For every right a person has to own property, subsequent duties are placed on them and others. As an example, owning a car means I have an exclusive right to drive, but I cannot drive as I please, anywhere I please, because laws and social norms prevent me from speeding down a highway. Owning a home means I can do what I will with the inside, again to a certain extent, but homeowner's association rules might govern what I can do to the outside.

According to Johnson (2007), property law in the United States has three main sources: common law, statutes, and the Constitution. Common law principals are based on judicial decisions, while state statues regarding property rights might be pulling in fifty different directions. Despite differences, legal precedent tries to ensure there is at least some commonality among jurisdictions. "No state law decision is binding on any other state, but it is common practice for state courts to look to other state courts as persuasive authority" (Johnson, 2007, p. 248). Constitutionally, the due process clause plays an important role in property rights debates, as it gives the government authority to take property for public purposes (for example, by eminent domain). Taken together, these sources of property rights often are viewed through another metaphor: the bundle of sticks.

The bundle of sticks metaphor (also sometimes referred to as the bundle of rights) stems from a realization that personal private property is more than only legal standing. Johnson (2007) traces the development of this metaphor, starting with Blackstone's classical liberal definition of private property that focused on securing individual autonomy and rights through owning a specific thing (sometimes called the "thinginess" of property). Typically, this specific thing was land, with which an individual could then ideally do what they would to secure for themselves economic freedom. However, as times changed, this notion of "real property" became outdated. "Interests in land were no longer the principal objects described by the law of property. The physicalist notion could not express all sorts of new property interests that were coming into being, especially intangible property such as business goodwill, trademarks, trade secrets, and shares of corporations—things that nobody could see or touch" (Johnson, 2007, p. 251).

Hohfeld (1913) took up this reconceptualization by deftly pointing out the legal and relational aspects of property rights. He does so by noting that legal concepts, property being one, often have both mental and legal aspects. Hohfeld delivers eight judicial correlates and opposites rooted in rights, powers, privileges, and immunities. All eight relations need not be covered here, but the fundamental takeaway from that groundbreaking work is that conceptual uncertainty leaves room for interpretations of the law (Cook, 1919). For example, a right correlates with a duty, as described above. It was Hohfeld who articulated these connections, arguing that most legal problems can be traced back to these eight correlates or opposites. As Johnson (2007) notes, it is largely from Hohfeld that legal scholars base their ideas on sociorelational aspects of the law, including property.

The primary contribution of this chapter is to show how personal connections to place brand identity can be seen through the lens of a property right. Again, property rights are a metaphor to understand how, personally, people can take on brand identities tied to distinct places (neighborhoods, cities, regions, states, etc.). The core part of this contribution is to shift the traditional, legalistic notion of property to a view that is more communal and relational in nature. This dichotomy is presented as legal-rational views of property (described above) versus socio-relational views (expounded upon below).

Typically, the bundle of sticks metaphor illustrates the interrelated nature of personal property. If I own a home, for example, I cannot build a toxic dump in the back yard simply because I own the home. As Shoked details (2011, p. 762), "Owning land is owning a part of a specific community. Removal of the community, just like removal of the land and walls, alters the nature of the property right. It does so in a different way that might be perceived as less intrusive, but it does so nonetheless."

It is part of the argument presented herein that there are certain aspects of property that everyone can own. For example, Groothuis et al. (2008) examine how two environmental activist groups took different positions when it came to installing windmills to generate electricity. One concern the authors note was a disruption to the viewshed based on the installation of the windmills, which, the other side argued, was worth the damage for the power-saving potentials then available to the community. According to their findings, based on a survey distributed in an Appalachian Mountain community in North Carolina, most respondents feared the technology would harm mountain views. Put simply: the view belongs to everyone as part of communal property. So who owns the view? No one, yet everyone. This is one example how property becomes relational.

According to Shoked (2011), even an individual property within a community belongs in some way to the community as a whole (hence the reason for homeowner's associations). Communitarianism is at the heart of this view of property. This is not the space to get into the debates about communitarian theories themselves, but the important part of this theoretical inquiry is to understand the foundations for seeing property rights as a means of community ownership rather than ownership in a vacuum. Such logic serves as the foundation for the sociorelational view of property that will be incorporated into Kavaratzis and Hatch's (2013) identity-based view of place branding.

## IDENTITY VIEW OF PLACE BRANDING

Government agencies at all levels are adopting and adapting place-branding strategies, usually in the name of increasing some kind of economic outcome—more tourists, more businesses, more residents, etc. Given the movement in the public sector toward New Public Management–style governance that encourages entrepreneurship and business-based practices, it is perhaps not surprising that public sector organizations are delving more and more into this branding realm (Eshuis, Braun, & Klijn 2013; Zavattaro, 2010).

As above, this section is not meant to serve as an exhaustive overview of the place-branding literature (see Lucarelli & Berg, 2011). Place branding can be understood as

> the broad set of efforts by country, regional and city groups, and by indus-
> try groups, aimed at marketing the places and sectors they serve. The intent
> of such efforts typically is to achieve one or more of four main objectives:
> enhance the place's exports, protect its domestic businesses from "foreign"
> competition (for sub-national places this may include those from other
> regions in the same country), attract or retain factors of development and
> generally position the place for advantage domestically and internationally
> in economic, political and social terms. (Papadopoulos, 2004, pp. 36–37)

Typically, there are two components that scholars examine when discussing place brands: identity and image. Place identity is what an organization works to construct about itself, while place image is what consumers picture in their minds (Govers & Go, 2009). Ultimately, it is consumers and users who determine the success of a place and its associated brand identity (Keller, 1993). The Kavaratzis and Hatch (2013) framework for how place brands are developed (and constantly redeveloped) is important given it combines both brand identity and brand image, showing how the two are inextricably linked.

Resident perceptions of place brand identity are often left out of extant liter-ature (Stylidis et al., 2014), favoring instead studies and inclusion of tourists/visi-tors (Wang & Chen, 2015). Typically, resident attitudes are considered in direct relationship to their views on tourism's impact on a local community (Lindberg & Johnson, 1997; Teye et al., 2002; Williams & Lawson, 2001). Hanna and Rowley (2011) note that residents should be seen as critical stakeholders in the place brand development process, as organizations cannot and should not communicate to residents in the same manner as local businesses and tourists. Residents are a crit-ical component to examine because, according to Wang and Xu (2015, p. 241):

> In the context of incoming tourism, it is considered that a destination's
> place identity will appeal to a resident if its identity attributes fit into his
> or her personal values. Therefore, for a city's tourism planners and manag-
> ers, one key to enhance a city's tourism should be to allow residents to
> incorporate the place identity attributes into their own self-concepts, so
> that residents' self-concept-related motives can provide a simple engine
> for their support for tourism development

The identity-based view of property given here, with its focus on the socio-relational aspects of property, is a way to incorporate identity, plus image, plus resident attitudes toward a place. The theoretical combination shows that resident views are crucial to branding success, given that residents often internalize feelings about their places. The root is empathy and value rather than pure economic exchange that often undergirds most place-branding research (Wang & Chen, 2015).

Kavaratzis and Hatch (2013) respond directly to what they call static views of identity. They argue that while scholars use the term and talk about its dynamism, there remains a reliance on a so-called tried and true way of experts distilling a brand identity, then having locals market and promote that seemingly new version of the place. This becomes problematic because branding disconnects how insiders see their place from how others view the place (identity and image). "Almost by definition, this approach limits the nature of branding to a communication-promotional tool with emphasis on visual strategies that might convey to others the place's identity. This can be noticed all too often in contemporary place branding practice, where the whole branding process is limited to the design of new logos and the development of catchy slogans," (Kavaratzis & Hatch, 2013, p. 74).

Their theoretical framework relies on the interplay of place culture, place identity, and place image. The process is ongoing and recursive. There is no linear pattern of consultation, communication, and evaluation. These all take place constantly with an eye toward resident perceptions of a place. This mirrors how Kalandides (2011) views the image-based aspects of place identity: as part of human identity, group identity, mental representations, group perceptions of the place, identification of a group within a territory, and as sense of character.

## PUTTING IT TOGETHER: HOW CONCEPTIONS OF PROPERTY CAN HELP UNDERSTAND PLACE IDENTITIES

This section combines thoughts from Tyson (2014) and Kavaratzis and Hatch (2013) to show how using a socio-relational view of property can influence our understanding of branding practices. The remainder of this section describes each circle and shows the linkages between each. As one can see, the process is cyclical, as one element cannot operate without the other. Everything a community does feeds back into itself. People either stay and build the community or flee for somewhere they see as a better fit. The borders, then, become porous as the community collapses. Individualism takes over, breaking down the social contract. The internal sense of place as property becomes important to understand functioning neighborhoods.

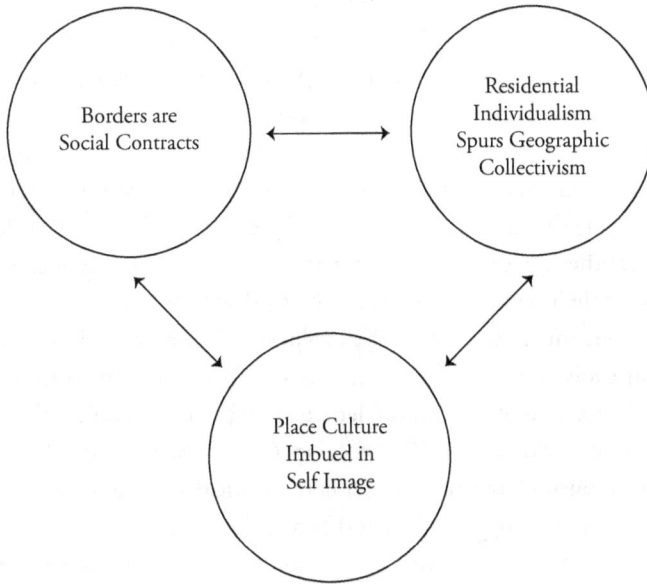

Figure 8.1. Metaphor of place brand identity as local property

## Borders Are Social Constructions

As Tyson deftly articulates (2014), borders are social constructions that take on real, important meanings. Oftentimes, borders are drawn and redrawn to appease various social and political interests. Gerrymandering congressional districts often is a visible application of this practice of border reconstruction. Neighborhoods, gated or not, also are physical manifestations of borders that separate "us from them." For example, Tyson details various cases of largely wealthy enclaves seeking their own municipal identities to move away from people they deem undesirable, usually for economic or racial reasons. Tyson argues that

> [p]eople care about property. They also care about where they live. Indeed, the regard for property is inextricably related to the regard for location. Whether through resisting annexation or calling for new municipal incorporations, local interest groups often use the tool of local govern- ment boundary law to express what they perceive as a fundamental right to protect their property values and express individual or collective self-determination through forming or moving to (or preventing their being subsumed by) a separate location or territorially based identity. (2014, p. 652)

This is not to say that all borders are fake. Indeed, borders are quite real in the sense that they are protected and policed. Eder (2006) points out that officers often stand guard along borders to prevent illegal crossing. He distinguishes between these kinds of hard facts, borders with a militarized or police presence, and soft facts, narratives and social constructions that often exacerbate differences between people. "Defining who we are and who the others are creates borders between groups of people that are as volatile as the discourses about them" (Eder, 2006, p. 255). This othering is the practice described in his recounting of areas seeking annexation or their own municipal identities (Tyson, 2014).

Van Houtum (2005) traces the evolution of border studies, noting that the field has evolved to include the term *boundary* studies. The early scholars of border studies focused on the lines of demarcation between peoples. Now, scholars recognize those "socio-spatial differences" (p. 672) in their studies. Political geographers, van Houtum continues, often take a critical approach, focusing on the negative consequences of boundary and border development. In essence, borders are meant to keep people out rather than welcome people in. Looking at the global refugee crisis of 2015, and to historical refugee crises, shows this pattern clearly. Van Houtum's (2005) sociospatial designation parallels the sociorelational view of property articulated earlier in the chapter. People take pride in where they live, so they often might take measures to keep populations they deem "undesirable" out.

Gated communities are a visible example of this practice. Low (2001) argues that gated communities are a response to urban politics and a prevailing discourse of fear. Historically, gated communities were meant as havens for the wealthy, and eventually they evolved into seemingly militarized zones with guards and gates (Low, 2001). In his study, Low interviewed homeowners who reported seeking a gated community largely because of a perception of urban crime in their cities, along with what Low called an increase in social diversity. As his interviews illuminate, this was either explicitly or implicitly about race differences. Seeking the shelter of a gated community gave homeowners at least the perception of increased safety even if statistical data about urban crime did not match these views.

Manzi and Smith-Bowers (2005) take a different approach, noting that along with this gate-as-protection element comes an often related notion that people living in these communities are discouraged from interacting with each other as neighbors. Using the lens of club goods, with a root in economics, the authors argue that gated communities have property that is both theirs and the community's inside. Club goods are a hybrid of public and private goods that enjoy mutual ownership and benefit. All the residents in a gated community, for instance, have access to the shared pool but not to each other's private homes. People choosing to live in a gated community simultaneously have a responsibility to themselves and to the sociorelational aspects of property rights. Neighbors get mad if another neighbor trashes the pool.

Neighborhood choice is all about putting up self-imposed borders. People live in areas that reflect their perceived sense of self (Levy & Lee, 2011). People take both practical and emotional factors into account when purchasing or renting a home. There is the idea of affordability and distance to the office, school, shopping, and more, coupled with houses and neighborhoods that simply "fit" the person (Levy & Lee, 2011). The tangible items are important, but "it is the residents who collectively set the tone, and it is this collective 'tone' that gives the place its identity and attracts others to the place" (Levy & Lee, 2011, p. 257).

Put simply, borders are social constructions that give people a sense of identity. People identify with their nations, states, cities, and neighborhoods. Borders serve as a way to physically and emotionally construct who belongs on the inside and who remains on the outside. It is this notion of place that people take as part of their personal identity. To them, it might sound better to tell people they live in City X rather than City Y even though the two share a geographic border. What they do not share is a perceptual border, so place is personal.

## Residential Individualism Spurs Geographic Collectivism

The second element of the framework in Figure 8.1 above speaks to how individuals come together to protect their place. This makes sense, especially when longevity in a place enters the equation. The longer someone stays in a place, the more likely they are to develop a strong sense of community, care about the community, and be hesitant to leave (Kasarda & Janowitz, 1974). This, then, means the person identifies fully with the place. They will protect their borders, sometimes to grave ends, such as the Trayvon Martin shooting in a Florida neighborhood. Alterations to this sense of place become personal when we see place brands through the lens of personal, sociorelational property. This is what Manzi and Smith-Bowers (2005) meant with their use of club goods to understand how individuals come together to protect a shared identity. We can often see this in full view after communities suffer tragedy. In Orlando, for example, residents donned Orlando Strong shirts, stickers, buttons, and more after the mass shooting at the Pulse Nightclub in 2016. The community came together to show that we are one, despite the large, spread-out population. Everyone felt protective of Orlando.

Oyserman, Coon, and Kemmelmeier (2002) trace the intellectual roots of individualism and collectivism. The two terms might seem opposite but actually have a long history of compatibility. As Love (2008) articulates, we can distinguish between the capital-I Individual who is independent and self-driven, and the lower-i individual who sees themselves as part of a greater collective. While good things can come of this distinction, Love (2008) details the conflict people often feel when pressured to be fiercely independent and self-reliant while living in a society governed by social norms. "Thus, although the ideal of American Individualism presents itself as an ideology of empowerment, it most often serves as a means of alienation and marginalization" (Love, 2008, p. 425). Love (2012) distinguishes between kinds of individuals: atomistic, institutional, fragmented, and integrated. Love places an atomistic and institutional individual on a continuum of sorts, with institutional individuals tied to each other through core social purposes and atomistic individuals existing in the same space yet with few, if any, social ties. Atomistic individuals could come to feel alienated, while institutional individuals also can be constrained by rules, regulations, or group norms.

Individuals, Love (2012) reminds us, are "discrete and unitary" (p. 368) at the same time. A person's physical being may change, but the soul and spirit remain the same through time. With this in mind, Love (2012) suggests moving toward a view of the individual as integrated. Citing Mary Parker Follett, Love explains that integrated individuals are socially embedded, aware of their situation, and constantly redefining themselves based on these social situations. They are not stuck within an institution and its rules and regulations. If they do not like something, they will work to change it together with others of similar minds. Without these relationships, the individual becomes more fragmented with few, if any, connections (Love, 2012).

It is this sense of connection and reconnection that applies here. In terms of place brands as identity, people find themselves tied to a neighborhood (Tyson, 2014), a city, a state, a nation. People will come together if those concepts are part of their core identities. Someone might, for example, consider themselves a Floridian more than a part of a local community so fight instead for issues at the state level rather than a local one. The same logic can apply for nationalism as is often seen. Fragmented individuals will not feel the same sense of connectedness as integrated peers. It is when people become fragmented that places can fall into disrepair. Not feeling part of a community leads to apathy. Detroit is a clear example of a community that lost hope then gained it back when trying to recover from economic collapse.

### Place Culture Imbued in Self-Image

The final aspect of the framework indicates how someone's identification with a particular place becomes part of their self-identity. This should not be surprising, given we often see this regarding nationalism and in other arenas. College sports allegiances are one popular place this occurs. Scholars have found that "the more an individual sees him or herself as being connected, in some way, to a team, the greater the value of the team's brand for that person" (Boyle & Magnusson, 2007, p. 498). At the core of their argument is social identity theory, whereby individuals see themselves as part of a group with similar interests (Stets & Burke, 2000). People can see themselves as part of the in-group or the out-groups (ibid.). People can gain benefits from the whole without doing much, if they choose. Such is the problem with the commons.

In terms of place branding, this in-group/out-group distinction manifests in who lives in a place and who does not. Tyson (2014) articulates this with his explanation of municipal identity and the machinations people can take to keep people in or out. "The residence or home of a person thereby determines a strong part of the person's self, distinguishing strongly between the We (in-group, e.g. residents ... ) vs Them (out-group, e.g. non-residents)" (Zenker & Beckmann, 2013, p. 8). As Zenker and Beckmann explain, those in the in-group have more knowledge about the place and can take its brand to heart. The out-group, which might include potential new residents, new business owners, and tourists, for example, often might have a stereotyped view of the place. In Orlando, for example, the overwhelming image is of a land of theme parks. The local tourism brand is fine, yet the city's and region's focus on innovation and economic growth is less well known and not part of the out-group image of Orlando and Central Florida (Zavattaro & Fay, 2018).

Tourists, too, go through the same social identity process before choosing a place to vacation (Ekinci et al., 2013). People enjoy a certain lifestyle and how that fits with their social conceptions of themselves. As of this writing (2016), Iceland has become an incredibly popular tourist destination. Through concerted efforts, officials in Iceland have increased their tourism outputs to 31 percent in 2015 from 18 percent in 2010 (Iceland Tourism Board, 2016). Since 2010, the number of locals working in the tourism industry has increased by nearly 37 percent (ibid.). This is massive growth, and people want to know what the hype is about and do not want to miss out on the hottest destination brand. Ekinci et al. (2013) call this lifestyle congruence, whereby visiting a place such as Iceland fits with someone's self-perception of their lifestyle.

Lindstedt (2011) explains how this identity-based view of brand construction happens at a local level. She explains there is a difference between, yet also a relationship between, the identity *of* the place and identity *with* the place. The former relates to how one place differs from another, while the other is how a person *perceives* the place to differ from another. Sometimes there is not much difference except for a few amenities and a name that might "sound" better to in-groups. People link certain meanings to places, and they do so through manageability, continuity, goal support, and distinctiveness (Lindstedt, 2011). Manageability refers to a person's self-perceived ability to handle the social and physical demands of the place. Here, people take into account items such as economic standing, crime level, built environment, accessibility, etc. People want to live in a place they perceive as manageable; negative perceptions affect economic drivers.

Continuity encompasses two dimensions Lindstedt (2011) calls place-referent and place-congruent. Place-referent means how well a person can continue as themselves if part of a place. This is an emotional affect, thus hard to measure. Place-congruent meanings are those that are generic from place to place yet attach to a person's self-perception. If a place's attributes do not match the self, that person is going to choose another location. Goal support is how well a place can provide resources a person can use to meet his or her goals. Whereas the first two were more emotional, goal setting is concrete: either a place has the resources or it does not. Finally, distinctiveness means how people can use their place to set themselves apart from others. The term *American*, for example, commonly means someone from the United States rather than Canada, Mexico, Central America, or South America. The term is so strong that others in the Americas have been essentially pushed out of being American in any form. Valuation is both social and economic, so Lindstedt (2011) recognizes the importance of both in terms of distinctiveness.

In sum, people go through steps to formulate a place as part of their core identities. When a place changes—either through planned interventions or unplanned occurrences—a person's self-perception also can shift. They will reevaluate manageability, continuity, goal support, and distinctiveness and make a decision to remain or leave. Sometimes this is easier said than done, but people want to be in a place that matches how they feel. This then feeds back into their willingness to come together to help the place beyond their individual needs, which relies upon someone's self-image and how tightly woven that is to the place. This self-image relates to a person's perception of their monetary property value and their intrinsic property values.

## CONCLUSION AND DISCUSSION

The purpose of this chapter is to use property as a metaphor to understand how a person's place becomes part of their overall identity. A theoretical model was developed to show the relationships between physical property, perception of a place, and collective action to preserve that place identity and, thus by extension, self-identity. There are practical implications of this relationship for place brand managers. First, managers who want to come in and distill a place brand without taking local (in-group) information into account often face failure (Kavaratzis & Hatch, 2013). Locals become attached to their neighborhood when it provides them physical, economic, and social resources (Lindstedt, 2011), so telling someone how to think or feel sets up potential failure. Second, there is a need to recognize the important role that human emotions play in place branding *beyond* economic ends. For many managers, the ultimate goal is economically driven. A consumer is going to pick your product, your place, your restaurant, etc. and not another. You make money, someone else does not. What many do not realize is that there is an emotional aspect also important to that decision. Therefore, managers need to balance economics and emotions when undertaking brand campaigns. Finally, managers can understand that people's desire to be involved (citizen engagement, often a normative value in public administration) depends upon how they are treated. This means that administrators need to see themselves as empathetic facilitators (Zanetti & King, 2013) integrated into the community (Love, 2012) rather than part of the formal power structure. It takes a reexamination of the role of government and administrators but one that is done in collaborative public management settings.

The chapter's theoretical nature opens up avenues for future testing of the relationships posited. I conclude, therefore, with some questions for future research:

1. How do managers ensure that the local voice is *meaningfully* included in place branding processes? Does this change when the process is done internally rather than by a hired consultant? How do locals even hear about branding endeavors? Are local roles specified—parent, single individual, business owner, etc.? How might these role conceptions influence a person's view of the collective?

2. How does a person experience changes to a city? To a neighborhood? How are these internalized and made part of the self, if at all? What does that person do with the new self-perception—stay, go, form a new collective, yearn for the past?

3. Do people see the emotional value of property, or do they think largely in economic terms? Do individuals realize the direct emotional tie between a place's identity and their own self-perception? Does this factor when choosing to live in a place or visit one? If so, how? If not, why not?

4. Are there factors missing from the theoretical model? What might modify these relationships, for good or ill? Could the relationships be linear rather than cyclical? If so, does that change the way people relate to places?

## REFERENCES

Boyle, B. A. & Magnusson, P. (2007). Social identity and brand equity formation: A comparative study of collegiate sports fans. *Journal of Sport Management, 21(4)*, 497-520.

Brown, S., & Campelo, A. (2014). Do cities have broad shoulders? Does Motown need a haircut? On urban branding and personification of place. *Journal of Macromarketing, 34(4)*, 421–434.

Cohen, M. D., March, J. G., & Olsen, J. P. (1972). A garbage can model of organizational choice. *Administrative Science Quarterly, 17(1)*, 1–25.

Cook, W. W. (1919). Hohfeld's contributions to the science of law. *The Yale Law Journal, 28(8)*, 721–738.

Cornelissen, J. P. (2005). Beyond compare: Metaphor in organization theory. *Academy of Management Review, 30(4)*, 751–764.

Cornelissen, J. P., & Kafouros, M. (2008). Metaphors and theory building in organization theory: What determines the impact of metaphor on theory? *British Journal of Management, 19*, 365–379.

Cornelissen, J. P., Kafouros, M., & Lock, A. R. (2005). Metaphorical images of organization: How organizational researchers develop and select organizational metaphors. *Human Relations, 58(12)*, 1545–1578.

Eder, K. (2006). Europe's borders: The narrative construction of the boundaries of Europe. *European Journal of Social Theory, 9(2)*, 255–271.

Ekinci, Y. et al (2013). Symbolic consumption of tourism destination brands. *Journal of Business Research, 66(6)*, 711–718.

Eshuis, J., Braun, E., & Klijn, E. (2013). Place marketing as governance strategy: An assessment of obstacles in place marketing and their effects on attracting target groups. *Public Administration Review, 73(3)*, 507–516.

Govers, R., & Go, F. (2009). *Place branding: Glocal, virtual, and physical identities, constructed, imagined, and experienced.* New York, NY: Palgrave Macmillan.

Groothuis, P. A. et al (2008). Green vs. green: Measuring the compensation required to site electrical generation windmills in a viewshed. *Energy Policy, 36(4)*, 1545–1550.

Hanna, S., & Rowley, J. (2011). Towards a strategic place brand-management model. *Journal of Marketing Management, 27(5–6)*, 458–476.

Hohfeld, W. S. (1913). Some fundamental legal conceptions as applied in judicial reasoning. *The Yale Law Journal, 23(1)*, 16–59.

Iceland Tourism Board (2016). Tourism in Iceland in figures May 2016. Retrieved from: http://www.ferdamalastofa.is/static/files/ferdamalastofa/Frettamyndir/2016/juni/tourism_-in_iceland_in_figures_may2016.pdf.

Johnson, D. R. (2007). Reflections on the bundle of rights. *Vermont Law Review*, *32*, 247–272.

Kalandides, A. (2011). The problem with spatial identity: Revisiting the "sense of place." *Journal of Place Management & Development*, *4(1)*, 28–39.

Kasarda, J. D., & Janowitz, M. (1974). Community attachment in mass society. *American Sociological Review*, *39(3)*, 328–339.

Kavaratzis, M., & Hatch, M. J. (2013). The dynamics of place brands: An identity-based approach to place branding theory. *Marketing Theory*, *13(1)*, 69–86.

Lakoff, G., & Johnson, M. (2003). *Metaphors we live by*. Chicago, IL: University of Chicago Press.

Levy, D., & Lee, C. (2011). Neighbourhood identities and household location choice: estate agents' perspectives. *Journal of Place Management and Development*, *4(3)*, 243–263.

Lindberg, K., & Johnson, R. L. (1997). Modeling resident attitudes toward tourism. *Annals of Tourism Research*, *24(2)*, 402–424.

Lindstedt, J. (2011). Place, identity, and the socially responsible construction of place brands. *Place Branding and Public Diplomacy*, 7(1), 42-49.

Love, J. M. (2012). From atomistic to interwoven: Utilizing a typology of i/ Individualisms to envision a process approach to governance. *Administrative Theory & Praxis*, *34(3)*, 362–384.

———. (2008). The rugged individualist club. *Administrative Theory & Praxis*, *30(4)*, 424–449.

Low, S. M. (2001). The edge and the center: Gated communities and the discourse of urban fear. *American Anthropologist*, *103(1)*, 45–58.

Lucarelli, A., & Berg, P. O. (2011). City branding: A state-of-the-art review of the research domain. *Journal of Place Management and Development*, *4(1)*, 9–27.

Lynn Jr., L. E. (1982). Government executives as gamesmen: A metaphor for analyzing managerial behavior. *Journal of Policy Analysis and Management*, *7(4)*, 482–495.

Manzi, T., & Smith-Bowers, B. (2005). Gated communities as club goods: Segregation or social cohesion? *Housing Studies*, *20(2)*, 345–359.

Morgan, G. (2006). *Images of organization*. Thousand Oaks, CA: Sage.

Nonaka, I. (1994). A dynamic theory of organizational knowledge creation. *Organization Science*, *5(1)*, 14–37.

Oyserman, D., Coon, H. M. & Kemmelmeier, M. (2002). Rethinking individualism and collectivism: Evaluation and theoretical assumptions and meta-analyses. *Psychological Bulletin*, 128(1), 3-72

Papadopoulos, N. (2004.) Place branding: evolution, meaning, and implications. *Place Branding*, *1(1)*, 36–49.

Penner, J. E. (1996). The "bundle of rights" picture of property. *UCLA Law Review, 43,* 711.

Sementelli, A. J., & Abel, C. F. (2007). Metaphor, cultural imagery, and the study of change in public organizations. *Journal of Organizational Change Management, 20(5),* 652–670.

Shoked, N. (2011). The reinvention of ownership: The embrace of residential zoning and the modern populist reading of property. *Yale Journal on Regulation, 28(1),* 91–149.

Stets, J. E., & Burke, P. J. (2000). Identity theory and social identity theory. *Social Psychology Quarterly, 63(3),* 224–237.

Stylidis, D. et al (2014). Residents' support for tourism development: The role of residents' place image and perceived tourism impacts. *Tourism Management, 45,* 260–274.

Terry, L. D. (1997). Public administration and the theater metaphor: The public administrator as villain, hero, and innocent victim. *Public Administration Review, 57(1),* 53–61.

Teye, V. et al (2002). Residents' attitudes toward tourism development. *Annals of Tourism Research, 29(3),* 668–688.

Tsoukas, H. (1993). Analogical reasoning and knowledge generation in organization theory. *Organization Studies, 14(3),* 323–346.

Tyson, C. (2014). Municipal property as identity. *Penn State Law Review, 118(3),* 647–696.

Van Houtum, H. (2005). The geopolitics of borders and boundaries. *Geopolitics, 10,* 672–679.

Wang, S., & Chen, J. S. (2015). The influence of place identity on perceived tourism impacts. *Annals of Tourism Research, 52,* 16–28.

Wang, S., & Xu, H. (2015). Influence of place-based senses of distinctiveness, continuity, self-esteem and self-efficacy on residents' attitudes toward tourism. *Tourism Management, 47,* 241–250.

Williams, J., & Lawson, R. (2001). Community issues and resident opinions of tourism. *Annals of Tourism Research, 28(2),* 269–290.

Zanetti, L. A., & King. C. S. (2013). Reflections on theory in action: Transformational public service revisited. *Administrative Theory & Praxis, 35(1),* 128–143.

Zavattaro, S. M. (2013). Expanding Goffman's theatre metaphor to an identity-based view of place branding. *Administrative Theory & Praxis, 35(4),* 511–529.

———. (2010). Municipalities as public relations and marketing firms. *Administrative Theory & Praxis,* 32(2), 191-211.

———. (2014). *Place branding through phases of the image.* New York: Palgrave Macmillan.

———. (2010). Municipalities as public relations and marketing firms. *Administrative Theory & Praxis, 32*(2), 191-211.

Zenker, S., & Beckmann, S. C. (2013). My place is not your place—Different place brand knowledge by different target groups. *Journal of Place Management and Development, 6(1),* 6–17.

# 9 Intellectual Property and Fairness across Borders
## A Capabilities Account

GREGORY R. PETERSON

In 1997, the South African government passed the Medicines and Related Substances Control Amendment Act, a law that allowed parallel importing of needed medicines, most notably high priced AIDS drugs vital to treating the many citizens suffering from the epidemic sweeping the country. The law alarmed international drug manufacturers, who feared that compulsory licensing and generic substitution would follow, and a bitter dispute ensued between the United States and South Africa over the intellectual property rights involved. While the United States championed corporate property rights, South Africa argued that the nature of the AIDS epidemic created conditions where humanitarian concerns trumped the property rights of drug manufacturers. The South African infection rate neared 20 percent, and the needed AIDS medications would normally cost $1,000 per month, almost half the annual income of the average South African (Fisher & Rigamonti, 2005, p. 3; see, e.g., Russell, 1999). The Agreement on Trade-Related Aspects of Intellectual Property Rights (TRIPS) had only been recently signed by World Trade Organization members in 1995, and although drug manufacturers argued that the treaty protected their claim that they and only they controlled importation of their patented medicines, allowing them to exclusively set country-specific pricing, the South African government argued otherwise. The public dispute led to the 2001 Doha Declaration, which broadly supported South Africa's particular position, including the provision of compulsory licensing of pharmaceuticals in emergency conditions.

The issue of affordable pharmaceuticals is but one of several flashpoints concerning intellectual property rights (IPR) and international trade. Global food production relies heavily on proprietary seeds, pesticides, and herbicides produced by companies such as Monsanto, which alone controls 90 percent of the global market for corn and soybeans. Countries that are most developed (MDCs) typically possess a comparative advantage in intellectual property control and creation, and it is typical for MDCs to "export" such property to intermediate

147

and less-developed countries (ILDC) which then manufacture products that are shipped both to MDCs and other ILDCs. MDCs complain bitterly about the lack of intellectual property protections in ILDCs, losing billions of dollars annually due to copyright piracy and violation of patent law. ILDCs, and those countries that are least developed (LDCs) complain about high costs and adequate access. Both the United States and Europe have been eager to secure stronger intellectual property protections, seeking bilateral trade agreements that, among other things, further that end.[1]

Both sides cite criteria of fairness. While illegal copying is described as theft, MDCs are accused of greed and callous exploitation of their weaker neighbors, who often perceive themselves to have little choice but to agree to strong IPR protection in exchange for improved trade status in other areas. Behind each side are theories of intellectual property that serve more strongly one side or the other, often seen as pitting the rights of the creators of intellectual property versus the welfare of those who use or consume it. In the case of pharmaceuticals, the stakes can be very high indeed, but the stakes more broadly concern basic issues of international development, pitting MDC corporate profits against the pace and very goals of development in ILDCs and LDCs. If drugs were cheaper, it is argued, many more lives could be saved or improved; if sophisticated software were more widely available on a legal basis, the pace of development in a variety of sectors could quicken.

The present chapter provides a brief overview followed by a proposed philosophical framework for thinking about IP in an international context. Although the proposal is little more than a sketch, it provides a potentially useful alternative to existing approaches and, at the very least, highlights the significant issues at play. In particular, I argue for a version of the capabilities approach pioneered by Amartya Sen and Martha Nussbaum that relies on joint considerations of both individual expression/social recognition and welfare defined in terms of a threshold level of capabilities (Sen, 1999, 2009; Nussbaum, 2000, 2007). Although a number of prominent accounts allow at best a modest role for considerations of welfare, I argue in favor of its relevance, especially given the disproportionate role played by multinational corporations in the profit and protection of intellectual property.

## PROPERTY AND INTELLECTUAL PROPERTY: DEFINITIONAL ISSUES

Although it is common to think of physical objects, especially land, as the *locus classicus* of what we think of as property, claims regarding intellectual property extend back to Greek and Roman times, and both the patent and copyright systems have their roots in the intellectual and technological ferment of the early modern period (for a brief review, see Moore, 2001, pp. 9–13). As a concept, intellectual property in particular raises the basic question of what we mean when we call something "property," for while I can point to a particular object as my property in what seems an intuitive way, I cannot do so with intellectual property. In an influential article, Honoré (1961) listed eleven "incidents" of property, which included such rights as the "right to possess," the "right to use," and the right to the "income of the thing." It is an easy step to then understand property as a "bundle of rights," where the notion of property is defined simply in terms of the associated rights in a specified legal or moral framework. Commonly, property ownership is seen to entail, with some provisos, the rights of exclusive use and alienation: to claim that an object such as an automobile is mine is to claim that I and only I can use it unless I grant permission, and if I have the right of alienation, I have the right to sell or gift that object for whatever price or benefit I see fit. Once sold or bequeathed the object is no longer mine, implying as well that I am no longer responsible for it.

Intellectual property rights can be perplexing in part because the intuitions behind such principles as exclusive use do not readily apply. As is most obviously the case with consumable objects such as food and fuel, use implies exclusion, and for me to use (eat) food implies that you cannot do so. But, as is much commented on, intellectual property is nonconsumable and nonrival. My "use" of Prince's song "Raspberry Beret" does not consume it: if I possess the CD or digital copy I can listen to it as many times as I want. It is also nonrivalrous: my owning a copy does not prevent anyone else from owning a copy, and my benefiting from the use of intellectual property does not prevent anyone else from also benefiting. In the case of medicines, the intellectual property concerns not the exact materials present in each and every pill or vaccine, but rather the structure of the materials and/or the processes involved in their manufacture. If I were to manufacture my own medications in my own backyard lab, no one would be harmed in the normal sense of the word. If I manufacture the drug on my own, the ability of the inventor to use and sell the drug is not diminished, although the demand for the drug will be lessened by one individual. Consequently, if there are harms involved in violations of intellectual property, it would seem that they primarily involve counterfactual claims of lost income or, as I shall argue later, reputational impacts when the originating source is not credited. The nonrivalrous and nonconsumable characteristics of intellectual property make it therefore considerably different from physical property, entailing a significantly different harm/benefit profile.

## PROPERTY: MORAL AND LEGAL JUSTIFICATIONS

Property rights may be justified on both moral and legal grounds, and it is common to understand the latter as being grounded in the former: once we recognize that individuals have a *right* to own objects, and we recognize that such a right is both serious and capable of being violated by others, the grounds are set for legal justification. Property rights may be private, collective, communal, or corporate, and justification of such rights may, as Jeremy Waldron (1988) argues, entail either that some but not necessarily all have rights to property (special property rights) or they may entail that all are entitled to some level of property ownership (general rights), or both.[2] Utilitarian justifications of private property claim, somewhat paradoxically, that rights of private property ownership benefit human well-being, at least in the aggregate. On the utilitarian account aiming to maximize aggregate happiness or satisfaction, property institutions are justifiable precisely because they maximize in such fashion, and social/legal regimes protecting property create, it is claimed, more happiness than their alternatives. Versions of this argument can be found in the classical sources of David Hume, Jeremy Bentham, and John Stuart Mill, and Harold Demsetz among others employs the explanatory structure of neoclassical economics to buttress this claim.[3] The form, if not the content, is the same as Adam Smith's invisible hand argument: it is by pursuing one's own self-interest that the common good is achieved.

Such welfarist/utilitarian arguments contrast with entitlement/rights-based arguments, and the primary historic sources have been claims of property rights based on first occupancy, associated primarily with assertions of national discovery of new lands (e.g., Pufendorf, 1991/1673, p. 84), rights based on the exertion of labor as argued by John Locke, and rights based on the history of entitlement and transfer as developed by Robert Nozick (1974). As non-welfarist accounts, the implication of these approaches is that such rights hold even when aggregate welfare suffers as a result. As applied to pharmaceuticals, if I have absolute intellectual property rights to a drug that I invented through my own labor, I have the right to sell that drug or to choose not to, and I have the right to sell that drug at whatever price I deem fit. Famously, Locke introduced provisos that hedged against harmful impacts of property rights, requiring that "enough, and as good" be left for others, and that property rights do not allow hoarding and thus spoilage of what could otherwise be used profitably by others (Locke, 2003/1689, 2.31; 5.33). Robert Merges also argues for the existence of a third "charity proviso" to be found in Locke's *First Treatise*, paragraph 42 (Merges, 2011, pp. 61–63). Locke's specific theory thus seems to blend rights-based and welfare-based considerations, and much debate concerns how those considerations are weighted and interpreted.

Although rights based on first occupancy currently do not find strong support, it should be noted that there exist parallels to first occupancy in intellectual property, and this concerns in particular the status of intellectual property "objects," especially mathematical formulae and physical laws. If intellectual objects are inventions, then first occupancy principles would not apply: *Finnegan's Wake* did not exist before James Joyce wrote it, and it exists only because of the labor, effort, and creativity that Joyce put into it. But mathematical formulae and physical laws, along with other possible subjects of intellectual property, are commonly thought to be discovered rather than invented. While it seems well-nigh impossible that the particular novel *Finnegan's Wake* could have been written by anyone but Joyce at the time that he wrote it, the same is not true for mathematical formulae and physical laws, and the labor put into their discovery varies considerably. Indeed, if the truths of mathematics and science are discovered rather than invented, the labor involved is arguably analogous to the labor involved in the discovery of new lands, which is often no trivial thing. This point is of some importance, because U.S. patent law prohibits patenting of mathematical formulae and natural laws, but it also enforces (as distinct from copyright law) patents against those who have discovered an idea or process independently.

Welfare-based justifications and rights-based justifications are sometimes argued to be accompanied by a third sort of justification, what might be called a realization-based justification as developed in different ways by Hegel and/or Kant.[4] On the Hegelian account, property ownership and manipulation is a necessary step in the development of my own self-consciousness, and if I am to fully develop as a human being, then I must have not only the opportunity but also the reality of owning and managing property. On this account, property becomes an extension of myself, and it is partly through mastering the responsibilities associated with the care, maintenance, and development of property that I mature as a human being. Kant's account is in some respects similar, emphasizing the relation of property and freedom and the link between property and steadfastness of will. Merges (2011) employs the example of Michelangelo and a block of marble: Michelangelo can exercise his freedom and steadfastness of will as an artist only if he can reliably expect the block of marble to be under his control without worrying about whether someone else will take the marble away, attempt to convert it into flooring, or use it to commence work on a competing sculpture project. Importantly, whereas entitlement theories tend to be theories of special property rights, consistent with property inequality and some owning property and some not (but possibly subject to Lockean provisos), realization theories justify general property rights in addition to whatever special rights might be conferred. Depending on the form of realization and what we count as contributing to welfare, realization theories may also just be seen as a special case or subset of welfare theories, a point of some importance for a capabilities-inspired approach.

## INTELLECTUAL PROPERTY: MORAL AND LEGAL JUSTIFICATIONS

I have already noted how these general justifications of property may touch on the specific claims of IP rights, and it is not hard to see how, at a general level, these three forms of justification may be applied. That being said, there is an important difference between justifying IPR in general, and justifying existing IPR as found in national and international law. American IP law in particular is of some importance due to its international reach, and it provides quite different protections depending on whether an idea is protected by copyright, trademark, patent, or as a trade secret or plant variety. I have already noted one important feature of patents, which preclude not only copying but profit from independent invention, and both copyrights and patents have term limits that are more easily justifiable on some theories than others. Any moral theory is thus likely to involve as much critique as endorsement of current patent regimes, whether in the United States or elsewhere.

A second important consideration is that while most moral theories rely on the image of the lone artist and inventor creating great works of art or new technological marvels, in the patent world corporations are the significant players, and in international trade this picture is complicated by the interests and needs of the states involved. To some extent, it may be argued that a corporation's protection of its property rights coincides with that of its employees. If an engineer consents to the terms of employment with a large corporation, agreeing to give up the property rights to any inventions made by the engineer in exchange for job security and a satisfactory salary among other possible benefits, then it is in the interest of the engineer that her or his company do well, and this would include the company maximizing the benefits from its property rights. Similarly, the interests of a state negotiating a treaty will often align both with those of the corporation which contributes to its GDP and the engineer-employee who is also a citizen of the state. But the fact that the interests of all three—engineer, corporation, and state—can align does not mean that they always do align. What is in the interest of the corporation is not necessarily in the interest of the engineer, and the corporation can fire or lay off the engineer while retaining the property rights to the inventions created while the engineer was under employment. Similarly, the interests of corporation and state do not necessarily align: a corporation whose property rights enable it to corner the market may end up impairing competition and citizen well-being; a state may choose to waive property rights for purposes of international good will or to improve bilateral relations.

In a relatively early and influential article, Hettinger (1989) raised a number of important issues with the idea of intellectual property and how it is cashed out in the American system of IPR. Hettinger understands the justification of the patent system in terms of plausible, goal-oriented tradeoffs. Individuals or corporations that apply for a patent take a significant risk, since by so doing they make public what had previously been private knowledge, and by making it public the patent holder gives competitors the opportunity to copy, reverse-engineer, or create competing alternatives that may have benefited from such public access. When the patent expires in twenty years or so, the right to exclusive use is lost, and the idea that lay at the basis of the patent can then be used by others. Such public access to innovation is beneficial to economic and technological progress. By contrast, trade secrets do not provide such a benefit. While a society might benefit from the products that a business produces, as long as the secret is successfully kept others cannot capitalize on the knowledge.

Although Hettinger is sympathetic to Locke's labor argument, he questions whether the moral desert owed to someone for their intellectual labor is necessarily monetary in character or entails ownership. Hettinger observes that there are many things we might say that people deserve, and money is only one possibility. A proper reward for the labor involved in intellectual effort may not be money but simply praise or social recognition. Although Hettinger does not cite this example, scientific discovery is a relevant example, since scientists do not own the mathematical proofs and formulae or the physical laws that they discover. Einstein thus did not own the equations at the heart of relativity theory, but for his effort and insight he garnered considerable social recognition and praise.

Defenses of intellectual property predominantly rely on adapting the historic justifications of property to the intellectual sphere. Merges, for instance, relies on a modified combination of justifications from Locke, Kant, and Rawls. Rejecting traditional interpretations that Locke's theory is based on a concept of mixing (in the modern sense) labor with property, Merges argues that Locke's theory is about *adding* labor to a thing, and it is this adding, this extension of the self, that confers property rights. Merges ties this to Kant's connection of ownership and freedom as outlined above, but he also gives weight to the Lockean provisos, so that property rights according to Merges imply a balancing of individual rights and communal welfare. Merges sees Rawls's account of distributive justice in terms of the difference principle as providing a solution here.

By comparison, Moore (2001) places a greater reliance on Locke, but his focus is on the intuition behind the first proviso, that enough and as good be left for others. Moore here invokes an interpretation in terms of Pareto superiority: between two options A and B, option A is better than option B if and only if at least one person is better off in option A than B and no one is worse off in A than in B. Importantly, Moore understands this in terms of opportunity costs that are determined at the time of invention and not later. Suppose, Moore argues, Crusoe and Friday are alone on an island, and Crusoe desires to appropriate some object. For Crusoe to have a right to that object, Friday must not be made worse off by Crusoe's appropriation, not only now but also in the future because of the opportunities lost due to Crusoe's appropriation (2001, pp. 86–87). Moore's argument implies that if, for instance, Crusoe stakes out a land claim, Crusoe has a property right to that land only if Friday is not made worse off by it. If the land Crusoe sought to claim was the only source of fresh water on the island, this would invalidate the land claim. But the land claim would also be rendered invalid on Moore's account if the land claim didn't make Friday worse off now but worse off in the future in a way that could be anticipated at the time of appropriation. If, for instance, there were multiple sources of fresh water at the time of the land claim, but it was known that the other sources were increasingly unreliable, this would count against Crusoe's claim. But what would not count against it is if, for all they knew, the other water sources were reliable, but they only later discovered that they were not.

Although these simple examples involve only individuals in something like the state of nature, Moore primarily aims his account at the level of property institutions and their legal support at the national and international level. He is critical of the rule-utilitarianism that he sees as underlying the current American system of copyright and patent protection, which justifies intellectual property rights because of their long-term societal benefits. Although Moore's account is in principle welfarist, cashed out in terms of harms and benefits, it is also deontological, and Moore argues for a revision of property law that grants greater rights to inventors than is currently the case in many respects but weaker in a few. On the one hand, he favors expansion of copyright protection, advocating for among other things the elimination of the fair use clause and elimination of ownership sunsets. But he opposes the ban on independent invention in current patent law, as this violates the principle of Pareto superiority. He nevertheless favors sunsets on patent rights, again on Pareto grounds: if the duration of the patent is too long, then someone would eventually be made worse off by the property right claim.

Merges and Moore thus provide essentially deontological arguments supporting property rights. What of utilitarian ones? Utilitarian arguments are rendered difficult by virtue of the fact that a full utilitarian argument must not only assess real world impacts but also, counterfactually, the impacts different property regimes would have if only they were implemented. To some degree, this can be addressed through comparative economic analysis: with nearly two hundred countries in existence, a wide variety of property regimes exist that can serve as the basis of economic comparison. What do these comparisons tell us?

For simplicity, I follow here the analysis of Maskus (2012) and the literature he cites (see also Fink & Maskus, 2005). Examining within-nation effects, a study by Moser (2005) found positive, industry-specific correlations of patent protection and innovation, although other studies reveal a more mixed reality for software (Maskus, 2012). Internationally, the impacts of intellectual property protection appears to depend on the level of development. Schneider (2005), comparing nineteen developed and twenty-eight developing countries, found a positive correlation for patent protection and innovation in MDCs, but a negative one for LDCs, and similar results were found by Chen and Puttitanun (2005) and Park (2005). A study by Allred and Park (2007) examining data at the level of firms found a positive impact for intellectual property rights when per capita income was higher than $1,000, but only a marginally positive impact when per capita income was lower. Although causality in such studies is difficult to determine, Maskus concludes that patents help ILDCs and MDCs, but the benefits are much weaker for LDCs, if they exist at all.

In considering the impacts across nations, it is important to keep the international dimensions of trade in mind, and the way that international protections and enforcement of international IP rights can and apparently do have differential effects. When countries engage in trade, they may benefit equally or unequally, and scenarios can be envisioned where one country benefits and the other does not or is even impacted negatively. Of course, states that act rationally will avoid negative impacts, but not all outcomes are anticipated, especially when externalities such as environmental impact are included. The comparative studies are thus not simply an examination of the impacts of IP regimes taken individually, but a snapshot of participation in a partly national/partly international system of IP protection. Notably, all of these studies were conducted after the establishment of TRIPS, and studies have also been conducted specifically on the impacts of that agreement. Maskus himself concludes that, overall, the impact of TRIPS has been beneficial, and he cites positive impacts for high-growth countries such as South Korea, Taiwan, Israel, and Singapore (2012, p. 30; Ivus, 2010). Nevertheless, it is important to recognize the criticisms as well. Stiglitz (2008; Stiglitz and Charlton, 2005) has argued against strong intellectual property rights, both on economic and philosophical grounds. Arguing that knowledge is a public good, he cites evidence on negative impacts of patent protection in the biotechnology sector and anecdotal evidence of the impacts of the WTO and TRIPS on specific countries, including the issues surrounding pharmaceuticals already noted. A further issue concerns the nature of the economic data itself. Country-level assessments that examine GDP impacts or similar measures do not necessarily equate with the measure of aggregate happiness, well-being, or preference that informs a genuine utilitarian calculus. If a fortunate few become fabulously wealthy while the majority remain in dire poverty, GDP measures would still mark this as a net gain even though the utilitarian calculus would not (cf. Sen, 1999). Even if the data cited by Maskus do accurately reflect across the board population benefits, there is the further uncomfortable fact that the poorest of the poor, those living in least-developed countries, seem to be benefiting marginally or not at all. That this is so is consistent with an optimal utilitarian outcome as long as those in LDCs constitute a minority, revealing the harsh price a utilitarian philosophy can exact.

These considerations leave the utilitarian argument in not very good shape. Based on the evidence cited, the utilitarian would likely have to conclude that if the choice is simply between the existing IPR regime and no intellectual property rights at all, existing IPR provides a better net outcome, but one that does not benefit the least advantaged and which has important strings attached. The utilitarian is not well equipped to consider alternative scenarios simply due to the complexities of international trade. If one is concerned not simply with aggregate outcomes but with rights, whether they be the property rights of the inventors or the subsistence rights of the least advantaged, there are reasons to have strong reservations with the utilitarian approach. Is there a better alternative?

## A JOINT WELFARE-FULFILLMENT ACCOUNT

### The State of Plenty

A standard move in the political philosophy literature is to begin with a putative state of nature. This is the approach of the classic contract theorists—Hobbes, Locke, and Rousseau—and state-of-nature scenarios are attractive in part because of their simplicity, enabling the philosopher to abstract from features of contemporary society that might not be considered fundamental. Moore's Crusoe and Friday thought experiment is one such adaptation of the state-of-nature simplification to considerations of intellectual property. It may be the case, however, that what is important about intellectual property is best illumined from the opposite perspective. I will call this the State of Plenty.

Imagine the following scenario: you are living sometime in the distant future, and in this distant future there is no want and all material needs can be instantly satisfied. Such a future is similar to that envisioned for life on Earth in the *Star Trek* universe, the economy of which is based on matter transformers that can instantly produce any material item that one needs or desires. Of course, the *Star*

*Trek* universe is not a perfect State of Plenty: matter transformers may break down or not be immediately available, and presumably they require energy to work and do not violate the laws of physics; they are not perpetual energy machines. So the State of Plenty requires something a bit more than *Star Trek*: we might imagine that, at birth, everyone is given a magic wand, and this magic wand is indestructible, does not require an energy input, and can produce whatever one needs. Thus, one need not go hungry, lack shelter, or suffer from medical maladies. Life is good.

Is ownership of property important in the State of Plenty? Admittedly, even in the State of Plenty there will be some scarcity, and this will undoubtedly contribute to the desire to own certain kinds of things and thus a system of property. I can always own land because I can create some more, and we might fancifully imagine being able to create one's own planet if scarcity of land is a concern. But if I want a *particular* piece of land, say a nice flat adjoining Central Park in New York City, that is another story. And if I want *the* Mona Lisa and not just some magical replica, that too is another story, and similar considerations hold for items that have personal importance attached to them, such as family heirlooms. Items that are unique because of their location or history will remain scarce, even if material needs no longer are a concern. Other considerations may have more to do with privacy than with direct claims of ownership, and such concerns would be specific to certain kinds of property, for instance, homes and items such as toothbrushes. In the State of Plenty, my toothbrush is nothing special—I can always create another one—but I nevertheless don't want others using it, for practical hygiene reasons. Similarly, there may be nothing special about my house—I can create many houses—but I nevertheless don't want people walking in uninvited at 3 a.m. Whether this amounts to a theory of property is an open question, since individuals who rent have the same rights, but this object-related limitation on use is one of the hallmarks of property.

Whether realization-based reasons persist is another matter, and I suspect one subject to conflicting intuitions. It may still be the case that ownership is part of maturational development, but it is less obvious how this is manifested when I can instantly replace any object with its replica. Of course, there may be projects I am working on, my block of marble, that I do not want interrupted, but if I can instantly recreate the block of marble just as I last left it, would the "theft" then be of great importance to me?

While there may exist variation in intuitions, I would suggest that, with a few exceptions, both ownership and property would be of much less importance to us in the State of Plenty, and that it is, at least in part, scarcity and need that drives much of our concern over these issues, as Hume originally observed in his *Enquiry Concerning the Principles of Morals* (1975, p. 184). We might still think labor is important as a property claim. Suppose I live in the State of Plenty, and I make violins, just for fun. Suppose that making violins is slow and difficult work, and that after I have made a violin, someone walks up and takes it. I grant that this *might* matter to me because of my historical connection to *that* violin, though I would also be perplexed why someone would take a violin that they could just create themselves. But suppose that making violins was easy for me. I choose not to make them by magic, but I'm still very good, and I can produce, incredibly, twenty a day. Does it still matter to me if someone took one, given that we both live in the State of Plenty? Would I not want to simply give them away anyway, out of the joy of making? In the State of Plenty, why else would I make them?

With these considerations, we can perhaps begin to see the implications for intellectual property. In the State of Plenty, we can ask, would we want IPR? Again, welfare considerations are irrelevant. Suppose I write a novel, design a new kind of computer chip, or create a form of life that has never existed. I could insist that others not copy my invention and that they buy it from me, but what would be the point? I already have everything that I need materially, and so does everyone else. If anything, I would want my work of art or invention disseminated widely, and I would likely encourage others to copy the invention freely and, if they like it, to spread the word. Because IP is nonrival, the uniqueness considerations affecting material property (*that* piece of land or the original Mona Lisa) would not apply. What *would* still likely be of value would be what we might call *reputational value*: the expectation that I receive credit for the work that I did, even if I do not receive any material reward. In the real world, of course, reputation has both material and nonmaterial rewards attached to it. The fact that I created a beautiful piece of music, even if disseminated freely, may lead others to purchase other pieces of my music or attend my concerts. In the real world, reputation has extrinsic, material rewards. But I suspect that reputation would matter even in the absence of those rewards, and in the State of Plenty, we would be happy to have our work disseminated widely, but unhappy if others disseminated our work under their name. There is a sense in which reputation has intrinsic value beyond material rewards, and this has some importance for how we construe IPR.

## Implications of the State of Plenty

Let us now return to the real world from the State of Plenty. What the thought experiment reveals, I propose, is that when it comes to IPR, there are two considerations, one of reputation and one of material welfare. When creating intellectual property, we want above all to be recognized for our efforts, and we desire the nonmaterial reputation that accompanies it. These reputational effects are an intrinsic value of our labor and invention, and they are conferred even in cases of discovery of physical laws and mathematical formulae where material reward from IPR is not currently available. It is noteworthy how the "incidents of property" listed by Honoré by and large do not apply to reputational rights. "Moral rights" of property as protected in the European Union which provide for limitations on use after alienation may be an implication of reputational rights, but it is doubtful that such rights exist, and I won't pursue that argument here.

Unlike those fortunate beings living in the State of Plenty, those of us living in the real world are concerned not only with reputation but also with material benefit. For most of us, property rights matter because they impact well-being, and if I am able to secure IPR for my inventions, I have the opportunity to benefit, perhaps considerably. The reason that Locke's labor theory of property is so persuasive to us, I would suggest, is partly because labor confers ownership in a reputational sense ("I made that chair and made it well!"), and partly because labor involves opportunity costs that impact material well-being. It is possible that I labor on a work of art or a new vaccine for the sheer pleasure of doing so or out of some sense of the common good, but most of us also want to be materially rewarded for such efforts precisely because, if we had not so labored, we could have labored on something else that *would have been* financially rewarding. Under conditions of scarcity, laboring involves real material risks, and laboring under expectations of rewards when none are forthcoming can be disastrous.

Given this, it follows that the material conditions attached to property rights are not intrinsic rights that are only then protected by law, but rather legal conventions that are invented precisely because of considerations of welfare.[5] A welfare-based approach has the most potential to make sense of a number of intuitions regarding the existing system of IPR, including the justification of sunsets imposed on both copyrights and patents. Recognizing that IPR should be based on the dual criteria of reputation and welfare also has significant implications for how we regard the status of corporate IPR. Although corporations have "reputations," such reputations do not have moral weight, and the concern for corporate reputation is merely economic in character. Strictly speaking, corporations do not invent; individuals invent, and corporations facilitate invention by bringing teams of talented individuals together and enabling them to work effectively. To the extent that corporate patents are justifiable, they are justifiable precisely to the extent that they improve welfare in a just and fair manner. But what kind of welfare criteria do we use to evaluate IPR systems?

Two welfare-based approaches have so far been canvassed. Utilitarianism can plausibly provide justification for IPR, and it may even justify the existing international IPR, but it does so at considerable cost, since it is willing to sacrifice the welfare of those living in LDCs, and utilitarianism lacks the resources to sufficiently address issues of unfair distribution generally. In this respect, Moore's criterion of Pareto-superiority at first seems an improvement over the strictly utilitarian approach, as it avoids the issues associated with mere aggregation. But there are two important problems with Moore's approach that I will mention only briefly here. First, some of the specific implications that Moore deduces from his own theory, such as the limitations on fair use, are problematic. These implications follow in part from Moore's stipulation that opportunity costs be determined at the time of acquisition or invention rather than later, and this has significant and undesirable implications for later welfare considerations. While Moore does endorse sunsets for patents (but not copyrights), he leaves open their duration, thus creating further problems. A second and more abstract problem concerns the criterion of Pareto-superiority itself, and it is notable that Moore struggles to explain, for instance, how patents are justifiable, since competitors are (almost always) made economically worse off every time a patent is improved (c.f., Moore, 2000, ch. 6).

What is needed, I propose, is a threshold-based account of well-being, such as that found in the capabilities approach of Sen and Nussbaum. The capabilities approach can be considered a version of an objective list account of well-being, and Nussbaum has argued on behalf of a list of ten basic capabilities that, she argues, should be the subject of legal protection. Both Nussbaum and Sen make a distinction between capability and functioning, and Nussbaum in particular argues for a political obligation tied to capability but not for functioning. Put differently, I must have the opportunity to flourish (function fully along one of several dimensions), even if specific actions I take—my choice of career, voluntarily engaging in risky sports such as skydiving—may forestall my actual flourishing. There is thus a threshold level that serves as the basis of rights and access to goods and services. Intuitively, the capabilities approach captures the notion that chronic hunger and malnourishment, inadequate access to health care, and educational disadvantage all prevent the capability, the opportunity to live a decent life. The moral and political obligation is thus tied to making sure I have the *capability* to flourish, but whether I *choose* to do so, especially once I reach adulthood, is another story; some respect for autonomy is built into the approach.

How might the capabilities approach inform thinking about intellectual property? It is noteworthy that the capabilities approach incorporates something close to the two criteria for intellectual property: reputation and welfare. Nussbaum lists property ownership among the basic capabilities to be protected, and she seems to have in mind the kind of reasons put forth by Kant and Hegel: owner-ship of property is part of self-realization and maturation, and she argues for the importance of property ownership for poor Indian women on these as well as economic grounds (2000). Property is thus grounded partly on nonmaterial considerations and partly on welfare considerations, but the welfare considerations are mainly of concern for those below the threshold level. The key question, then, is: How does a legal regime of IPR, including corporate IPRs, impact those below threshold, both domestically and internationally, while at the same time giving credit where credit is due (respecting reputation)? I do not pretend that there is an easy answer to this, and it would require the kind of difficult economic assessment required of utilitarianism. Such an approach might well employ the criteria of Pareto-superiority supported by Moore, but only up to the threshold level of well-being: a property regime that improves the life of those below threshold but makes the well-off modestly worse off economically, but not so worse off to fall below threshold, could be supported in the capabilities approach even though it would not be in Moore's approach.[6]

## CONCLUSION

I concede that this proposal is but a sketch, and significant details would need to be worked out to make it plausible. My own intuition is that while the current IPR regime can be improved on, very radical tampering is impractical and imprudent. But even modest shifts, especially with respect to how IPRs possessed by wealthy multinationals based in MDCs are enforced in LDCs, can have major impacts on the well-being of the least advantaged, eventually enabling them to be creators and inventors in their own right. As even this brief survey reveals, the current international IPR system has both strengths and weaknesses, and philosophical reflection can aid in both understanding what intellectual property is and how best it should be justified. In particular, starting with a State of Plenty rather than a State of Nature can yield significant insight into how we justify IPRs and how we balance the interests of inventors with those of consumers and citizen well-being.

## NOTES

1. I use *ILDC* here to refer to countries such as Brazil or China that are now widely considered to occupy a middle space between what has in the past been the comparatively simple distinction of more developed and less developed countries. I reserve the term *LDC* for *least* developed countries, countries such as Angola or Bangladesh that constitute the "bottom billion" of the world's population (Collier, 2007).

2. For the distinction of private, collective, communal, and corporate, see Waldron (1988, pp. 38-48); for the special/general distinction, see Waldron (1988, ch. 5).

3. Hume's argument can be found in *A Treatise Concerning Human Nature*, 3.2.2.2–8, The views of Bentham and Mill can be found in MacPherson (1978), which includes excerpts from Bentham's *Principles of the Civil Code* and Mill's *Principles of Political Economy*, Book II.1–3, 11; for an argument and narrative based more straightforwardly on economic cost-benefit analysis, see Demsetz (1967). Although Mill argued on behalf of private property, he could also be a critic. For a discussion, see Ryan (1984).

4. See Kant (1996/1797), Hegel (1991/1821). For an analysis and development of Kant's view, see Merges (2011); for Hegel's, see Waldron (1988).

5. This would seem to imply that in the state of nature there would still be reputational rights but no property rights otherwise, contra Locke. As Locke himself realized, however, the status of property rights in the state of nature is more complicated than first appears, assuming that moral realism of some form holds. If principles of respect for others' well-being holds in the state of nature, then there are reasons to not engage in actions that reduce their well-being, including theft of personal belongings. Problems arise when there is not, as Locke supposed, enough and as good for everyone. Under conditions of scarcity, there may not be enough food for both Crusoe and Friday to survive. It might be argued that if Friday has the last supply of coconuts on the island, he has a right of self-preservation if Crusoe attacks him. But this is not the same thing as saying that he has exclusive right to the coconuts, even if he had labored upon them. It would be difficult to claim that Crusoe should simply acquiesce and give up life in recognition of the dire situation that only one can survive. But if a particular ethic were to assert that, it is doubtful that the argument would be based on property rights as opposed to other considerations, such as the wrongness of killing.

6. Some will no doubt be alarmed by the suggestion that it is permissible to make the well-off worse off in order to improve the lot of those below threshold, but this is of course the basis of progressive taxation. It is important to note that the capabilities approach in the conception of Nussbaum and Sen and as I envision it here is not strictly egalitarian and allows, at least in principle, considerable variation in wealth consistent with the meeting of capabilities. Peter Singer (1972; 2004) has famously argued on behalf of significant individual level aid to the poor, initially arguing for the principle that if we can prevent something bad from happening without sacrificing anything of "comparable moral importance," we should do it. Both Singer and his opponents have since put forth arguments that this would entail bringing those who are well-off to a level of well-being that is, in capability terms, just above threshold. I would suggest, however, that this would be deeply undesirable on a capabilities approach for the simple reason that, even in MDCs, life is risky, and even an individual in the upper middle class with modest life savings may find him or herself suddenly without a job or direly ill. On the capabilities approach, I would

suggest, no one is served by making the middle class poor, but society is likely poorly served by an intellectual property regime that, *ceteris paribus*, creates billionaires in the midst of extreme suffering when that suffering could be partially alleviated by alternative IPR regimes.


REFERENCES

Allred, B. B., & Park, W. G. (2007). Patent rights and innovative activity: Evidence from national and firm-level data. *Journal of International Business Studies, 38(6)*, 878–900.

Chen, Y., & Puttitanun, T. (2005). Intellectual property rights and innovation in developing countries. *Journal of Development Economics, 78(2)*, 474–93.

Collier, P. (2007). *The bottom billion: Why the poorest countries are failing and what can be done about it.* New York, NY: Oxford University Press.

Demsetz, H. (1967). Toward a theory of property rights. *The American Economic Review, 57(2)*, 347–359.

Fink, C., & Maskus, K. E. (2005). *Intellectual property and development: Lessons from recent economic research.* New York, NY: the World Bank and Oxford University Press.

Fisher, W. W. I., & Rigamonti, C. P. (2005, February 10). *The South African AIDS controversy: A case study in patent law and policy.* Retrieved from http://cyber.law.harvard.edu/people/tfisher/South%20Africa.pdf.

Hegel, G. W. F. (1991). *Elements of the philosophy of right.* (A. W. Wood, Ed.). Cambridge, UK: Cambridge University Press.

Hettinger, E. C. (1989). Justifying intellectual property. *Philosophy & Public Affairs, 18(1)*, 31–52.

Honoré, A. M. (1961). Ownership. In A. Guest (Ed.), *Oxford essays in jurisprudence.* London, UK: Oxford University Press.

Hume, D. (1975). *Enquiries concerning human understanding and concerning the principles of morals.* New York, NY: Oxford University Press.

———. (2005). *A treatise of human nature.* New York, NY: Barnes & Noble.

Ivus, O. (2010). Do stronger patent rights raise high-tech exports to the developing world? *Journal of International Economics, 81(1)*, 38–47.

Kant, I. (1996). *The metaphysics of morals.* (M. Gregor, Trans.). New York, NY: Cambridge University Press.

Locke, J. (2003). *Two treatises of government and a letter concerning toleration.* New Haven, CT: Yale University Press.

Macpherson, C. B. (1978). *Property: Mainstream and critical positions.* Toronto, ON: University of Toronto Press.

Maskus, K. E. (2012). *Private rights and public problems: The global economics of intellectual property in the 21st century*. Washington, DC: Peterson Institute for International Economics.

Merges, R. P. (2011). *Justifying intellectual property*. Cambridge, MA: Harvard University Press.

Mill, J. S. (2008). *Principles of political economy with chapters on socialism*. New York, NY: Oxford University Press.

Moore, A. D. (2001). *Intellectual property and information control: Philosophic foundations and contemporary issues*. New Brunswick, NJ: Transaction Publishers.

Moser, P. (2005). How do patent laws influence innovation? Evidence from nineteenth-century world's fairs. *The American Economic Review, 95(4)*, 1214–1236.

Nozick, R. (1974). *Anarchy, state, and utopia*. New York, NY: Basic Books.

Nussbaum, M. (2007). *Frontiers of justice: Disability, nationality, and species membership*. Cambridge, MA: Harvard University Press.

Nussbaum, M. C. (2000). *Women and human development*. New York, NY: Cambridge University Press.

Park, W. G. (2005). Do intellectual property rights stimulate R&D and productivity growth? Evidence from cross-national and manufacturing industries data. In J. Putnam (Ed.), *Intellectual property rights and innovation in the knowledge-based economy* (9:1–9:51). Ottawa, ON: Industry Canada.

Pufendorf, S. (1991). *On the duty of man and citizen according to natural law*. Cambridge, UK: Cambridge University Press.

Russell, S. (1999, May 24). New crusade to lower AIDS drug costs. *The San Francisco Chronicle*, p. 1.

Ryan, A. (1984). *Property and political theory*. New York, NY: Basil Blackwell.

Schneider, P. H. (2005). International trade, economic growth, and intellectual property rights: A panel data study of developed and developing countries. *Journal of Development Economics, 78(2)*, 529–547. https://doi.org/10.1016/j.jdeveco.2004.09.001.

Sen, A. (1999). *Development as freedom*. New York, NY: Alfred A. Knopf.

Singer, P. (1972). Famine, affluence, morality. *Philosophy & Public Affairs, 1(3)*, 229–243.

———. (2004). *One world: The ethics of globalization*. New Haven, CT: Yale University Press.

Stiglitz, J. E. (2008). Economic foundations of intellectual property rights. *Duke Law Journal, 57(6)*, 1693–1724.

———, & Charlton, A. (2005). *Fair trade for all: How trade can promote development*. New York, NY: Oxford University Press.

Waldron, J. (1988). *The right to private property*. New York, NY: Clarendon Press.

# 10 NIMBY, NAMBY, and UAVS

## The Drone Revolution

TIMOTHY M. RAVICH

Some of the greatest technological accomplishments during the last century have turned traditional notions of property law upside down. Examples include radio broadcasting, GPS, outer space exploration and planetary landings, railroads, subsurface oil and gas extraction, and the internet. Manned aviation is arguably the most widely experienced and compelling example of the legal and social challenge to reconciling technological advances with centuries-old understandings of property ownership and use. As detailed in Stuart Banner's *Who Owns the Sky: The Struggle to Control Airspace from the Wright Brothers On*, since approximately the mid- to late 1800s, manned aviation specifically has disrupted the Roman concept that one who owns land also owns the skies above it. Laws first developed for the jet age generally establish five hundred feet above ground level as the extent of private property ownership (at least in urban areas). But, now, innovations in *unmanned* aviation and the nearly ubiquitous opportunity to fly at low altitudes are impacting existing conceptions of property and challenging the notion that private property ownership can exist at all "above the grass."

In some measure, the operation of nanotechnology-driven airplanes presents nothing new, stirring age-old and foreseeable legal and social controversies, albeit in a new context. For example, the operation of a drone can spark disputes between neighbors, as when a private citizen in Kentucky self-identified as the "drone slayer" shot down a drone flying over his property. But, increasingly, the proliferation of small hand-held airplanes is generating controversies at low altitudes and in unexpected areas, including over university campuses, under bridges, through banquet halls, and above government buildings and dignitaries. Consequently, the use and ownership of drones is confronting lawmakers and jurists with unprecedented jurisdictional and common law questions involving aerial trespass and invasions of privacy.

Consider the 2016 case of *Huerta v. Haughwout*, for example. There, federal regulators sought to prosecute two private citizens for flying drones only a few feet above the ground. One of the drone operators uploaded a fourteen-second video on YouTube showing the firing of a handgun attached to his small eighteen-inch-long drone. The second remote pilot posted a four-minute-long YouTube video sardonically titled "This is how to roast your holiday turkey." It shows a drone flying no more than eight feet off the ground with some kind of flame-throwing contraption attached to it and spewing intense streams of fire to scorch a turkey carcass on a spit nearby. While a federal judge permitted the FAA to investigate and serve subpoena on these operators, he questioned the extent of the government's authority in light of 1940s-era Supreme Court precedent holding that "the landowner owns at least as much of the space above the ground as he can occupy or use in connection the land." The court posited: "Must this foundational principle vanish or yield the moment that person sets any object aloft no matter how high in the airspace outside one's home?"

This chapter evaluates this question qualitatively, by discussing the legal antecedents underlying how—and if—regulators should manage the latest innovation to disrupt traditional property rights—unmanned aerial systems (UASs). This chapter begins by setting out the controversy posed by the flight of UAS and follows with a discussion of the historical tension between manned (e.g., on board piloted) aviation operations, on the one hand, and property law, on the other hand. After defining the modern national airspace system, the chapter then sets out the seminal property law and takings cases that lawyers and courts are revisiting in the modern era of unmanned aviation. Finally, this chapter concludes by discussing ways in which the next generation of drones and similar flying contraptions will challenge and reconstitute the property laws that governs them.

For further reading, this chapter is excerpted, adapted, and drawn from Commercial Drone Law: Digest of U.S. and Global UAS Rules, Policies, and Practices (American Bar Association 2017), *Airports, Droneports, and the New Urban Airspace*, 44 Fordham Urban Law Journal (2017), and ACRP 11-01/ Topic 08-03, *Evolving Law on Airport Implications by Unmanned Aerial Systems* (2017), a report supported by the National Academy of Sciences, Engineering, and Medicine, Airport Cooperative Research Program.

## DEFINING UAS

Fundamentally, drones are automatic, automated, autonomous, semiautonomous, remotely piloted, and optionally piloted airplanes. Of numerous shapes and sizes, fixed-wing aircraft and quadcopters are the most common kinds of drones. They are manufactured by sophisticated producers such as Northrup Grumman in tandem with suppliers from around the world as well as by aviation amateurs with home-built kits working out of home garages. The smallest drones are nano-, micro-, and mini- battery-powered gadgets that are compact and lightweight enough to fit in the palm of a hand. Oppositely, the largest drones are automobile-sized machines that are weaponized and equipped with decision-making avionics that effect lethal decisions based on inputs transmitted from ground stations thousands of miles away.

In all, like so many other ubiquitous devices wired (or wireless, as the case may be) into the "Internet of Things," drones are widely accessible and relatively inexpensive. In fact, starter drones sold by online retailers such as Amazon cost only a few hundred dollars and come standard with artificially intelligent software and sensor suites that are managed remotely on ordinary smartphones and tablets. Drones enable anybody to fly anywhere at any time with astounding agility.

Working in three dimensions, drone users can ascend, hover, and maneuver over railroad tracks, act as poachers targeting endangered wildlife, or invade film sets, for instance, as effortlessly as they can fly indoors, in subway tunnels and banquet halls. Indeed, the global inventory of drones includes civilian, combat, and tactical aircraft that serve countless ground, sea, air, and outer space operations.

Among the "dirty, dull, and dangerous" jobs drones perform or support are aerial photography, zoning and urban planning, public safety, border management, coastal security and maritime patrol, search and rescue, traffic surveillance, weather monitoring, pipeline monitoring, forest fire monitoring, first responder medical support, and critical infrastructure inspection. By operating virtually, autonomously, or remotely, drones maneuver more nimbly than manned craft and reduce and optimize the economic and human costs of flight. For example, using high resolution, multispectral, thermal, and hyperspectral sensors on flight-capable platforms, farmers engage in "precision agriculture" to assess yield and crop health—a data-driven approach that is far more efficient than manual, ground-based processes reliant on the naked eye. But for all the beneficial uses of drones, conflicts between drone operators and private landowners grab the biggest headlines in the United States and abroad, creating an inhospitable regulatory environment for drone producers and users.

## CONTROVERSY

In April 2014, the United Kingdom's Civil Aviation Authority prosecuted a man who flew his drone into restricted airspace over a nuclear submarine facility; two years later, a British Airways flight reportedly collided with a drone in what might have been the first such incident involving a major airline. Meanwhile, on the other side of the Atlantic Ocean, a drone whizzed above tennis players at the U.S.

Open in New York before slamming into an empty seating area. And the United States Department of Transportation imposed a $1.9 million civil penalty against a company for conducting sixty-five unauthorized operations in some of the nation's most congested airspace and heavily populated cities. In fact, by March 2016, the Federal Aviation Administration reported receiving more than one hundred drone "incidents" or sightings a month from pilots, citizens, and law enforcement.

While the practical significance of drone sightings or "incidents" is unclear, the likelihood that consequential conflicts involving drones and ground-based operations may intensify is plausible given the Federal Aviation Administration's projection of seven million drones by 2020. Deconflicting these anticipated unmanned operations in a national airspace system originally designed for manned flight presents unprecedented regulatory challenges. And yet, ironically, controversies involving unmanned aviation and traditional property laws predate and inform the drone era.

## THE INTERSECTION OF AVIATION AND PROPERTY LAW

The nineteenth-century case *Guille v. Swan*, 19 Johns. 381 (N.Y. Sup. Ct. 1822) was one of the first cases requiring lawmakers to balance aviation and property. There, the operator of an air balloon crash landed into a private garden in New York. "When the balloon descended [the balloonist called for assistance and] more than two hundred persons broke into [the] garden through the fences, and came onto the premises [to his rescue], beating down [the garden's] vegetables and flowers." The landowner sued for damages and won, convincing the court that the balloonist was liable because the damages caused by his trespass were foreseeable as a matter of law:

> Ascending in a balloon is not an unlawful act ... but, it is certain, that the aeronaut has no control over its motion horizontally; he is at the sport of the winds and is to descend when and how he can; his reaching the earth is a matter of hazard. He did descend on the premises of the plaintiff below, at a short distance from the place where he ascended. Now, if his descent, under such circumstances, would, ordinarily and naturally, draw a crowd of people about him, either from curiosity, or for the purpose of rescuing him from a perilous situation; all this he ought to have foreseen, and must be responsible for.

*Guille* reflected an early view of aviation as an ultrahazardous activity for which owners, operators, and manufacturers were strictly liable. This reactionary impulse to resist groundbreaking innovations is as alive in private property owners today with respect to drones as it was decades ago with respect to airplanes and airports.

In fact, landowners in the early era of manned aviation not only believed flying posed extremely high risks to people and property on the ground, but also regarded the ground-based infrastructure necessary to support flight itself as inconsistent with the use and enjoyment of private property. In the 1920s-era case *Dysart v. City of St. Louis*, 11 S.W. 2d 1045 (Mo. 1928), for example, a Missouri taxpayer attempted to stop the development of a publicly funded airport. Airports could never serve any general or public good, the petitioner claimed:

> It will afford a starting and landing place for a few wealthy, ultra-reckless persons, who own planes and who are engaged in private pleasure flying. They may pay somewhat for the privilege.
>
> It will afford a starting and landing place for pleasure tourists from other cities, alighting in St. Louis while flitting here and yon. It will offer a passenger station for the very few persons who are able to afford, and who desire to experience, the thrill of a novel and expensive mode of luxurious transportation.
>
> The number of persons using the airport will be about equal to the total number of persons who engage in big-game hunting, trips to the African wilderness, and voyages of North Pole exploration.
>
> In the very nature of things, the vast majority of the inhabitants of the city, a 99 percent majority, cannot now and never can, reap any benefit from the existence of an airport. True, it may be permitted to the ordinary common garden variety of citizen to enter the airport free of charge, so that he may press his face against some restricting barrier, and sunburn his throat gazing at his more fortunate compatriots as they sportingly navigate the empyrean blue. But beyond that, beyond the right to hungrily look on, the ordinary citizen gets no benefit from the taxes he is forced to pay.

The Supreme Court of Missouri rejected this view, however, recognizing that, by 1928, "[it was] unquestionably true that the airplane [was] not in general use as a means of travel or transportation, either in the city of St. Louis or elsewhere; [but] *it never will be unless properly equipped landing fields are established*."

In the same year, in *Hesse v. Rath*, 164 N.E. 342 (N.Y. App. 1928), a case factually similar to *Dysart*, Judge Benjamin N. Cardozo, then a New York appellate judge, announced that "[a]viation today is an established method of transportation." The eventual U.S. Supreme Court Justice also accepted the inevitability of airports and air transportation and cautioned contrary views:

The city that is without the foresight to build the ports for the new traffic may soon be left behind in the race of competition. Chalcedon was
called the city of the blind, because its founders rejected the nobler site
of Byzantium lying at their feet. The need for vision of the future in the
governance of cities has not lessened with the years. The dweller within the
gates, even more than the stranger from afar, will pay the price of blindness.

While courts in Missouri and New York and elsewhere around the nation litigated
the question of whether the development of an airport constituted a valid municipal purpose, other states such as Florida embraced aviation activities proactively.
For example, the Florida Legislature enacted Ch. 13569, General Acts of 1929,
authorizing municipal corporations to purchase (including by way of a right of
condemnation), establish, construct, and operate airports and landing fields.
Courts upheld such laws on constitutional grounds, including in *State v. Dade
County*, 27 So. 2d 283 (Fla. 1946), in which the Supreme Court of Florida stated:

> [T]his Court knows that air transportation is one of the great innovations
> of the age, that Miami is potentially one of the greatest air distribution points
> in the World, and that Florida is the port of entry for air transportation from
> South and Central America, the West Indies, and Africa.
>
> It is quite true that there were no Jules Verns [*sic*] or Wright Brothers in
> the Constitutional Convention to portend the marvelous changes the future
> had in store, but it was not intended by those present that the dead hand of
> the past should shape the destiny of the future. Constitutional mandates
> are wise in proportion to the manner in which they respond to the public
> welfare and should be construed to effectuate that purpose when possible.
> The law does not look with favor on social or progressive stalemates ... [and]
> extension of political controls should keep pace with physical changes, and
> collective ingenuity should not be hobbled by the Constitution in a way to
> be outclassed by collective design to overreach and serve a selfish purpose.

Between the time of these court decisions and the end of World War II, private,
public, and commercial aviation was becoming routine, so much so that state
courts, again such as the Supreme Court of Florida in the decision of *Brooks v.
Patterson*, 31 So. 2d 472 (Fla. 1946), rejected claims founded in nuisance and
trespass in connection with airplane operations:

> The City should be mindful at all times of the admonition which comes
> to us from the days of the Roman Empire, "*sicutere tuo ut alienum non
> laedas*"—so use your own property as not to injure another's.

That aviation is as much a part of modern civilization is as the railroad, steamship and automobile as a means of transportation of both freight and passengers is too obvious for serious discussion.

The place which aviation now occupies was envisaged, probably initially, by Alfred Lord Tennyson in his prophetic dream which we find recorded in his frequently quoted poem, 'Locksley Hall,' when he wrote: "For I dipt into the future, far as human eye could see; Saw the vision of the world, and all the wonder that would be; Saw the heavens fill with commerce, argosies of magic sails; Pilots of the purple twilight, dropping down with costly bales."

Today, a world without airports and airplanes is unimaginable. But the question of where the newest airplanes can fly, particularly in the middle area between privately owned air space and the public navigable airspace is unsettled.

## WHERE TO FLY—THE NATIONAL AIRSPACE SYSTEM (NAS)

Understanding *where*—the airspace—the law currently permits flight is central to understanding the challenge posed by, potentially, millions of drones flying in the future. The term *airspace,* standing alone, is not defined in the Federal Aviation Regulations. Rather, regulators speak in terms of "controlled airspace" and "navigable airspace." In a regulatory sense, then, "controlled airspace" is "an airspace of a defined dimension within which air traffic control service is provided to . . . flights in accordance with the airspace classification." The national airspace system is segmented into two categories of airspace or airspace areas: regulatory (Class A, B, C, D, and E airspace areas, restricted and prohibited areas) and

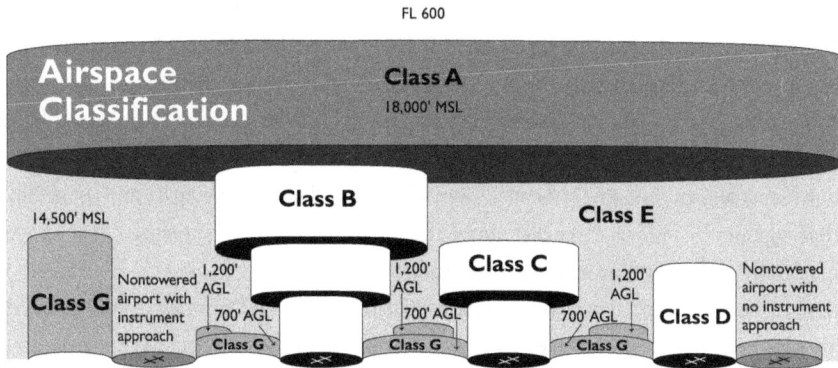

Figure 10.1. FAA airspace classification

nonregulatory (military operations areas ["MOAs"], warning areas, alert areas, and controlled firing areas). Within these two categories, there are four types of airspace: controlled, uncontrolled, special use, and other airspace, extending to outer space (flight level 60,000 feet ["FL 600"]). The Federal Aviation Administration has illustrated the segmentation of *controlled* airspace as follows, where different operational rules exist within different spheres of airspace over land, for instance, Class B airspace—resembling an upside-down wedding cake— includes airspace from the surface to 10,000 feet surrounding the nation's busiest airports in terms of passenger enplanements.

In this classification scheme, the legal controversy introduced by drone operations is more jurisdictional than technological. Where drones are permitted to fly is a critical issue whose resolution both depends upon and is limited by legal precedent established in the middle of the last century with respect to manned airplane operations.

## AIRSPACE AND GOVERNMENT TAKINGS

The so-called drone revolution brings home the point that the skies are not an unlimited resource but a finite one. Allowing airplanes to fly in the airspace above private property necessarily requires regulators to limit and balance airspace rights with ground rights. The Fifth Amendment, a guarantee that the government will not take private property without just compensation, is a natural starting point. Its application in the modern era of aviation was tested in the 1940s with the advent of modern military and commercial aviation.

Until that time, the Roman doctrine of *cujus est solum ejus usque ad coelom*—"whoever owns the soil, it is theirs up to Heaven"—controlled air and property rights. That changed when the Supreme Court of the United States decided *United States v. Causby*, 328 U.S. 256 (1946). There, a North Carolina farmer sued the federal government for inverse condemnation. Essentially, the landowner contended that the activities of Army and Navy bombers and fighter airplanes—taking off and landing at an airfield close to his barn—deprived him of his private property rights. More specifically, heavy bombers, transports, and fighter airplanes repeatedly flew at low altitudes and landed along a "path of glide" that was a mere eighty-three feet above the farmer's property, sixty-three feet above his barn, and eighteen feet above the highest tree on his property. He claimed that light and noise from the airplanes not only terrified his family but caused his chickens to kill themselves from fright, effectively destroying his commercial chicken farming business on his private property. The federal government argued that its airplane operations had not effected a deprivation or taking of the farmer's property under the Constitution.

Government lawyers defended the flights on the basis of the Air Commerce Act of 1926. Under that law, Congress vested the national government with "complete and exclusive national sovereignty in the air space," reserving to American citizens "a public right of freedom of transit in air commerce through the navigable air space of the United States." The "navigable air space" included "airspace above the minimum safe altitudes of flight prescribed by the [Federal Aviation Administration]." Thus, according to the government, the flights at issue were merely an exercise of the right of travel through the airspace within the minimum safe altitudes for flight established under the Air Commerce Act. Moreover, the flights could not and did not effect a taking because they occurred within the navigable airspace without any physical invasion of the farmer's property. At most, the government argued, only incidental damage occurred as a consequence of authorized air navigation.

The Supreme Court of the United States sided with the farmer—but only to a point. It concluded that the airplane landings were perhaps no more (or less) of appropriation of the use of private property as a more conventional entry upon it:

> We would not doubt that if the United States erected an elevated railway over [the farmer's] land at the precise altitude where its planes now fly, there would be a partial taking, even though none of the supports of the structure rested on the land. The reason is that there would be an intrusion so immediate and direct as to subtract from the owner's full enjoyment of the property and to limit his exploitation of it. While the owner does not in any physical manner occupy that stratum of airspace or make use of it in the conventional sense, he does use it in somewhat the same sense that space left between buildings for the purpose of light and air is used. The superadjacent airspace at this low altitude is so close to the land that continuous invasions of it affect the use of the surface of the land itself. We think that the landowner, as an incident to his ownership, has a claim to it and that invasions of it are in the same category as invasions of the surface.

Notably, in this context, the flights in *Causby* were not unauthorized but allowed, and the farmer's only remedy was monetary, in an amount that corresponded to the nature of the taking, including whether it was temporary or permanent. In reaching this holding, the Court abandoned historical notions of unlimited air rights above private property rights and instead recognized a public navigational easement above private property for the use of aviators: "The flight of aircraft is lawful 'unless at such a low altitude as to interfere with the then existing use to which the land or water, or the space over the land or water, is put by the owner, or unless so conducted as to be imminently dangerous to persons or property lawfully on the land or water beneath.' "

Justice William O. Douglas, writing for the *Causby* majority, reasoned that "[t]he airplane is part of the modern environment of life" where ancient doctrines of airspace ownership such as *ad coelom* "ha[d] no place in the modern world. The air is a public highway. . . . Were that not true, every transcontinental flight would subject the operator to countless trespass suits." *Causby* thus marked a reboot of putatively fixed property law doctrines, accepting as routine the concept of machines flying in the sky—above and through columns of airspace above privately owned parcels of land. But, at what altitude did a private property owner's air rights end and the navigable air space begin?

*Causby* did not answer this question, leaving many low-altitude-airspace-related issues unresolved. Mid-1940s-era regulators had not enacted air traffic rules placing the airspace needed for takeoff and landing within the public domain. Therefore, the Supreme Court was not asked to evaluate the validity of any regulation prescribing any specific altitude as the minimum safe altitude or the "immediate reaches above the land." As such, *Causby* did not define a precise altitude beneath which airplanes (whether government- or privately operated) could not fly over private property—an issue brought front and center by innovations in drone technology.

## AERIAL SURVEILLANCE: AT THE INTERSECTION OF PROPERTY AND PRIVACY RIGHTS

Gone are the days when private property rights extended up to Heaven. And, thanks to drones, gone too are the days when sustained flight was not possible below the navigable airspace at altitudes as low as eighty-three or sixty-three or eighteen feet as in *Causby*. Now, quadcopters and micro-drones fly and hover and loiter at any altitude—above farm animals, over a neighbor's swimming pool, or even indoors, say, in the "airspace" above a cocktail reception or in a classroom. In this sense, drone operations implicate a subspecies of property rights: privacy. While current local, state, and federal laws respecting drone surveillance are unsettled and emerging, operators and regulators may be guided by court opinions of the last century balancing low altitude airplane operations with private property and personal dignity rights.

*Olmstead v. United States*, 277 U.S. 438 (1928), was one of the first cases to consider and reject a shift in the nation's property laws to accommodate high-tech innovations. In the 1928 decision, the Supreme Court of the United States evaluated whether the federal government's intercept of private telephone conversations with wiretaps attached to telephone wires on public streets violated the Fourth Amendment's prohibition of unreasonable government searches and seizures. *Olmstead* applied a traditional and simple rule to find that the government acted lawfully: No physical trespass, no search.

This strict property-based approach was overruled in the 1967 decision of *Katz v. United States*, 389 U.S. 347 (1967), however. There, the high court considered the constitutionality of eavesdropping devices attached to public telephone booths. "[T]he Fourth Amendment protects people, not places," Justice Potter Stewart famously wrote, supplanting the *Olmstead* trespass doctrine with an analytical framework requiring courts to consider whether the subject of a search had a "reasonable expectation of privacy." In this legal regime, proof of an actual or physical trespass was no longer necessary or sufficient to establish a violation of the Constitution's Fourth Amendment. Courts applied this rule to aerial surveillance more than twenty years later when the Supreme Court of the United States decided three important cases construing Fourth Amendment protections in the navigable airspace.

First, in the 1986 decision of *Dow Chemical Co. v. United States*, 476 U.S. 227 (1986), a chemical company refused a request by the Environmental Protection Agency for an on-site inspection of its plant. Elaborate security around the perimeter of the complex barred ground-level public views of the area. Thus, the EPA, instead of seeking an administrative search warrant, employed a commercial aerial photographer using a standard precision aerial mapping camera to take photographs of the facility from various altitudes, all of which were within lawful navigable airspace. The chemical company learned of the surveillance and brought suit in federal district court, alleging that the EPA's actions violated the Fourth Amendment. But on appeal, the Supreme Court of the United States allowed the aerial photography, distinguishing between the protected immediate surroundings of a private home ("curtilage") and public spaces:

> [T]he open areas of an industrial plant complex with numerous plant structures spread over an area of 2,000 acres are not analogous to the "curtilage" of a dwelling for purposes of aerial surveillance; such an industrial complex is more comparable to an open field and as such it is open to the view and observation of persons in aircraft lawfully in the public

airspace immediately above or sufficiently near the area for the reach of cameras. We hold that the taking of aerial photographs of an industrial plant complex from navigable airspace is not a search prohibited by the Fourth Amendment.

But as was made clear in *California v. Ciraolo*, 476 U.S. 207 (1986), also decided in 1986, *Dow* did not mean that law enforcement were prohibited from conducting aerial surveillance of private property.

In *Ciraolo,* local police acted on an anonymous tip and flew a private fixed-wing aircraft at an altitude of one thousand feet over a residence where they spotted a homeowner growing marijuana. They sought and obtained a search warrant based on this naked eye observation. The homeowner successfully moved to suppress the evidence adduced against him, but ultimately lost on appeal when the Supreme Court of the United States held that the inspection was not an unreasonable search in contravention of the Fourth Amendment. True, the overflight was of property within the "curtilage" of the house, a fence shielded the yard from observation from the street, and the occupant had a subjective expectation of privacy, but the high court stated that such an expectation was not reasonable and not one "that society is prepared to honor."

While acknowledging that an aircraft was an unknown type of "of future 'electronic' developments that could stealthily intrude upon an individual's privacy" at the time that *Katz v. United States* was decided, the *Ciraolo* court emphasized that no physical trespass had occurred and the police were in a public place, the navigable airspace, where "they had a right to be." Consequently, law enforcement were free to inspect the yard from that vantage point just as they would have been free to inspect the backyard garden from the street if their view had been unobstructed. In language reminiscent of *Causby*, the court recognized widespread acceptance of manned flight in the navigable airspace as an influential factor in its decision to allow the surveillance:

> In an age where private and commercial flight in the public airways is routine, it is unreasonable for respondent to expect that his marijuana plants were constitutionally protected from being observed with the naked eye from an altitude of 1,000 feet. The Fourth Amendment simply does not require the police traveling in the public airways at this altitude to obtain a warrant in order to observe what is visible to the naked eye.

Finally, *Ciraolo* was followed three years later by *Florida v. Riley*, 448 U.S. 445 (1989), a case in which the Supreme Court of the United States considered whether a search occurred when local police officers flew a helicopter, consistent with aviation regulations, at a mere altitude of four hundred feet above a residential greenhouse to observe marijuana plants through a small break in the roof. The Supreme Court of Florida initially decided that helicopter surveillance at four hundred feet constituted a search for which a warrant was required. The Supreme Court of the United States disagreed, however, quoting *Ciraolo* for the proposition that the police traveling in the public airways do not need to obtain a warrant "in order to observe what is visible to the naked eye."

For the better part of the last century, *Causby, Dow, Ciraolo,* and *Riley* have provided an important framework within which to relate constitutional and common law protections to private and public aviation operations. Regulators have not definitely or uniformly extended these precedents into the modern drone age, however. Several states such as Arkansas, for example, prohibit the use of drones to commit voyeurism. Using a drone to commit "peeping tom" activities in Mississippi is a felony. Under anti-paparazzi rules, California prohibits entering the airspace of an individual without permission to capture an image or recording of that individual engaging in a private, personal, or familial activity. Florida prohibits the use of a drone to capture an image of privately owned property or the owner, tenant, or occupant of such property without consent if a reasonable expectation of privacy exists. Nevada prohibits the weaponization or use of a drone within a certain distance of critical facilities and airports without permission. Tennessee prohibits the use of drones over the grounds of a correctional facility. Texas makes it a misdemeanor to operate a drone over a critical infrastructure facility if the drone is not more than four hundred feet off the ground. Virginia requires law enforcement agencies to obtain a warrant before using a drone for any purpose, except in limited circumstances. Meanwhile, the federal government, with complete sovereignty over the nation's *navigable* airspace, only just finalized an introductory set of rules for small (under fifty-five pounds) commercial drones on August 29, 2016.

Consequently, today, a patchwork of drone-centered ordinances and legislation has emerged beneath the altitudes considered in these cases while last-century understandings of trespass under *Olmstead* and twentieth-century formulations of a "subjective expectation of privacy" under *Katz* are in flux. To be sure, analyzing twenty-first-century aerial innovations with eighteenth-century conceptions of property law is bound to be problematic and a confrontation between state drone laws and the preemptive effect of federal aviation regulations is inevitable.

PROPERTY LAW AND TECHNOLOGY: WHERE OLD MEETS NEW

Thirty years ago, in his dissenting opinion in *Riley*, Justice William Brennan presented a hypothetical situation prophetic of modern drone operations and the limitations of property law:

> Imagine a helicopter capable of hovering just above an enclosed courtyard
> or patio without generating any noise, wind, or dust at all—and, for good
> measure, without posing any threat of injury. Suppose the police employed
> this miraculous tool to discover not only what crops people were growing
> in their greenhouses, but also what books they were reading and who their
> dinner guests were. Suppose, finally, that the FAA regulations remained
> unchanged, so that the police were undeniably "where they had a right
> to be." Would today's plurality continue to assert that "[t]he right of the
> people to be secure in their persons, houses, papers, and effects, against
> unreasonable searches and seizures" was not infringed by such surveillance?
>
> Yet that is the logical consequence of the plurality's rule that, so long
> as the police are where they have a right to be under air traffic regulations,
> the Fourth Amendment is offended only if the aerial surveillance inter-
> feres with the use of the backyard as a garden spot. Nor is there anything
> in the plurality's opinion to suggest that any different rule would apply
> were the police looking from their helicopter, not into the open curtilage,
> but through an open window into a room viewable only from the air.

In fact, today, drones have become the "miraculous tool" that Justice Brennan imagined. The law has remained unsettled as to where public or private operators "have a right to be" or who has the authority to say, however.

In addition, drone operations pose a complex problem beyond where to fly and who, among local, state, and federal officials, should regulate that flight. The equipment deployed on over-the-counter drones is incredibly invasive, including high-definition cameras and live-streaming imaging sensors. The law has yet to catch up with these advances on the ground even as the availability of "smart" devices become common and public attitudes about privacy (e.g., Facebook) change in comprehensive ways. The 2001 case of *Kyllo v. United States*, 533 U.S. 27 (2001), illustrates the technological challenge posed by the prospect of ubiquitous drone ownership and use.

In *Kyllo*, law enforcement aimed a thermal imager at a private home from a public street to detect heat linked to marijuana production. Writing for the majority, the late Justice Antonin Scalia wrote, "We think that by obtaining sense-enhancing technology any information regarding the interior of the home that could not otherwise have been obtained without physical 'intrusion into a constitutionally protected area,' constitutes a search—at least where (as here) the technology in question is not in general public use." Thus, Justice Scalia established a rule further entangling the concepts of technology-assisted searches and trespass: "[W]here the Government uses a device that is not in general public use to explore details of the home that would previously have been unknowable without a physical intrusion, the surveillance is a 'search" and is presumptively unreasonable without a warrant."

A plain reading of *Kyllo* would disallow the use of drones for Fourth Amendment purposes because flying sensors and cameras allow exploration of "details of the home that would previously have been unknowable without a physical intrusion." However, drones might satisfy the parameters of *Kyllo* insofar as they are increasingly "in general public use." *Kyllo* thus raises more questions than it answers, including: Are property rights enabling or disabling a socially useful technology? Is the innovation of unmanned aviation interfering with traditional property laws to such an extent that drones should be disallowed altogether? Or can the technology itself drive a solution and facilitate these concerns? For the moment, it appears that lawmakers and jurists are working toward the harm rather than working backward from problems (actual or perceived) to enduring solutions.

## CONCLUSION: FROM NIMBY TO NAMBY

Unmanned aerial vehicles give aviators of all backgrounds and intentions access to the airspace like never before. Correlatively, traditional conceptions of property law, including privacy rights, lag far behind innovations in aviation. While drones portend many social benefits, their operations also are creating unprecedented conflicts. "Not above my airspace" has replaced the traditional refrain "not in my backyard." Complicating matters is the fact that existing legal regimes appear ill-equipped to manage the anticipated exponential increase in drone ownership and use. For now, surface owners' airspace rights extend up to an altitude of four hundred or five hundred or one thousand feet in accordance with court opinions such as *Causby, Dow, Ciraolo,* and *Riley.* Meanwhile, the privacy of landowners is no longer protected by rigid rules against trespass under *Olmstead,* but instead by elastic analyses of subjective expectations, which, under *Katz,* ambiguously, does not reach airspace where operators "had a right to be." Taken together, these legal precedents appear to be outdated and confusing in the new era of unmanned aviation, neither fully protecting private property rights nor encouraging an important new industry fully.

That said, the common law is demonstrably adaptable if not trailblazing. Reconceptualizing property law to adapt to innovative uses of low-altitude airspace is possible when and if the relevant technology demonstrates safe and reliable operations in that space. Amazon, for example, has proposed segmenting and reserving airspace below five hundred feet for commercial drone operations in the following illustration, which carves out a special zone in the national airspace—between four hundred and five hundred feet above ground level—exclusively for drone operations (van Wagenen, 2015).

Alternatively, one scholar has called for exclusionary rules—new, technology-agnostic laws that give landowners definite rights to exclude drones (or anything else) from the airspace directly above their land, up to the navigable space line where the public highway for air travel begins (Rule, 2015). Regulators, meanwhile, seem to be moving in the direction of regulating all airspace from the soil up. While these approaches are as possible as they are partisan, they underscore how imperative democratic processes are to achieving a principled, negotiated arrangement between property ownership and drone use.

"Good fences make good neighbors," Robert Frost's poem "Mending Wall" tells of the role of boundaries. True, yesterday's two-dimensional physical fences are today's software-driven "geo-fences" restricting drones from flying into certain airspace. But in any case, in circumstances involving dramatic technological change, the best solution may be legislative, as courts (demonstrably) are and should be places of last resort on issues as practical as who—or what—can fly where.

## REFERENCES

Banner, S. (2008). *Who owns the sky: The struggle to control airspace from the Wright brothers on.* Cambridge, MA: Harvard University Press.
Brooks v. Patterson, 31 So. 2d 472 (1947).
California v. Ciraolo, 476 U.S. 207 (1986).
Causby v. United States, 328 U.S. 256 (1946).
Dow Chemical Co. v. United States, 476 U.S. 227 (1986).
Dysart v. City of St. Louis, 11 S.W. 2d 1045 (Mo. 1928).
Federal Aviation Administration. (2016). UAS Sightings Report. Retrieved from: www.faa.gov/uas/law_enforcement/uas_sighting_reports/.
Florida v. Riley, 448 U.S. 445 (1989).
Guille v. Swan, 19 Johns. 381 (N.Y. Sup. Ct. 1822).
Hesse v. Rath, 164 N.E. 342 (N.Y. App. 1928).
Hunt, R. H. (1948). Aviation and airports in Florida. *Florida Law Journal, 72,* 73.
Huerta v. Haughwout, 2016 WL 3919799 (D. Conn. 2016)

Katz v. United States, 389 U.S. 347 (1967).

Kyllo v. United States, 533 U.S. 27 (2001).

Madrigal, A. (2012). If I fly a UAV over my neighbor's house, is it trespassing? *The Atlantic*. Retrieved from: www.theatlantic.com/technology/archive/2012/10/if-i-fly-a-uav-over-my-neighbors-house-is-it-trespassing/263431/.

Olmstead v. United States, 277 U.S. 438 (1928).

Ravich, T. M. (2017). ACRP 11-01/Topic 08-03, Evolving Law on Airport Implications by Unmanned Aerial Systems.

———. (2017). Airports, Droneports, and the New Urban Airspace. *Fordham Urban Law Journal 44*, 587.

———. (2017). Commercial drone law: Digest of U.S. and global UAS rules, policies, and practices. American Bar Association.

———. (2015). Commercial drones and the Phantom Menace. *Journal of International Media and Entertainment Law, 5*, 175–215.

———. (2009). The integration of unmanned aerial vehicles into the national airspace. *North Dakota Law Review, 85*, 597–622.

Rule, T. A. (2015). Airspace in an age of drones. *Boston University Law Review, 95*, 155–208.

State v. Dade County, 27 So. 2d 283 (Fla. 1946).

Talanova, J. (2015). Drone slams into seating area at U.S. Open. Retrieved from: www.cnn.com/2015/09/04/us/us-open-tennis-drone-arrest/.

Van Wagenen, J. (2015). Amazon proposes new ATM model for commercial UAS Ops. Retrieved from: www.aviationtoday.com/av/topstories/Amazon-Proposes-New-ATM-Model-for-Commercial-UAS-Ops_85676.html#.VyemqfkrJhF.

# CONCLUSION
## The Future of Property

GREGORY R. PETERSON, ANN E. DAVIS, AND STACI M. ZAVATTARO,

We started this volume with stories of how property rights and images of property pervade our world. We hope each chapter gave readers ideas for more questions related to property in contemporary governance, as many of today's most salient policy disputes have some kind of property element. We see women calling for lawmakers to "keep your hands off my body" when it comes to reproductive rights. Scientists rely on commons arguments when discussing the effects of global warming. Songwriters want to protect their intellectual property in a world where streaming music reigns. Celebrities protect their brands and will sue when they perceive someone tarnishing that image. These are all, at the core, debates about property.

Taking a governance lens as we have done in this volume shows the importance of property in this way. We cannot and should not escape its importance, but we ask: Where do we go from here? We could think of worlds in the future where technology has shifted so radically that we now need a whole new definition of property. The sharing economy already is slowly taking us down that path. On the other hand, will some things stay the same? It is sometimes tempting to think that, despite the historical durability of property as an institution, the future will be different, and that as human society grows more prosperous, the need for or desirability of property institutions will simply wither away. Such was the vision of Karl Marx, who saw in the communalism of the early church and the radical practices of the Paris Commune a precursor of the final stage of society yet to come, a stage where the notion of property itself becomes obsolete, transcended by the social and technological advances of those who follow us. Such futures, however, are difficult to imagine, and even the boldest science fiction often recognizes limits to the human capacity to share. At our cores, we will probably remain self-maximizing individuals who will cling to the notion of what's mine is mine. Yet we also need to recognize the importance of community. Seeing property through a governing lens can begin to alter those conversations and perhaps, one day, policies and practices.

So we ask again: Where do we go from here? We break down our answer in philosophical and practical terms.

## PHILOSOPHICAL PROBLEMS RELATED TO PROPERTY'S EVOLUTION

Central to the idea of this volume is the claim that no one discipline "owns" property as a subject matter. Property is central to law and economics, but the underpinnings of property are ultimately philosophical, and property in its distribution, institutionalization, and protection is inevitably political. Property, both the concept and the reality, has a history. It also has a future that is as unpredictable as the technological and social changes that impact the development of new property regimes. Still, what is the payoff of an interdisciplinary approach? How do contributions from other disciplines affect one's own, and how should interdisciplinary reflection on property influence existing or future property regimes? Who benefits? Who *should* benefit?

One way to think about this question is to frame it in terms of a dilemma. On the one hand, we might be inclined to think property is in some sense a natural phenomenon, and while culture inevitably has its role, some might still conclude that there are economic laws that govern the emergence of property regimes and their resultant patterns, much as economists sometimes think of the laws of supply and demand as natural laws, the violation of which can only be temporary until the realities undergirding human nature and social structures reassert themselves. If property is natural in this sense, then it might seem that academic study of property at best serves to make apparent what these natural laws are. Given that these laws are natural, there is little we can do to change them. At best, we can admire them and perhaps take advantage of our knowledge of them from time to time.

On the other hand, we might be moved to think that property is not a natural phenomenon at all but rather a mere construction, varying from culture to culture and time to time with no particular rhyme or reason. On this account, there are no "laws of property" that hold across time and space, only particular instances of notions of property across cultures, the particularity of which renders generalization impossible. Any academic study of property is, therefore, to paraphrase Ernest Rutherford, merely an exercise in stamp collecting (Birks, 1962). With such accounts, it is frequently thought that norms are also thoroughly culture-bound, so the academic study of property amounts to nothing more than admiring the stamps we are able to collect.

At the time of this writing, the Federal Communications Commission (FCC) is weighing whether to allow marketers to leave messages in cellphone voice boxes without the phone ringing or providing cellphone owners the opportunity to block the messages. The issue is at heart a property issue: Who owns a cellphone voice box, and what does it mean to own a "voice box" that is not in any sense a physical box but a piece of software, the location of which is, in a sense, inside your phone, but in reality an abstraction describing a network of data connections, the physical location of which may change regularly? To what extent do appeals to property and ownership in such a context depend on some "natural" basis of property, and to what extent is property in such a context a "mere" construct? Thinking through the classic nature/construct divide, we submit, clarifies the significance of the chapters contributed to this volume, and it emphasizes as well our interdisciplinary approach to property.

## PROPERTY AS NATURAL

Although the idea that property is natural taps into a deep tradition of thought within Western philosophy, the claim is hardly one of univocal agreement, and one only has to look to the writings of idealist philosophers such as G. W. F. Hegel and utilitarians such as J. S. Mill to appreciate the diverse ways that property regimes can be justified (cf. Ryan, 1987; Waldron, 1988). This difficulty is compounded by the fact that the term *natural* is considerably ambiguous, and modern meanings of natural differ in important respects from premodern ones, a distinctive difference lying in the modernist's rejection of any role for teleology in naturalistic explanation (Brooke, 2009). That being said, the natural law tradition of property that culminates in Locke's *Second Treatise* has proven to be deeply influential, and remains the first touchstone for contemporary justifications of property.

Roots for the appeal to nature can be found in Aristotle's *Politics*, Book I of which begins with, by the standards of the day, a naturalistic account of the origin of society that includes property as an integral element in familial and eventually social life. For Aristotle, the claims for property emerge as a result of household function, the tools we own serving as crucial instruments for the sustaining of life. Notoriously, Aristotle's account of property includes a defense of slavery, based, it would seem, on the capacity to own, for the slave is not "by nature his own but another's man ... and he may be said to be another's man who, being a human being, is also a possession. And a possession may be defined as instrument of action, separable from the possessor" (*Politics* I.4). Yet, not all forms of property ownership are legitimate, and Aristotle later condemns the practice of usury as an improper sort of activity (*Politics* I.10).

Although Aristotle's comments on property are comparatively brief, they are instructive both for what they claim and the conception of nature that they presuppose, ultimately linked to human functioning and thus to human flourishing. Yet while Aristotle's own account has considerable influence, it is the broadly Christian background that sets the backdrop for the early modern accounts of property. Thus, Hugo Grotius's seventeenth-century account of property and ownership, developed in *De Jure Belli* and *Mare Liberum*, begins with the theological claim that the Earth as a whole is the common property of humankind, bequeathed to us through common descent from the biblical Adam. Human beings jointly have a right to use nature for their own purposes, just as the theatergoer has a right to any of the seats still empty in the theater (*De Jure Belli*, II.2.II.1). The further claim to private property is based on agreement, subject to a proviso of absolute necessity for those who fall upon hard times (II.2.VI.2–4). On these grounds, Grotius endorsed private property on land but not at sea, opposing the British claim to ownership of the Atlantic, a matter of bitter dispute at that time with the Dutch.

Although Grotius famously suggested that the principles of natural law held even if the "wicked" assumption that God did not exist turned out to be true, the theological backdrop to the debate continued to be influential, undergirding the more optimistic tone of Locke's own version of the social contract. For Locke, the claim of Grotius and also Pufendorf (1991) that the Earth itself is common property by natural law but that private property was a matter of agreement and thus convention posed a problem, for if private property were a matter of convention, the convention could easily be changed by a monarch to benefit the crown at the expense of the people. But if private property itself is grounded in natural law, how does one justify the transition from theologically gifted common property to private? Locke's famous solution was to appeal to labor. If I own anything, I own my own actions, and when I mix my actions with the soil, such mixing transforms material to property. What makes a parcel of land *mine* is the effort I put into cultivating it and making it productive, with the implication that failure to cultivate deprives one of the ownership claim. Locke included further provisos: ownership was contingent on others having "enough and as good" left for others, and wasting one's resources—allowing one's stockpile of acorns to rot—similarly places limits on an ownership claim. For Locke, then, the claim to private property is grounded in natural law, and any effort to deprive an individual of property rightly earned by a monarch or any other party is morally illegitimate.

Although Locke's account has been deeply influential, the particular arguments he used to justify private property remain much debated. While both Grotius and Locke could presuppose a theological framework for their work, such presuppositions are no longer widely shared, and even those deeply indebted to Locke's general claims have doubts about the specifics of his labor theory (Nozick, 1974; Waldron, 1988). Further, describing such arguments as appeals based in "nature" or what is "natural" seems by itself to do little work. For Aristotle, nature was teleological, and so it might be thought to make sense within the confines of his framework that slaves be considered property since it is their "nature" to be so. But whatever vestige of teleology was still present in Grotius's day was largely gone by Locke's time, and it is even less present now. If nature is no longer conceived to be purposeful in the way that the ancients supposed, to what extent does it matter that property is in some sense "natural," and what does it even mean to make such a claim?

While contemporary philosophers have largely abandoned traditional appeals to natural law as a ground for property rights, the question of whether or not our conceptions of property are in some sense natural has shifted to the social and natural sciences. Harold Demsetz's (1967) "Towards a Theory of Property Rights" is revealing in this respect. Demsetz argues that private property emerges when the benefits of internalizing costly externalities outweighs the costs of doing so, and he appeals to then-available historical narratives of the evolution of property rights among Native Americans to make his case. Drawing in particular on Eleanor Leacock's *The Montagnes "Hunting Territory" and the Fur Trade*, Demsetz argues that, in the case of Native American communities impacted by the trade, we can see the transition from communally oriented property rights to privately oriented ones as the economic value of beaver pelts drove attention to the boundaries of hunting territory. Prior to the advent of the fur trade, overhunting of beavers was a real but relatively minor issue, an externality that could be ignored. But this ceased to be the case once Europeans arrived with their insatiable demand for fur, and the shift to a private property regime, according to Demsetz, serves communal interests as well, arguing that the privatization of property is the more efficient solution to externalities than that provided by communal property arrangements.

Demsetz's story is not quite one of natural law—history, culture, and contingency all play important roles, but his line of reasoning is very much in the tradition of Adam Smith and later neoclassical economics. On such an account, there may be no gene or set of genes that prime us to make private ownership claims, but the basic principles of economics joined with the assumption of human self-interest—*homo economicus*—necessarily lead to the institution of private property as a means of internalizing the costly externalities that inevitably arise as humankind populates the planet.

The neoclassical economist's assumption of human self-interest as a sole motivator in the economic sphere, let alone in life more generally, has since fallen on hard times (Camerer & Fehr, 2006; Henrich et al., 2004; Kahneman, 2011), but the search for some deeper, natural grounding of an instinct for property rights has persisted. Biologists observe the wide range of property-related behaviors that occur among nonhuman animals. Marking and defense of territory is a common behavior, especially among mammalian predators, and a wide range of animals, from termites to beavers to bower birds, create artifacts designed for their (largely) exclusive use. Among our closest evolutionary relatives, chimpanzees make and use tools, although they do not seem to consider these as property subject to exclusive use. Food sharing among chimps is extremely rare, occurring only in the aftermath of hunts of monkeys that provide a protein-rich meal for the group. Chimpanzees can be trained to barter tokens for goods, including desired tools with which to procure food, but such behavior seems largely confined to the laboratory and is absent in the wild (Brosnan, Grady, Lambeth, Schapiro, & Beran, 2008; Savage-Rumbaugh, Rumbaugh, & Boysen, 1978). Reciprocity as a behavior, however, is more widespread, and primates and monkeys both develop dense grooming networks based on mutual benefit (Cheney & Seyfarth, 1992).

A common strategy in psychology is to study the behavior of children on the assumption that if a behavior is primarily the result of nature rather than culture, we should find it at early stages of development before culture can have a significant impact. Fasig and colleagues (2000) found that children as young as eighteen months could make self-versus-other ownership distinctions, while Friedman and Neary (2008) found that two-year-olds readily attributed ownership based on who first possessed an object. A few studies have also examined Locke's labor theory. Beggan and Brown (1993) found that if forced to choose between ownership claims of an original owner and someone who subsequently put creative labor into the object, the majority of both adults and children, in this case fifteen- and ten-year-olds, opted in favor of first possession. In three- to four-year-olds, however, creative labor appears to make the greater claim, with a majority prioritizing creative labor over first possession (Kanngiesser, Gjersoe, & Hood, 2010).

A distinctive line of reasoning concerns the endowment effect, the phenomenon of people typically placing greater value on objects of use if they are in their possession rather than what they would normally be willing to purchase them for. First observed by Richard Thaler (1980), Daniel Kahneman and colleagues (1990) performed a now-classic experiment in which subjects valued a new coffee mug differently depending on whether they were initially given the mug and offered the opportunity to sell it as opposed to being given the opportunity to buy it. Importantly, the endowment effect does not seem to be a mere laboratory artifact, and Kahneman and colleagues hypothesized that it could be understood as a form of loss aversion that explains market phenomena such as the reluctance of struggling homeowners to sell their home at a loss. The endowment effect might be understood as a mere and perhaps unfortunate psychological quirk, but it is plausible to think that it is linked to ownership and an intuitive possessiveness over things owned. This line of reasoning has been pursued by Huck et al. (2005), who have developed a mathematical model showing that the endowment effect may be an evolutionarily advantageous trait, since individuals who emotionally overvalue their possessions would have a bargaining advantage over those who don't (see also Frank, 1988). Thus, our intuitions regarding property and ownership might not be merely a matter of cultural happenstance but the result of prolonged evolutionary pressures that have shaped our behavioral proclivities in subtle but strong ways.

While these science-based arguments have a certain plausibility, they also have important limits. Although the early presence of behavioral biases in young children is consistent with the claim that the behaviors in question are the primary result of biological factors, the argument is far from conclusive in the absence of genetic evidence, especially when the sample comes exclusively from children raised in Western cultures. This problem is more apparent in the much more extensive literature on the endowment effect, and there we find that, while the endowment effect does appear in children and not only adults (Harbaugh, Krause, & Vesterlund, 2001), evidence indicates that it is also subject to cultural variability. Among the Hadza of Kenya, those not exposed to Western culture do not display the endowment effect in contrast to those who have been so exposed (Apicella, 2014), and Maddox et al. (2010) have shown that the effect is smaller in Asians than it is among Westerners (see also Morewedge & Giblin, 2015 for a review).

The problems facing traditional natural law arguments for property rights and the ambivalent evidence from the sciences do not conclusively establish that property is not "natural," whatever we may mean by that term. It is possible that stronger philosophical arguments may be found or more persuasive scientific evidence may be discovered. But these problems do suggest that, however we think of property, it is doubtful that we can explain or justify particular conceptions of property merely by an appeal to nature. Social construction of some sort would seem to be involved.

## PRACTICAL PROBLEMS RELATED TO PROPERTY'S EVOLUTION

It is sometimes thought that social construction forms a sort of double opposite to claims based on nature. Not only does the fact that something is constructed imply (so it is argued) that the something in question is not natural (and presumably is therefore artificial in some sense), but in virtue of its being constructed it is also understood to be therefore unreal. Deconstructionist archaeologies are commonly thought to have this aim: if one can show that X is the result of some historical process, one can show that X is "merely" a construct emerging out of the social conditions of a particular place and time, and since only what is natural is real, if it turns out that something is a construction (and therefore not natural), it must therefore be unreal as well. One finds this line of argument sometimes in analyses of both race and gender, and some conclude from the arguments supporting the claim that because race or gender are not the result of our biological natures, they should therefore be understood to be mere constructs with no genuine ontological status (on race, cf. Appiah, 1995, 1996; James, 2017; Zack, 1993, 2002; for gender, see Bach, 2012; Mikkola, 2017). Following this line of reasoning, if it is established that property is not in some sense natural, we therefore must conclude that property is a constructed fiction.

Such arguments are likely too simple in the cases of both gender and race, and they are too simple in the case of property as well. Problematic here is both the automatic contrast between nature and construct and the identification of construction and fiction. While some constructs are fictions not found in nature, not all constructs are, and to the extent that it makes sense to talk about natural objects, whether they be quarks or rivers or mountaintops, it also makes sense to speak of how we construct our concepts to talk about them. That we have constructed a concept of quarks does not imply that there are no quarks, and more careful authors are aware of these issues. In her history of the concept of the modern fact, for instance, Poovey (1998) charts the rise of the concept and its links both to the rise of early statistical data and the use of such data for political ends. On Poovey's analysis, the modern fact has both a beginning and an end, but she is also careful to distinguish the historical analysis of concept from the ontological and epistemological assessments to be made both by us and by our historical predecessors.

However we regard the relation of natural objects and conceptual constructions, it is clear that our constructions exist only because we have constructed them, and it is a further question as to how we regard the reality of such constructions. These include what are commonly labeled social facts, and such social facts are peculiar in both their seeming dependence on our belief in them and the very real causal impact they wield because of such joint belief. Money is the classic example, since the power and influence of money is both indisputable and dependent on our collective belief in its power and influence. If our belief in the power of money fades, as was the case with currencies of the American Confederacy or the Weimar Republic, the power of the currency fades with it. The phenomenon of property more generally also appears to share this feature: even if there exists some biological predisposition for an endowment effect, it would only be manifest if I asserted my ownership in a social context, and my assertion would only have impact if I could persuade or coerce others to assent to my assertion.

Searle's (2010) account of social ontology may prove particularly helpful here, as Searle provides a way of thinking about social constructions that affirms their social reality rather than dismissing them as mere fictions. For Searle, social objects are the result of speech acts, specifically a form of speech acts that he refers to as status function declarations. In short, property exists because we jointly declare it exists, and the jointness of the declaration is an important feature of the ontological status of property, explaining its causal force and persistence beyond the action of any single individual. Searle perspicaciously speaks of such social facts as institutional facts, and this is an important point to recognize for two reasons. First, institutions are ways that people and societies organize themselves, and to speak of property as an institution is not simply to speak of my particular claim to land that I have mixed my labor with, but a way that I organize myself and am indeed compelled to organize myself with respect to other members of my society. Second, institutions are both dynamic and culturally specific, and the continued existence of an institution is dependent on the credence that a community gives to it, while a shift in institutions can be understood, in Searle's terms, as a shift in collective intentionality.

Searle provides, therefore, an alternative to the mere constructionist perspective that moves swiftly from the identification of X as construction to the conclusion that X is a fiction. Social constructions are real and have causal effects precisely because of the joint intentionality supporting them. That being said, Searle's account has issues, and we note here three. First, as Searle portrays the matter, institutions as created by our status function declarations are heavily dependent on Searle's own very specific account of free choice and rationality, and this creates a brittleness to his social ontology that need not be the case (Searle, 1992). Second, Searle's account of the moral dimensions of societal disagreement and change appears incomplete and on some points open to challenge. On Searle's account, moral frameworks are themselves institutions, deriving their power from the web of status function declarations that constitute society.

For Searle, many of these form a tacit background, providing desire-independent reasons for action. Raised in a society constituted by thick obligations to kin, Searle's framework entails that, once I know that someone is a close relative, I have obligations to that person independent of my desires to help or not. Given that status function declarations are societally dependent, this would seem to imply a strong moral relativism to his account, but Searle affirms a grounding of at least negative rights, constituted as the sort of freedoms from interference enshrined in U.S. Bill of Rights and other early modern documents, in an account of human nature that appears independent of any particular societal arrangement (Searle, 2010). Searle's own brief account leaves many questions open, and his dismissal of those rights traditionally classed as positive rights, such as a right to education or access to health care, has important implications for how we think of the many difficult questions at the frontier of property rights, environment, and technology, among other areas.

The issue of moral disagreement and competing institutions indicates a third problem with Searle's framework, in that it does not provide much insight more generally as to how and why the joint intentionality underlying institutions changes or how we regard the ontology of institutions during that time of change. How many people, after all, are needed for joint intentionality, and how does such joint intentionality spread across both time and place? Searle may legitimately indicate that these are the sorts of questions with which the social sciences are best equipped to deal, but we note here the relevance of Hacking's (1999; 2007) understanding of social constructions as a form of kind-making subject to feedback loops. As Hacking argues, diagnoses such as autism are partly rooted in biology, but the conceptualization of autism has been subject to change over time as the label has become claimed by different constituencies, including those who have been so diagnosed. Hacking's insight has application beyond the domain of psychological diagnosis, and it would not be surprising if we could understand the evolution of property regimes in part by the dynamics of such feedback loops.

## GOVERNANCE, CAPABILITIES, AND PROPERTY AS INSTITUTION

The present volume does not aim to solve issues of the relation of nature and construct, but we believe that reflecting on the issues surrounding traditional ways of thinking about the nature/construct relation illuminates some of the significance of the chapters contributing to this volume. Here, we suggest, the concept of governance plays a key role. Although the title of the volume includes the term *governance*, the reader may note that most authors do not use the term explicitly, and this reflects the interdisciplinary character of the volume. It may also reflect something intrinsic to the notion of property itself. In the Lockean tradition, at least, governance and property are deeply intertwined, and for Locke the primary purpose of the state is to protect and defend the property rights of its citizens. A traditional volume on political science and property would likely include governance as a key term, and chapters of such a volume would no doubt proceed with in-depth analyses of the governmental structures and procedures that structure the legal frameworks governing property. And while this volume certainly includes its share of that sort of analysis, implicit in the volume is a broader approach to governance, one that understands governance not only in terms of formal institutions but in terms of informal ones as well. Certainly, property regimes are in no small part the result of formal governance institutions, and the fate of climate change and the future of drone technology, for instance, hinge on how formal institutions governing these domains and their associated property rights evolve.

Property rights are, arguably, embedded in networks of informal institutions, and it is often these informal institutions or changes therein that drive the change in the formal institutions. One can see this in current and ongoing conflicts over issues of piracy and intellectual property rights, and the historical contributions to this volume hint, and sometimes more than hint, at the role such informal institutions play. Respect for property is not merely a matter of formal law; understanding property regimes as the result of both formal and informal institutions of governance can help us understand how and when property regimes change, as well as determining what sorts of property regimes are viable and what sorts are not.

While many property regimes are viable, not all of them are just, and both formal and informal forms of governance inevitably embody—institutionalize—particular forms of (in)justice. In the introduction to this volume, we referred to the capabilities approach as one way of thinking about questions of justice in relation to property, and Peterson notes in his contribution to this volume the productive role that the capabilities approach can play in thinking about intellectual property specifically. The capabilities approach arguably provides a way of thinking about the fairness of property regimes without either simplistically reducing to a Lockean (or Grotian) natural law on the one hand or a mere constructionism on the other. On the capabilities approach, property rights are measured in terms of their ability to contribute to our ability to flourish and live well, and Nussbaum argues that the contribution is significant enough to consider property rights as an element of those basic capabilities for which we all, governments included, have societal responsibilities. Nussbaum is also careful to note that the particular manifestations of the capabilities to be protected may vary from culture to culture, and so we might expect the particularity of justifiable property rights to vary over time and geography.

Indeed, one of the central challenges of the twenty-first century concerns how best to translate property rights in an ever-increasingly globalized economy across vastly different cultures with their own distinctive governmental arrangements and developmental status (cf., e.g., Hassoun, 2012; James 2012). In this respect, Zavattaro's engagement with property as metaphor is especially perspicacious, given that any traditional conception of property we start with must inevitably be extended to meet the demands of the twenty-first century.

The points we make here would require fuller treatment—indeed, a full book in itself—to work out. We raise them here not because we think the arguments to be without weakness or the conclusions to be indubitably true, but because we believe reflection on these points underlies a core theme of this volume, which is the importance of maintaining and developing inclusive, interdisciplinary approaches to property that help us to not only understand the past but also to plan well for the future. Too often, we think of property as primarily a branch of a specific discipline such as legal studies or, perhaps, economics or political science. The study of property, a concept with such everyday use that we are tempted to think it easy to understand and employ, is surprisingly subtle, and its history is surprisingly complex. Property is deeply intertwined with law across cultures, but law has a history, and the history of property law is as complex as the cultures from which it arises.

The historical chapters by Davis, Brown, Fraley, and Leuchter reveal this complexity but also reveal patterns in the ways in which property regimes emerge as the result of both informal and formal modes of governance, patterns that are to some degree intelligible to us today. Such scholarship requires expertise in both history and law, and often other fields such as economics as well. Among other things, understanding the history well, tracing the in-depth particularities, and not simply gliding over the centuries with flaccid generalizations is important to see how dichotomies that seek to neatly separate what is nature and what is a construct break down.

The contributions in this volume that engage the intersection of property, environment, and technology drive home this point even more forcefully. The natural world of Locke and Grotius was static in conception, land once owned could always be owned because it would always be there, unchanged, and it was thought that real property constituted by land had a permanence that later financial instruments lacked. Yet our modern understanding of the Earth is anything but static: Earth and sea and stream are all continuously changing, ebbing and flowing, and their ebb and flow are not independent of the property institutions we construct, which causally impact even the Earth's climate as a whole. Especially in the case of the environment, what is natural is deeply intertwined with our constructions that alter the land in innumerable ways. Understanding this well requires even further expertise in biology, geology, and ecology, among other disciplines, and understanding the further dimensions involved in technological innovation such as drones requires further expertise yet. In this respect, the contributions in this volume by Richards, Consalo, McGuire, and Ravich are all deeply important, not only for what they reveal, but also for making us appreciate what is yet left out.

Indeed, what is left out of this volume points even more to the importance of interdisciplinary approaches to property. While Peterson's chapter on intellectual property reveals the extent to which concerns about justice must draw not only on the best of contemporary philosophy but also deep knowledge of dimensions of computer technology, biotechnology, and international trade, Zavattaro's writing illustrates the way that cognitive linguistics, in this case the work of Lakoff and Johnson, influences our understanding of the metaphorical domain of property both in the theory and practice of place branding, illustrating along the way how fields such as public administration also have a role to play in our understanding of property and its relation not only to abstract concepts of rights but more intimate conceptions of identity. Both chapters indicate the richness of fields that could be included in a productive discussion and exchange.

We do not consider this a weakness of the current volume—all books must end—but rather an invitation to further rich discourse, intellectual cross-fertilization, and the testing of ideas across disciplines, perhaps even contributing to the development of new ones.

## FINAL COMMENTS

Who owns the "voice box" that visually sits as an icon on every smart phone? Does ownership as a concept even make sense to describe something that is not simply in one location—"in your smartphone"—but whose reality is smeared across telecommunications networks? And yet, we think of smartphones as *our* smartphones, and the messages that are "stored" on our smartphones as *our* messages. Issues of property and ownership are not going away, and if anything the issues will continue to press on us, sometimes with increasing urgency, in the face of ongoing technological, environmental, and societal change. But as Pasteur famously observed, fortune favors the prepared mind. We cannot fully predict the changes that will impact the property regimes of the future, but we can prepare for them, and the tools we have to do so are better now than at any previous time. It is our hope that the current volume has in its own small way contributed to that effort, and that the contributions here represent not an ending of conversations once held on the banks of the Hudson but rather a beginning of many conversations with partners yet to be discovered.

## REFERENCES

Apicella, C. L., Azevedo, E. M., Christakis, N. A., & Fowler, J. H. (2014). Evolutionary origins of the endowment effect: Evidence from hunter-gatherers. *American Economic Review, 104(6)*, 1793–1805.

Appiah, K. A. (1995). The uncompleted argument: DuBois and the illusion of race. In L. Bell & D. Blumenfeld (Eds.), *Overcoming racism and sexism*. Lanham, MD: Rowman & Littlefield.

———. (1996). Race, culture, identity: Misunderstood connections. In K. A. Appiah & A. Gutmann (Eds.), *Color Conscious*. Princeton, NJ: Princeton University Press.

Aristotle. (1998). *Politics*. (E. Barker & R. F. Stalley, Trans.). New York, NY: Oxford University Press.

Bach, T. (2012). Gender is a natural kind with a historical essence. *Ethics, 122(1)*, 231–272.

Beggan, J. K., & Brown, E. M. (1993). Association as a psychological justification of ownership. *The Journal of Psychology, 128*, 365–380.

Birks, J. B. (1962). *Rutherford at Manchester*. New York, NY: W. A. Benjamin.

Brooke, J. H. (2009). Should the word nature be eliminated? In J. Proctor (Ed.), *Envisioning nature, science, & religion* (pp. 312–336). West Conshohocken, PA: Templeton Press.

Brosnan, S. F., Grady, M. F., Lambeth, S. P., Schapiro, S. J., & Beran, M. J. (2008). Chimpanzee autarky. *PLoS ONE, 3(1)*, e1518. https://doi.org/10.1371/journal.pone.0001518.

Camerer, C. F., & Fehr, E. (2006). When does "economic man" dominate social behavior? *Science, 311*, 47–52. https://doi.org/10.1126/science.1110600.

Cheney, D. L., & Seyfarth, R. M. (1992). *How monkeys see the world: Inside the mind of another species*. Chicago, IL: University of Chicago Press.

Demsetz, H. (1967). Toward a theory of property rights. *The American Economic Review, 57(2)*, 347–359.

Fasig, L. G. (2000). Toddlers' understanding of ownership: Implications for self-concept development. *Social Development, 9(3)*, 370–382.

Frank, R. H. (1988). *Passions within reason: The strategic role of the emotions*. New York, NY: Norton.

Friedman, O., & Neary, K. R. (2008). Determining who owns what: Do children infer ownership from first possession? *Cognition, 107*, 829–849.

Grotius, H. (2004). *The free sea*. (R. Hakluyt, Trans.). Indianapolis, IN: Liberty Fund.

———. (2005). *The rights of war and peace*. (R. Tuck, Ed.). Indianapolis, IN: Liberty Fund.

Hacking, I. (1999). *The social construction of what?* Cambridge, MA: Harvard University Press.

———. (2007). Kinds of people: Moving targets. *Proceedings of the British Academy, 151*, 285–318.

Harbaugh, W. T., Krause, K., & Vesterlund, L. (2001). Are adults better behaved than children? Age, experience, and the endowment effect. *Economic Letters, 70*, 175–181.

Hassoun, N. (2012). *Globalization and global justice: Shrinking distance, expanding obligations*. New York, NY: Cambridge University Press.

Henrich, J. P., Boyd, R., Bowles, S., Camerer, C., Fehr, E., & Gintis, H. (2004). *Foundations of human sociality: Economic experiments and ethnographic evidence from fifteen small-scale societies*. New York, NY: Oxford University Press.

Huck, S., Kirchsteiger, G., & Oechssler, J. (2005). Learning to like what you have ? Explaining the endowment effect. *The Economic Journal, 115(505)*, 689–702. https://doi.org/10.1111/j.1468-0297.2005.01015.x.

James, A. (2012). *Fairness in practice: A social contract for a global economy*. New York, NY: Oxford University Press.

James, M. (n.d.). Race. *The Stanford encyclopedia of philosophy* (Spring 2017 Edition). Retrieved from <https://plato.stanford.edu/archives/spr2017/entries/race/>.

Kahneman, D. (2011). *Thinking, fast and slow*. New York, NY: Farrar, Straus, and Giroux.

Kahneman, D., Knetsch, J. L., & Thaler, R. H. (1990). Experimental tests of the endowment effect and the Coase theorem. *Journal of Political Economy, 98(6)*, 1325–1348.

Kanngiesser, P., Gjersoe, N., & Hood, B. M. (2010). The effect of creative labor on property-ownership transfer by preschool children and adults. *Psychological Science, 21(9)*, 1236–1241.

Locke, J. (2003). *Two treatises of government and A letter concerning toleration*. New Haven, CT: Yale University Press.

Maddux, W. W., Yang, H., Falk, C., Adam, H., Adair, W., Endo, Y., . . . Heine, S. J. (2010). For whom is parting with possessions more painful?: Cultural differences in the endowment fffect. *Psychological Science, 21(12)*, 1910–1917.

Mikkola, M. (n.d.). Feminist perspectives on sex and gender. In E. N. Zalta (Ed.), *The Stanford encyclopedia of philosophy* (Summer 2017 Edition). Retrieved from https://plato.stanford.edu/archives/sum2017/entries/feminism-gender/.

Morewedge, C. K., & Giblin, C. E. (2015). Explanations of the endowment effect: An integrative review. *Trends in Cognitive Sciences, 19(6)*, 339–348.

Nozick, R. (1974). *Anarchy, state, and utopia*. New York, NY: Basic Books.

Poovey, M. (1998). *A history of the modern fact: Problems of knowledge in the sciences of wealth and society*. Chicago, IL: University of Chicago Press.

Pufendorf, S. (1991). *On the duty of man and citizen according to natural law*. Cambridge, UK: Cambridge University Press.

Ryan, A. (1987). *Property*. Minneapolis, MN: University of Minnesota Press.

Savage-Rumbaugh, E. S., Rumbaugh, D. M., & Boysen, S. (1978). Linguistically mediated tool use and exchange by chimpanzees. *Behavioral and Brain Sciences*, *1(4)*, 539–554.

Searle, J. (1992). *The rediscovery of the mind*. Cambridge, MA: MIT Press.

———. (2010). *Making the social world: The structure of human civilization*. New York, NY: Oxford University Press.

Thaler, R. H. (1980). Toward a positive theory of consumer choice. *Journal of Economic Behavior and Organization*, *1*, 39–60.

Waldron, J. (1988). *The right to private property*. New York, NY: Clarendon Press.

Zack, N. (1993). *Race and mixed race*. Philadelphia, PA: Temple University Press.

———. (2002). *Philosophy of science and race*. New York: Routledge.

# CONTRIBUTORS

R. Ben Brown is a lecturer with a continuing appointment in the legal studies program at the University of California Berkeley where he is also an affiliated scholar with the Center for the Study of Law and Society. His research and teaching interests are United States legal and Constitutional history and the history of property law. He holds a JD from Vanderbilt University and a PhD from the University of Michigan. His dissertation examined the ending of the common property regime of open range grazing in the southern United States in the nineteenth century. His latest article published in *Radical History Review* was "Free Pigs and Free Men: Closing the Southern Range and the American Property Tradition."

Karen Z. Consalo, Esquire, is a lecturer in the department of legal studies at the University of Central Florida. In addition to teaching at UCF, Professor Consalo serves as an adjunct professor of law at Barry University School of Law and teaches in the environmental studies department of Rollins College. She has numerous publications in law reviews, journals, and professional publications, including the *Florida Bar Journal*, the *Florida Planning Magazine, Stetson Law Review, Florida State Journal of Land Use and Environmental Law*, and the *Barry University School of Law Environmental and Earth Law Journal*. Since 2000, Professor Consalo has worked as an attorney in both the private and public sector and is currently the managing partner of The Consalo Law Firm, P.A. She advocates for smart urban and suburban development.

Ann E. Davis is associate professor of economics at Marist College in Poughkeepsie, N.Y. She has served as chair of the department of economics, accounting, and finance, and was the founding director of the Marist College Bureau of Economic Research. She earned her BA in American studies at Barnard College in New York City, MA in economics at Northeastern University in Boston, and PhD in economics at Boston College. She has also published in a range of academic journals on topics in economic history and methodology, such as the *Journal of Economic Issues, Science and Society*, the *Review for Radical Political Economics*, and the *Cambridge Journal of Economics*, as well as numerous book chapters. She served as director of the National Endowment for Humanities Summer Institute "Meanings of Property," in June 2014. Her recent books include *The Evolution of the Property Relation: Understanding Paradigms, Debates, and Prospects*, and *Money as a Social Institution*.

Jill Fraley is an associate professor of law and director of the Center for Law & History at Washington and Lee University School of Law. She writes and teaches in the areas of property, environmental law, and legal history. Her work on the nature of possession has been relied upon by the distinguished treatise, *Thompson on Real Property*. She is currently completing a book on waste property and the development of boundaries in colonial America. She was a Fulbright Scholar in Ireland at Trinity College where she researched early Irish property law and the English colonization. She is a member of the board of the Appalachian Citizens Law Center, where her research contributes to both environmental and property cases. Ms. Fraley received her BA in history from Yale University, her JD from Duke Law School, and her LLM and JSD from Yale Law School, where she focused on American legal history.

Tyson Leuchter is an Honorary Research Fellow at Birkbeck, University of London. He received his doctorate from the History department at the University of Chicago in 2017. His dissertation, "The Most Sacred Right of All: Property, Public Debt, and Law at the Paris Stock Exchange, 1793-1825," examines one of the key institutions of nineteenth-century financial capitalism. It focuses on political discourse, theoretical and legal debates about the moral rightness and economic utility of public debts and futures contracts, and the legal travails of the Paris stockbrokers; Leuchter argues that the recurring disputes over the Exchange were central to the twin development of capitalism and modern law in France. His work has previously appeared in *Modern Intellectual History* and *La Révolution Française*. Currently, he is preparing a book manuscript, drawn from his dissertation.

Chad J. McGuire is an associate professor of environmental policy at the University of Massachusetts, Dartmouth, where he chairs the department of public policy and coordinates the graduate program in environmental policy. His work is focused on understanding environmental issues at the intersection of natural and human dimensions. Professor McGuire has worked on legal and policy issues related to fisheries, land use, and climate change. His recent work looks at how existing government policies influence public perceptions of risk. He is the author of three books and author or co-author of more than thirty academic articles and book chapters. He holds a BSc and MSc in environmental science from the University of Massachusetts, a JD from Thomas Jefferson School of Law, and a LLM from the University of San Diego School of Law specializing in environmental law.

Gregory R. Peterson is professor of philosophy and religion and director of the ethics lab at South Dakota State University. Author or coauthor of more than fifty journal articles and book chapters, he is also the author or editor of several books, most recently *Habits in Mind* (2017). While his early research focused on philosophy of religion, philosophy of science, and philosophical issues in cognitive science and the biology of cooperation, his current research focuses on virtue theory, political philosophy, applied ethics, experimental ethics, and democratization. In addition to his many publications, Dr. Peterson is the recipient of numerous grants and fellowships from the National Science Foundation, the National Endowment for the Humanities, and the John Templeton Foundation. In his spare time, Dr. Peterson enjoys hiking in national parks and running the occasional 5K race.

Timothy M. Ravich is assistant professor of legal studies at the University of Central Florida. He is an internationally recognized authority in aviation law and one of only thirty-seven lawyers in the state of Florida who is a board certified specialist in aviation law. His scholarship focuses on administrative law, civil litigation, and national security law through the lens of civil, commercial, and military aviation. He has published a course book, *Aviation Law after September 11th*, and written extensively in connection with aviation issues, including airline deregulation and passenger rights, aviation security and terrorism, and unmanned aerial vehicles ("UAVs" or "drones"). He is the author of the LexisNexis *Expert Aviation Series* and has contributed to Thomson Reuters/Aspatore Special Reports.

Donald G. Richards is professor of economics at Indiana State University, where he teaches courses in macroeconomics, international economics, and sustainable agriculture. He is the author of many articles and *Intellectual Property Rights and Global Capitalism* (M. E. Sharpe). His latest book is *Economics, Ethics, and Ancient Thought*.

Staci M. Zavattaro is an associate professor of public administration at the University of Central Florida. She has written several books about place branding in public administration, as well as edited volumes on social media, and another on academic success. Her work appears in journals including *Place Branding and Public Diplomacy*, *Journal of Place Management and Development*, *Administrative Theory & Praxis*, and *Administration & Society*. Her research interests include administrative theory, place marketing, and organizational communication. Palgrave Macmillan published her book regarding cities through phases of the image in 2014. She serves as editor-in-chief of *Administrative Theory & Praxis*.

# CONTRIBUTORS

www.ingramcontent.com/pod-product-compliance
Lightning Source LLC
Chambersburg PA
CBHW030734280326
41926CB00086B/1504